Cooking with Herbs

COOKING WITH HERBS

By Emelie Tolley and Chris Mead

Text by Emelie Tolley
Photographs by Chris Mead
Designed by Nancy Butkus Design

CLARKSON N. POTTER, INC., PUBLISHERS

To my nieces, Myra and Susan, for the joy they have brought to my life. And to Myra and Peter for so generously sharing their love.
E.T.

To Mary

And to Emelie, who did such a great job writing Herbs *and* Cooking with Herbs. *I have the easy job! And to all the people who found herbs before we did and made our work a lot of fun.*
C.M.

Also by Emelie Tolley and Chris Mead

Herbs: Gardens, Decorations, and Recipes

Photograph on page 9 © David Alossi
Photographs on pages 226–232 © Anne Pagniez
Recipes on pages 251–252 from *Marcella's Italian Kitchen.* Used by permission of Random House.
Recipes on pages 254–257, copyright © 1986 by Giuliano Bugialli.
All rights reserved. Used by permission.
Recipes on pages 281–282 © Latifa Bannani-Smires.
Used by permission.

Text copyright © 1989 by Emelie Tolley
Photographs copyright © 1989 by Chris Mead

Published by Clarkson N. Potter, Inc., 201 East 50th Street, New York, New York 10022 and distributed by Crown Publishers, Inc.

CLARKSON N. POTTER, POTTER, and colophon are trademarks of Clarkson N. Potter, Inc.

Manufactured in Japan

Library of Congress Cataloging-in-Publication Data

Tolley, Emelie.
Cooking with herbs.
Includes index.
1. Cookery (Herbs)   2. Cookery, American.
3. Cookery, International.   I. Mead, Chris.   II. Title.
TX819.H4T65   1988   641.6′57   88-19562
ISBN 0-517-57139-0

10 9 8 7 6 5 4 3 2 1

First Edition

We would like to thank all the people who have shared their time, expertise, and recipes with us: Those who are represented on the following pages as well as those who do not appear because space ran out.

Our gratitude goes, too, to those who helped make our task easier: Jacqueline Horscher-Thomas; Doreen, Fred, and Jackie Mead; Myra Oram; Albert Morris, Keith Varty, and Alan Cleaver; Nina Flinn and Hector Lombardi; Joe Ruggiero; Albert Hadley; Ronaldo Ferri; Anne Blackwell; Steven Aronsky; Sandra Kreinik; Sharon Donovan; Helen Jones; Lyndsey Veccios; Cobweb Antiques. And our deep appreciation to Nancy Butkus for her sensitivity to our concept of *Cooking with Herbs* and her creativity in transforming our pictures and text into a beautiful book.

Last, a very special thank-you to all those at Clarkson N. Potter, especially Pam Krauss, Nancy Novogrod, Gael Towey, Carol Southern, Missy Schueneman, and Jonathan Fox, who have helped, supported, and encouraged us along the way.

✿✿✿

Overleaf: **Sandi Wickersham Resnick's mixed herb bouquet.**

Contents

Introduction

A striking bouquet of sunflowers, *above*, sits in the corner of the dining room at La Bonne Étape in Provence. Bruce Zabov's delicious marjoram-infused mélange of chicken, potatoes, green beans, and tomatoes, *opposite*, photographed on his airy Louisiana porch.

It's hard to imagine a kitchen without a few cloves of garlic, a bunch of parsley, and jars of dried oregano, thyme, and rosemary. Whether or not we are aware of it, we all cook with herbs: it's a question of degree. Those of us who love to eat well won't cook without them. How could we eat summer's juicy ripe tomatoes without a generous sprinkling of fresh basil—unless, of course, we were tempted to try tender young borage leaves instead? We wander through the garden all summer long, gathering handfuls of aromatic herbs and envisioning how they will make just-caught fish, grilled meats, lush vegetables, and even desserts more appealing. As fall approaches we dry or freeze the harvest to enliven meals on cold winter days or transplant a miniature version of the garden to the kitchen windowsill.

When Chris and I wrote our first book, *Herbs*, it was intended as an introduction to these useful edible plants. We hoped to whet the appetite and entice readers to learn more about how herbs can add color to the garden; the ways they can be used to scent and decorate the house; and the zesty flavor they bring to foods. We discovered that many cooks planted their first herb garden in order to have their favorite herbs at hand, while gardeners were learning to use

With cocktails, Sue Ellen Lawton often serves a braunschweiger ball made from a German liverwurst-type sausage mixed with butter and herbs and then frosted with cream cheese.

⫷⫷⫷

Potted orange trees and herbs are scattered among the formal plantings at the Villa Villoresi near Florence.

herbs in the kitchen. Experienced chefs and novices alike seemed interested in cooking with herbs and were searching for new herbal recipes. So Chris and I took to the road again, visiting chefs and good cooks all over the United States and in England, France, Italy, Spain, and Morocco to discover how they use herbs today and to gather their best recipes. The result is a wonderful harvest of herbal drinks; fabulous appetizers; great ways with fish and vegetables, meats and poultry, pasta and bread; and dazzling desserts.

The sheer pleasure of taste is reason enough for the amazing surge of interest in cooking with herbs, but our increased awareness of healthy eating has also prompted us to enliven our foods with herbs rather than unhealthful amounts of salt or sugar. So has *nouvelle cuisine*; although its sometimes pretentious approach to food has given way to a more appealing and realistic style of cooking today, its legacy of using only the freshest herbs and finest produce remains. It inspired young American chefs to rediscover the bounty of our native produce, and in turn, these young innovators have shown us that just-picked vegetables, fresh fish, or a range-grown chicken, simply cooked and seasoned with herbs, can be as memorable as a traditional French dinner.

Moreover, Americans have become confirmed travelers, experiencing a wide variety of foods and flavors, and even those who stay at home are constantly exposed to articles about interesting foods and the people who cook them. We've developed sophisticated palates, stimulated by a wide range of the ethnic tastes we seek out in restaurants

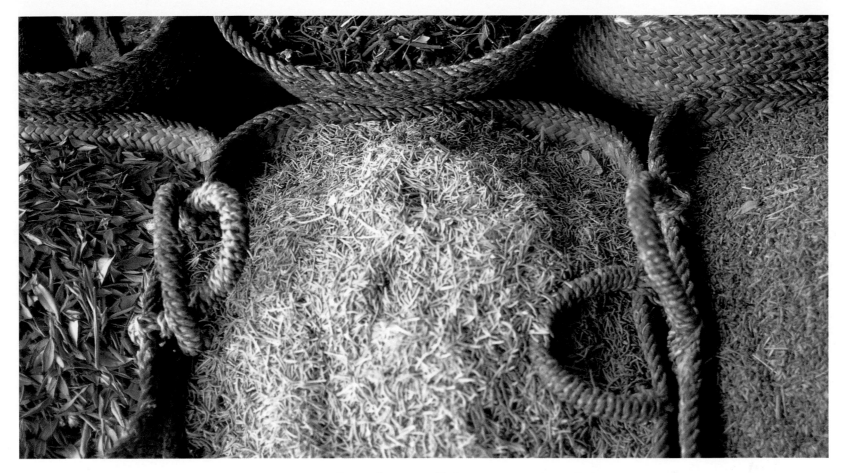

Baskets piled high with dried herbs and spices tempt shoppers in a Moroccan market.

or try to re-create in our own kitchens. It's not surprising that coriander, purslane, and lemon grass are almost as familiar these days as tarragon and rosemary.

Americans are also embracing their own culinary heritage. Amateur cooks and chefs are researching and preserving authentic regional dishes and old recipes that refer to overlooked herbs or forgotten ways of using them, then drawing upon them as inspiration for new dishes.

As you travel through this book with us, you'll discover that it's divided regionally but is not a regional cookbook in the expected sense. For we came to realize that true regional cuisine is not a set collection of traditional recipes

Bay thrives in the mild Italian climate. These beautifully shaped trees are silhouetted against the sky on the edge of the Adriatic at Ancona.

but is constantly evolving. It is revitalized by the integration of new ingredients and techniques, and its quality depends on the availability of local products and the spirit of those who cook it. Certainly each region and culture can be characterized by a specific taste, a "flavor chord" as the Coyote Cafe's Mark Miller calls it: basil and garlic remind us of Genoa; rosemary, garlic, and thyme conjure up images of fragrant Provençal dishes, and mint provokes memories of heady tea drunk in a Moroccan souk. And once you define a region's flavor character, you can bring the essence of that region to any food.

As you meet the cooks we visited both here and abroad, you'll see they've looked at their heritage and at herbs with a fresh eye. They've revived old-fashioned herbs such as lovage; experimented with exotic herbs like epazote; added herbs where none were traditionally used; refined and lightened recipes to meet today's needs; and used local produce to create their own indigenous cuisine. They've added herbs to everything from bread sticks to ice cream.

We discovered that the growing awareness of food has helped develop a group of young American chefs, professionals schooled in traditional cuisine but unfettered by its rules. Others have graduate degrees in fields such as archeology, but found they were happier in the kitchen. Many of our cooks became interested in food because their mothers or grandmothers were fabulous cooks, and eating good food and sharing it with friends had been an important part of their home lives. Some were artists who thought of cooking as another way of expressing their creativity through color, texture, and the endless possibilities of herb garnishes. All these cooks experiment with flavors and cooking methods, but they agree that the best meals start with the freshest produce, carefully seasoned and simply cooked—just the kind of food that appeals to us today.

A young Texan chef told us he loves to cook because it's a way of turning the necessity of eating into a great source of pleasure. We hope this book will inspire you to cook more, encourage you to try new recipes and foods, and help you to discover the pleasures of cooking with herbs—pleasures that are doubly sweet when they're shared with family and friends.

For this enticing vegetable plate, Molly Chappellet steamed green beans with sage, enhanced cucumbers with mint and bronze sage.

At the Carved Angel in England, guests are greeted by a bouquet of herbs arranged in a lovely porcelain compote.

California

California boasts fields of fragrant garlic; valleys of lush vineyards; stands of aromatic California bay laurel; groves of citrus, avocados, olives, and nuts; a bounty of fish from the sea; and acres of fertile farmland—all warmed by the temperate sunshine that encourages herbs and vegetables to grow year round. With such an embarrassment of riches, it's no wonder the new wave of American cooking started in California.

Innovative chefs such as Alice Waters and Michael McCarty chose the freshest foods and prepared them in the simplest way, focusing our senses on their inherent flavors. They were joined by European chefs like Wolfgang Puck, who found the variety and quality of foods in California much like those of Europe. These young chefs insisted on using herbs, vegetables, and fruits in season, when their flavors are at their peak, harvesting them while they are still

Freshly gathered produce rests on a garden bench at Mudd's Restaurant in California.

1

Paradise Farms' edible flowers, *above*, are grown organically.

Molly Chappellet's lush kitchen garden tumbles down the side of a hill to the Chappellet vineyard, *below.*

young and tender; and encouraged the cultivation of miniature vegetables and new European varieties. Seeking to be self-sufficient and knowing that proximity means freshness, they supported the development of local sources for herbs and edible flowers, goat cheese, lamb, and other ingredients.

Influenced by both classic cooking methods and *nouvelle cuisine*, the originators of California cooking have blended diverse culinary traditions into an entirely new approach to food. They have been inspired by the family cooking of the European countryside; they've assimilated the piquant flavorings favored by California's Mexican population; but above all they've been receptive to new ideas and new ingredients. Herbs play an important part in their creations—not the dried herbs of classic French cuisine, but bountiful handfuls of fresh herbs used with imagination. They experiment, allowing their instincts and sense of taste to govern how food and seasonings are combined in a given dish.

California's successful vintners, possessing an almost intuitive sense of the way food and wine enhance each other, have also helped direct attention to California food. Since herbs often provide the predominant flavor of a dish, vineyards such as Inglenook are making a conscious effort to understand the way herbs can affect the taste of a wine.

Perhaps nowhere else in the country are herbs so readily available and so important to the character of the cuisine. Their inimitable taste and freshness elevate California's simply cooked foods to a special dining experience.

At California's Domaine Chandon vineyard, chef Philippe Jeanty flavors his elegant lamb ravioli with marjoram.

UNDERSTANDING HERBS AND WINE

As Americans become more sophisticated in their use of herbs and spices, California winegrowers have begun to explore the ways herbs affect the taste of the wines served with them. Perhaps no one has delved into this relationship more thoroughly than Barbara Lang, Inglenook Vineyard's former culinary director, who set out to determine which wines and herbs were most compatible.

"A wine can complement or contrast with the dominant flavor in a dish," she explains. "For example, the pungency of rosemary would be an austere contrast to a buttery, full-bodied Chardonnay, while the subtle vanillin taste of tarragon would complement and enhance the wine's rich flavor. It's also important to consider the complexity of the wine. A simple wine may be improved by a complex dish with strong flavors that tone down its rough edges, while a wine of great complexity needs simple, elegant foods as a backdrop for the wine's subtle nuances. A young Zinfandel with 'rough edges' would stand up to the zesty taste of grilled lamb flavored with garlic, rosemary, and thyme. With a few years' aging, however, the mellowed wine would be overwhelmed by this robust combination; it will be better suited to the more delicate flavor of a roast leg of lamb with a thyme and wine sauce."

Barbara's husband, Kristof Ostlund, is the chef in the Inglenook dining room, located in a small house near the winery. A former civil engineer, Kristof discovered his cooking talents when helping out in the dining room at lunch. Now, he cooks for press and sales-related groups, carefully planning menus to implement Barbara's research and showcase a particular wine. Barbara says the best way to discover which wines you like best with different herbs is to conduct your own tasting. Prepare a neutral food like a chicken breast with a variety of sauces or stuffings, each flavored with a different herb. Taste each version with two red wines such as a Zinfandel and a Merlot and two white wines such as a Chardonnay and a Chenin Blanc, rating each pairing on a scale of 1 to 10.

Neat vineyards, *top and above*, flourish all through the Napa Valley, often side by side with lush plantings of herbs. Grilled pork tenderloin and a fruity merlot, *opposite*, are ready to be enjoyed in the shade of the vines.

GRILLED PORK TENDERLOIN WITH TARRAGON MUSTARD SAUCE

Loin of pork requires a different grilling method than steak or chops. Because the loin is thicker, you must use indirect heat and allow it to cook more slowly. If you do not have a grill, roast the pork in a 350°F oven for about 1½ hours, or until the internal temperature reaches 160°F. Serve with a Merlot; the sweet flavor of the tarragon will complement the fruity quality of the wine.

- 1 pork tenderloin, about 3 pounds
- Salt and freshly ground pepper
- ¼ cup olive oil

TARRAGON MUSTARD SAUCE
- ⅓ cup dry white wine
- 1 shallot, sliced
- 6 peppercorns
- ¼ cup coarse Dijon mustard, or to taste
- 1 cup heavy cream
- 2 tablespoons minced fresh tarragon, or 2 teaspoons dried
- Salt and freshly ground pepper

Barbara recommends a merlot to accompany the pork because the sweet flavor of the tarragon sauce complements the fruity quality of the wine.

Pat the pork tenderloin dry with a paper towel. Sprinkle with salt and pepper. Let sit on a plate at room temperature for 1 hour.

Build a fire in a grill using a generous amount of good-quality charcoal. When the charcoal is covered with a fine white ash, the fire is ready. Rake the coals evenly around the sides of the grill, leaving the center free of coals.

Rub the loin all over with the oil, then place it on the center of the grill. Cook the loin for approximately 35 to 55 minutes, basting occasionally during cooking. Cooking time will vary, depending on how hot the coals are; use a meat thermometer to check the pork for doneness; it should be taken off the coals when its internal temperature is 160°F. Let the tenderloin rest for 10 minutes before carving to allow the meat to reabsorb some of its juices and finish cooking.

While the loin is cooking, place the wine, shallot, and peppercorns in a 1-quart non-aluminum saucepan. Reduce over low heat until only 2 tablespoons remain, about 5 to 10 minutes. Remove from the heat and strain. Return the wine to the pan; discard shallot and peppercorns. Set aside until the loin is removed from the grill.

While the loin is resting, finish the sauce. In a small bowl, stir 2 tablespoons of the mustard into the cream; add the remaining mustard by teaspoonfuls according to taste. Stir the mustard mixture into the reduced wine. Add the minced tarragon and cook at a light simmer for 5 minutes over medium heat. The sauce should be slightly thickened. Add salt and pepper to taste.

Carve the pork into thin slices and nap with sauce.

SERVES 6 TO 8

Enclosing fish and seasonings in parchment before cooking helps the flavor of the herbs penetrate and keeps the fish moist.

SALMON EN PAPILLOTE

Serve with a Chardonnay; tarragon highlights the hint of vanillin oak aging imparts to the wine.

5 tablespoons unsalted butter

2 shallots, minced

½ pound fresh button mushrooms, sliced

1 tablespoon finely chopped fresh tarragon, or 1 teaspoon dried

2 tablespoons dry sherry

1 tablespoon Dijon mustard

3 thick salmon steaks, approximately 1 pound each

Salt and freshly ground pepper

1 lemon, cut in 6 wedges, for garnish

Preheat the oven to 425°F.

In a small skillet, melt 2 tablespoons of the butter over medium heat. Add the shallots and cook until soft, about 5 to 8 minutes. Add the mushrooms and sauté until they have just turned color. Add the tarragon, sherry, and mustard; cook for another minute. Remove from the heat and set aside.

Carefully bone the salmon steaks, dividing them in half lengthwise to make 6 servings. Do not remove the skin. Check to be sure all of the bones have been removed by pressing gently on the steak with your fingers. Place 1 piece of salmon skin side down on a cutting board and using a sharp, clean knife, butterfly the fish, cutting just to but not through the skin. Repeat with remaining salmon pieces wiping the blade after each cut.

Fold six 12 × 15-inch pieces of parchment paper in half lengthwise, and cut out 6 very fat parchment hearts about twice as long as the salmon steaks.

Melt the remaining butter. Unfold a parchment heart and brush one side of the heart with melted butter. Center a piece of salmon on half the heart. Spread a small amount of the shallot mixture over the fish and season to taste with salt and pepper. Fold the parchment over the salmon so the cut edges meet. Beginning at the point of the heart, fold the end up about 1 inch and crease the fold. Fold the next section partly over the first; continue folding small sections until the edges are sealed. Each fold should overlap the previous one. Repeat with the remaining 5 pieces of salmon and parchment paper.

Place the parchment packages on a baking sheet. Bake for 10 to 12 minutes. The parchment packages will puff and brown slightly. To serve, place a parchment package on a dinner plate and cut a small X in the top. Allow your guests to open the papillote and enjoy the wonderful aroma. Garnish with a lemon wedge.

SERVES 6

THE FRENCH LAUNDRY

The first time Don and Sally Schmitt visited Yountville, they fell in love with a wonderful turn-of-the-century building that started life as a bar. By the time the Schmitts discovered it, the bar, a victim of the Depression, had been turned into a French laundry. Several years later, the Schmitts heard the building was available, bought it, and remodeled it into one of the Napa Valley's most delightful restaurants.

In the intervening years, Sally was learning the restaurant business, overseeing a café and a less serious lunchroom in a local shopping complex. The once-a-month dinners she initiated, which featured braised meats and other simple, homey dishes she learned from her mother, soon earned her a dedicated following. On her days off, Sally experimented with Mexican and Chinese foods, so by the time she and her husband opened the French Laundry, her approach—although still simple—had become a bit more sophisticated. "The food here isn't trendy," she admits. "I like to give an old recipe a new twist by changing one or two ingredients." For example, rather than lemon and parsley, she might use orange and tarragon on broiled scallops. "I tend to use herbs one at a time. I like to single them out rather than combine them," Sally notes, "although I do sometimes mix in parsley or chives. They seem to go well with anything."

A charming herb garden just outside the restaurant's door offers guests a cool spot to enjoy a predinner aperitif or coffee after dessert. "The garden was a necessity," says Sally, "because when we first started you couldn't buy fresh herbs anywhere." The herbs are used only in season and never frozen or dried. "When the basil is gone," claims Sally, "I pull up the plants and wait until spring."

The deep-set windows in the kitchen of the French Laundry overlook the fertile vineyards and gentle hills of the Napa Valley.

CHICKEN IN LEMON AND MINT CREAM

The chicken breasts in this recipe should be just barely done. If possible, add the mint chiffonnade to the sauce at the last minute. It will keep its lovely green color best if not overheated or kept for a prolonged time. To make the chiffonnade, strip the mint leaves from the stem, hold them in a tight bunch; slice finely into thin strips.

2 tablespoons (¼ stick) unsalted butter

2 tablespoons vegetable oil

3 large chicken breasts, boned, skinned, and halved

Salt

½ cup dry white wine

SAUCE

3 tablespoons unsalted butter

3 tablespoons flour

2 cups light cream, or a mixture of 1 cup cream, 1 cup chicken stock

Salt and coarsely ground white pepper

Chopped zest of 1 large lemon

2 tablespoons lemon juice

¼ cup loosely packed fresh mint leaves, cut into chiffonnade

6 sprigs fresh mint or additional lemon zest for garnish

Preheat the oven to 300°F.

In a large skillet, heat the butter and oil over low heat until foamy. Add the chicken breasts and heat gently on both sides, just until they firm up a little; do not try to finish cooking. Transfer the chicken to a rectangular baking dish large enough to hold the breasts in a single layer. Sprinkle them with salt, pour the wine over them, cover with

A charming herb garden welcomes guests.

foil, and place in the oven. After 15 minutes, check the breasts for doneness; when pressed with your finger they should feel slightly firm, but not hard. When cooked, remove and let cool in their baking dish without refrigerating. Pour off the juices and reserve for the sauce.

To make the sauce, melt the butter over medium heat in a sauté pan large enough to hold the chicken pieces. Add the flour and mix with a wire whisk until smooth, then cook gently, stirring often, until the mixture turns golden brown, about 3 minutes. Immediately pour in

the cream and reserved chicken juices. Cook and stir until the sauce thickens and comes to a boil. Season to taste with salt and white pepper, then add the lemon zest. Add the lemon juice and return to a boil. The sauce should be thick enough to coat the chicken lightly, but should run off a spoon. If necessary, thin the sauce with a little more cream. (At this point sauce and chicken can be held for an hour or so. When ready to serve, reheat the sauce very gently.)

Just before serving, stir the chiffonnade of mint into the warm sauce. Add the chicken breasts to the sauce, cover, and warm them through over very low heat. Do not let the sauce boil at this point or you will overcook the chicken and lose the color of the mint.

To serve, place 1 breast on each plate, nap with a spoonful of sauce, and garnish with a mint sprig or lemon zest.

SERVES 6

Two of Diane's favorites: herbed peasant bread and muffins flavored with cheddar cheese, sage, and garlic.

A CALIFORNIA BAKER

The conservative California Club, established in 1862, had never had a woman in its kitchen until Diane Heiser Weber arrived in 1985. By that time she had proved her culinary talents and her stamina; but when Diane first tried to launch her career as a chef, few women were accepted in serious kitchens. Whenever she was able to talk her way into a job, "the rest of the kitchen lived for the sadistic amusement of seeing how long I would last," she recalls. Her male coworkers took great delight in taunting her, playing practical jokes, and standing idly by as she dragged hundred-pound bags of flour around the kitchen. "It was physically hard on me, but I was consistent, quiet, and responsible," she adds, "and when they realized I was serious, I was finally accepted."

Diane's specialty is baking, and while working as the pastry chef at Pastel's in Los Angeles, she met Gaston LeNôtre, the well-known French master pâtissier, who invited her to his school in Paris. Recently, she accepted that invitation and

learned the secrets of making wonderful crusty bread, rich chocolates, and a vast array of tempting pastries.

Because herbs aren't used as frequently in baking, Diane had little interest in them until a friend, Carole Seville, brought her bunches of aromatic herbs from her garden. "I realized they were beautiful just sitting in a pitcher of water," she says. "Then I discovered that herbal flavors were wonderful in sorbets, and edible flowers could be candied to decorate desserts and cakes.

Inspired, she rented an allotment near her apartment. About 250 Los Angeles gardeners share this large piece of land, each taking care of his or her own plot and contributing one hour a month to a general cleanup of the public space. The gardeners grow their herbs, vegetables, and flowers organically and trade their produce. Diane gets the rose petals for her sorbet from a neighboring gardener who grows old roses. "Try to pick them when they're in full bloom," she advises, "because that's when they're most fragrant and have the most flavor."

HEARTY PEASANT BREAD

This bread gets its special texture from a mixture of pastry, cake, and bread flours. Pastry flour is milled especially for use in pie crusts and other short pastries. It can be found in fine gourmet shops or health food stores, or you may be able to purchase it from a local bakery. Wheat germ, toasted and untoasted, is available in super-markets and health food stores. To toast your own, sprinkle some on a baking sheet and bake in a 350°F oven, shaking occasionally, until golden brown, about 5 minutes.

- 1 package active dry yeast
- ¼ cup warm water (105°–115°F.)
- 2¾ cups pastry flour
- 2¾ cups cake flour
- 5 cups bread flour
- 1 tablespoon salt
- 1½ teaspoons honey
- 1 cup less 2 tablespoons milk
- 1½ cups water
- 1 large egg
- 2 tablespoons vegetable oil
- ⅔ cup toasted wheat germ
- 2 sprigs fresh thyme (with blossoms, if possible)
- 2 sprigs fresh rosemary
  Untoasted wheat germ, for top

Dissolve the yeast in the warm water.

In a large bowl, combine the flours, yeast mixture, salt, honey, milk, water, and egg with a dough hook or by hand. When well mixed, turn the dough onto a floured surface and knead for 10 to 12 minutes. During the last 3 minutes of the kneading time, make a well in the dough and add the oil and the wheat germ; work in thoroughly. The dough should be smooth and elastic.

Place the dough in a large, lightly oiled bowl. Cover tightly with plastic wrap and allow to rise in a warm, draft-free place until doubled in size, about 1½ to 2 hours. Divide the dough in half and gently incorporate the thyme into the dough as you form it into 2 free-form round loaves. Pierce the center of each loaf top with a sprig of rosemary, inserting it as far as it will go. Cover lightly with a linen cloth and allow to rise an additional 30 minutes.

Preheat the oven to 375°F.

Just before baking, mist the bread with cool water and sprinkle on a small amount of untoasted wheat germ. Bake until golden brown, or until the bread sounds hollow when rapped with your knuckles, about 45 minutes to 1 hour.

NOTE: This bread cannot be made successfully in a food processor.

MAKES 2 LOAVES

Diane Weber picks old-fashioned roses for her sorbet in a neighbor's allotment.

ROSE PETAL SORBET

The delicate perfume of rose petals is as appealing in sorbet as it is in the garden. Be sure you use fragrant roses (the old-fashioned varieties are best) from bushes that have been grown without pesticides. Leftover syrup can be used to make other herb-flavored sorbets by substituting rosemary or mint for the rose petals in the recipe below.

Generous 1¾ cups Sugar Syrup (recipe follows)

2 to 3 cups fragrant rose petals

Juice of 1 lemon

Red food coloring (optional)

Frosted rose petals, for garnish (page 14)

In a medium bowl or jar, combine the sugar syrup with the rose petals and let stand overnight to infuse the syrup with the rose flavor.

The following day, strain the syrup into another bowl. Stir in the lemon juice and a few drops of food coloring if you want the sorbet to have a faint pink hue. Transfer the rose syrup to an ice-cream maker, then freeze according to the manufacturer's directions. Garnish with frosted rose petals, if desired.

MAKES APPROXIMATELY 1 PINT

SUGAR SYRUP

5 cups sugar

4¼ cups water

In a saucepan, combine the sugar and water. Cook over high heat, stirring with a wooden spoon, until the sugar has dissolved. Continue heating until the syrup comes to a full boil, then immediately remove the syrup from the heat and pour it into a large jar in which you can store it. Syrup will keep for up to 2 months in the refrigerator.

MAKES 6 CUPS

Subtly flavored rose petal sorbet is even more appealing garnished with frosted roses and petals.

A TASTE OF LAVENDER

It's hard to know whether Carole Seville likes herbs more for their beauty in the garden or their flavor in the kitchen. Hearing her talk about her herb garden, you know she loves it. A cookbook editor and freelance food writer, Carole also does PR for restaurants. Lately she's been able to combine her interests in food and gardening by planning and maintaining herb gardens for restaurants that want an on-site source of fresh herbs.

Carole is constantly on the lookout for new ways to use herbs. Before moving to California, she raised Nubian goats so she could make her own herbed cheese, rolling the fresh goat cheese in hyssop, lavender, and thyme, and raised sheep for their wool, which she colored with herbal dyes. The latest step in this constant quest for knowledge is a distilling machine for capturing the essence, or oils, of the herbs that grow so profusely in her garden. "There's always something more to learn," she claims.

PINK LAVENDER LEMONADE

Carole makes this lemonade with distilled lavender essence from her still, but the lavender "tea" in the recipe here gives equally good results. Dried hibiscus flowers can be purchased in herb and natural food stores or in ethnic markets where Mexican products are sold.

   5 cups water
1 ½ cups sugar, plus ½ cup additional if desired
   ¼ cup dried hibiscus flowers
   ¼ cup chopped fresh English lavender leaves
2 ¼ cups lemon juice
        Fresh lavender flowers, for garnish

In a saucepan, combine 2 ½ cups water with the sugar and the hibiscus flowers. Bring to a boil, stirring to dissolve the sugar. Simmer for a few minutes to extract the color of the hibiscus, then remove from the heat, stir in the lavender leaves, and allow mixture to cool with lid on.

Strain liquid into a large pitcher or jar, add the remaining water and the lemon juice, and stir well. Add more sugar if desired. Just before serving, add ice cubes. Pour into chilled glasses and garnish with a lavender flower.

SERVES 6 TO 8

Carole Seville likes to use lavender to flavor lemonade and applesauce.

AN EDIBLE BOUQUET

As unlikely as it may seem, it took a Beverly Hills hairdresser and a folk-artist-cum-nurse's-aide to turn the growing of edible flowers into a thriving business. Pam and Jay North started their first garden to grow vegetables for their pet monkeys, but ended up with more vegetables than the monkeys could eat. At first the Norths gave away the surplus, then they began to sell it. The direction of the business changed when an Italian chef asked them to supply him with basil. Checking the price, they realized there was more profit in basil than in vegetables, and they immediately expanded their herb operation. Another serendipitous call from a produce wholesaler looking for nasturtium flowers put them in the edible flower business. Although they had no nasturtiums growing in their gardens, the canyons around their house were filled with the colorful orange blossoms, so they accepted the order, then scurried out to forage the flowers to fill it.

A little research revealed that flowers had once been relatively common on dining tables. Intrigued with the idea of reviving an old idea and creating a new industry, the Norths have worked hard to reeducate people to the pleasure of using flowers in the kitchen, steadily increasing the number of varieties they grow. They also sell the blossoms of their herbs, which are decorative and often more intensely flavored than showier flowers like pansies. Jay warns against buying flowers for the table in a florist shop, because they have been doused with chemical sprays. He adds, "Make sure you know what you're eating. Not all flowers are edible; some, like lily of the valley and daffodils, are pretty but poisonous."

Pam knows many people are still timid about eating colorful flowers, but she's trying to change that. These days most of her cooking time is spent dreaming up new uses for their produce to inspire customers. She loves to recount a story about a female chef who ordered a bridal bouquet of edible flowers. At the reception, instead of tossing the bouquet to the bridesmaids, she threw it into the salad for everyone to enjoy.

To sugar edible flowers, paint them with a light coat of barely beaten egg white, dip in granulated sugar, then place on wax paper to dry.

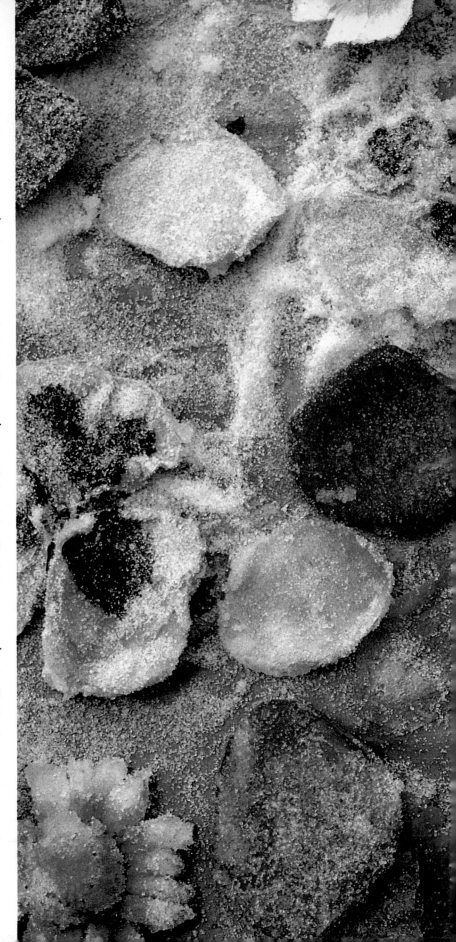

Nasturtium, a member of the watercress family, shares its relative's peppery tang.

NASTURTIUM BLOSSOMS WITH CRAB MEAT STUFFING

These brightly colored blossoms look pretty served on a bed of deep-green nasturtium leaves. If you are going to serve them as finger food, they will be easier to handle if you affix the flower to a small cracker with a dab of the cream-cheese mixture. Do not stuff the flowers more than 2 hours before serving.

24 nasturtium flowers

8 ounces whipped cream cheese, at room temperature

3 tablespoons dry white wine

3 tablespoon finely chopped fresh or canned cooked crab meat

1 ½ tablespoons finely chopped fresh chervil

Salt and white pepper

Remove the stems from the nasturtium flowers. Gently wash them, shake off excess moisture, and set on a cloth towel to dry.

In a bowl, beat the cream cheese, wine, crab meat, and chervil together until light and fluffy. Season to taste with salt and pepper. Place the mixture in a pastry bag fitted with a plain or serrated tip, and carefully fill the flowers. Refrigerate until ready to serve.

SERVES 6

COCONUT CALENDULA CAKE

2 cups sifted cake flour

1 tablespoon baking powder

¼ teaspoon salt

½ cup (1 stick) butter

1 cup sugar

3 egg whites

1 teaspoon vanilla extract

⅔ cup milk

Boiled White Icing (recipe follows)

1½ cups grated coconut

1 cup calendula petals

Preheat the oven to 350°F. Grease and lightly flour two 9-inch round cake pans.

Sift the flour, baking powder, and salt together and set aside. In a large mixing bowl, cream the butter and gradually add the sugar, continuing to beat until the mixture is light and fluffy. Beat in the egg whites, one at a time, stirring well after each addition. Add the vanilla.

Add sifted ingredients to the butter mixture alternating with the milk, stirring well after each addition. The batter should be very smooth. Divide batter between the 2 pans and bake for about 25 minutes, or until a cake tester inserted in the center of the layer comes out dry and without crumbs, and the cake has just begun to pull away from the sides of the pan. Cool the cake in the pans for 5 minutes, then turn the layers out onto racks to finish cooling.

Spread icing between layers and on tops and sides. Before the icing has set, sprinkle coconut and calendula petals over the top.

NOTE: If you like a stronger calendula flavor, chop an additional ¼ cup of calendula petals and steep them in the milk overnight. (Alternatively, you can heat the milk, pour it over the petals, and let it cool.) Strain the milk before stirring into the cake batter if you prefer.

MAKES 1 9-INCH CAKE

BOILED WHITE ICING

2 cups sugar

1 cup water

2 egg whites

1 teaspoon lemon juice

1 teaspoon vanilla extract

Place the sugar and water in a saucepan and cook over medium-high heat, stirring, until the sugar is dissolved. Stir down any crystals that may form around the sides of the pan. Bring to a boil and cook until the syrup reaches 240°F. on a candy thermometer, or it spins a very fine thread when dripped from the end of a spoon. Remove from the heat.

In a medium bowl, whip the egg whites until stiff but not dry. Add the hot syrup in a thin stream, whipping the whites constantly until the icing is cool and thick enough to spread. Beat in the lemon juice and vanilla, and use immediately.

MAKES ENOUGH FOR 1 9-INCH LAYER CAKE

❧

Pam uses chamomile blossoms to decorate a salad, *left*. To keep insects away from edible flowers, such as the calendula petals on the cake, *below*, Jay uses a spray made from garlic and onions.

THE CREATIVITY OF WOLFGANG PUCK

"California is one of the luckiest parts of the world for a cook," says Wolfgang Puck, the Austrian-born, French-trained chef who dispenses wonderfully creative food from his two Los Angeles restaurants, Spago and Chinois on Main. "There is more variety in fish on the East Coast," he admits, "but in California herbs and vegetables are fresh all year." Puck, whose dishes rely heavily on the freshness of his ingredients, is especially insistent on using fresh herbs because he feels the flavor of dried herbs dissipates as they age.

A garden just outside Spago helps keep the restaurant kitchen supplied with herbs and edible flowers, and Wolfgang has additional herbs and vegetables grown for him close by. The availability of all this fresh produce has influenced the menu. "Ten years ago we used truffles but they were out of character. Now we use the best thing available where we're living. Besides the herbs, vegetables, and California wine, we have local cheeses and they're even raising lamb in Sonoma. Food is simpler than before, but to make it right *and* simple is hard."

A salad of perfectly cooked lobster and a mixture of local greens and vegetables gets its distinctive flavor from a cilantro and mango vinaigrette.

❧

LOBSTER SALAD WITH CILANTRO-MANGO VINAIGRETTE

Cook the lobster for this salad shortly before serving; it is much more flavorful when served lukewarm or at room temperature than when chilled. Grilled salmon or sea bass can be substituted for the lobster, but it should not be overcooked.

COURT BOUILLON

- 2 carrots, scrubbed and sliced
- 2 celery stalks, sliced
- 1 leek, sliced
- 1 sprig fresh thyme
- 1 bay leaf
- 1 teaspoon salt
- ½ teaspoon freshly ground pepper
- 2 quarts water
- 2 cups dry white wine

- 2 lobsters, 1¼ pounds each
- 6 tablespoons walnut oil
- ¼ cup balsamic vinegar
- ½ mango, diced
- 2 shallots, diced, or 2 tablespoons chopped red onion
- ¼ cup diced red bell pepper
- ¼ cup whole cilantro leaves
  Salt and pepper
- 4 to 6 cups assorted salad greens (lamb's lettuce, small red-leaf lettuce, arugula, or whatever is available in the market)

Combine the court bouillon ingredients in a large pot. Bring to a boil over high heat and continue to boil for 20 minutes.

Add the lobsters to the court bouillon and return to the boil for 12 minutes or until done. Using tongs, remove the lobsters from the court bouillon, reserving the liquid for future use, if desired. When the lobsters are cool enough to handle, remove the meat from the shell. Slice the tail meat lengthwise. Set aside.

In a small bowl, mix the oil, vinegar, mango, shallots, bell pepper, and ¾ of the cilantro leaves; add salt and pepper to taste.

Divide the salad greens between 2 dinner plates and spoon ¾ of the vinaigrette over them. Arrange the lobster attractively on top of the greens, and spoon the remaining vinaigrette over. Garnish with the reserved cilantro leaves and the split body of the lobster, if desired.

SERVES 2

❧

Flowers and herbs share space with lobster and vegetables in the kitchen at Spago, where Wolfgang Puck's creativity extends beyond the preparation of the food to its presentation.

FRESH IDEAS FROM THE GARDEN

Kerry Marshall started growing vegetables as a child, so when he and Virginia Mudd got together to open a restaurant that would serve fresh, organically grown food, it seemed natural for him to take over the gardening end of the project. Named Mudd's, the restaurant has its own garden, which took constant tending and nearly eight years to mature into the colorful and bounteous haven it is today. Beneficial insects, like the praying mantis, were brought in to take care of garden pests, and the vegetables and herbs are rotated every four years to give the soil a chance to revitalize itself.

Mudd's chef, Jonathan Winslow, had known both Kerry and Virginia for a long time before he joined them at the restaurant. A self-taught chef who learned to cook from his Southern mother and sister, Winslow says the menu at Mudd's has been influenced by what he calls "new international" cooking. But the garden still dictates what's on the menu. "When you have everything growing outside, you don't use what's out of season," he says. Each day he wanders around the garden to see which foods are at their peak and which herbs will provide the seasoning. "I think of tastes. I pinch and smell the herbs as I walk around, then I work out what goes with what," says Jonathan. Menu specials are typed up each day after this walk. The masses of lavender growing in the garden were a challenge. "I wanted to use it so much," he confesses, "but lavender has such a strong, distinctive flavor, it must be handled with almost the same care as rosemary."

Kerry Marshall gathers nasturtiums from the organic herb garden, *opposite,* **to garnish the scallops,** *above.*

GRILLED SEA SCALLOP SALAD WITH NASTURTIUMS

At Mudd's, herbs and flowers are used freely as garnishes. They find the peppery flavor of nasturtium leaves and flowers a good substitute for watercress, which can't be grown in the restaurant garden.

This recipe uses the feet of the scallops, the tiny muscles that attach them to the shell, in the sauce. If you are buying shelled scallops, ask your fishmonger to include the feet if possible. If you cannot get feet, omit this ingredient.

20 sea scallops, with feet if possible

⅓ cup minced shallots

1 cup (2 sticks) unsalted butter, cut into small pieces

¼ cup dry white wine

2 tablespoons Champagne vinegar

¼ cup fish stock (page 23)

2 tablespoons fresh lemon juice

3 tablespoons chopped nasturtium flowers

1 tablespoon minced fresh Italian parsley

Salt and white pepper

½ cup olive oil

3 tablespoons white wine vinegar

6 cups assorted greens (oak leaf, arugula, dandelion greens, Marvel 4 Seasons, nasturtium leaves, etc.)

Nasturtium blossoms, for garnish

A prostrate rosemary plant hangs outside the restaurant.

❦

Remove feet from scallops and reserve for the sauce. Set scallops and feet aside.

Reserve 1 tablespoon of shallots for the dressing. Sweat the remaining shallots in 1 tablespoon of the butter over low heat until soft. Add the wine, Champagne vinegar, stock, and lemon juice. Reduce over high heat until just 2 or 3 tablespoons remain. Remove from the heat and whisk in the remaining butter bit by bit. Strain the sauce through a fine sieve and return to pan. Stir in the chopped nasturtiums, parsley, and scallop feet; season to taste with salt and white pepper. Keep warm.

Light a charcoal fire in the grill or preheat the broiler. The fire in the grill is ready when the coals are covered with a fine white ash. Coat the grill or broiler pan with vegetable oil to keep the scallops from sticking. Soak four 6-inch-long bamboo skewers in water for 10 minutes.

Thread 5 scallops on each skewer. Brush with 2 tablespoons of olive oil and grill over coals or in the preheated broiler for 1 or 2 minutes per side, depending on their thickness.

Make a vinaigrette with the remaining 6 tablespoons of olive oil and the vinegar. Toss the greens with the reserved 1 tablespoon of shallots and the vinaigrette. Divide them among four dinner plates, top each with a skewer of grilled scallops, and nap with the sauce. Garnish with additional nasturtium blossoms.

SERVES 4

❦

Fresh sorrel is an unexpected addition to this colorful pasta.

PASTA WITH FRESH SORREL AND FETA

The tartness of sorrel balances the creamy feta cheese in this recipe. Using extra-virgin olive oil and unsalted butter instead of cream allows the individual flavors to shine.

½ cup plus 2 tablespoons extra-virgin olive oil

2 garlic cloves, minced

¼ cup minced shallots

16 baby zucchini with blossoms attached if possible

24 *haricots verts* (thin green beans)

2 cups vegetable stock

¾ cup good-quality dry white wine

½ cup fresh corn kernels

4 tomatoes, peeled, seeded, and quartered

4 tablespoons (½ stick) unsalted butter

1 pound fresh tagliatelli or fettucine

1 cup crumbled feta cheese

Salt and freshly ground pepper

¾ cup julienned sorrel, loosely packed

Parmesan cheese

Fill a large pot with water and add 2 tablespoons of olive oil. Bring to a boil.

Heat the remaining ½ cup olive oil in a sauté pan over moderate heat. Add the garlic and shallots, and cook for 1 minute without browning. Add the zucchini and beans, and sauté for a few seconds, then remove vegetables and deglaze the pan with the stock and wine. Reduce by a third over high heat, about 3 to 4 minutes, then add the corn, tomatoes, and butter and continue cooking for another minute.

Meanwhile, cook the pasta in the boiling water until it is just al dente, 2 to 3 minutes. Drain. Place the pasta in a large serving bowl along with the feta. Add the vegetables and toss together. Correct the seasoning and add the sorrel. Sprinkle grated or shaved Parmesan over the top and serve immediately.

SERVES 4

GRILLED SALMON WITH LAVENDER BUTTER SAUCE

This sauce is equally good with broiled or poached salmon. It can be prepared slightly ahead and kept warm in a bain-marie. Don't add the lavender until just before serving or the flavor will be too strong, although the fresher the lavender, the milder its flavor and the more you can use. If you prefer a lighter sauce, use less butter, as indicated.

SAUCE

1 cup (2 sticks) unsalted butter, cut into small pieces

⅓ cup minced shallots

¼ cup dry white wine

¼ cup Champagne vinegar

¼ cup fish stock (recipe follows), or 2 tablespoons each clam juice and water

2 to 4 lavender flower heads, chopped

Salt and white pepper to taste

4 salmon fillets, about 6 ounces each

Olive oil

In a saucepan, melt 1 tablespoon of the butter over low heat. Add the shallots and sweat until soft. Add the wine, vinegar, stock, and half the lavender. Raise heat to high, and cook until liquid is reduced to 2 or 3 tablespoons. Remove from the heat and whisk in the remaining butter bit by bit. (Depending on your taste, you may not want to add all the butter.) Strain the sauce through a fine sieve; add the remaining lavender. Season to taste with salt and pepper. Keep warm.

Prepare a fire in the grill. When the coals are covered with a fine white ash the fire is ready. Rub the salmon fillets with a little olive oil and place on the grill. Cook, basting occasionally with olive oil, approximately 3 to 5 minutes per side. The fish should be firm but not dry. Serve with the sauce on the side.

Prepare the stock in a large sauté pan. Heat the oil and add the vegetables and herbs. Sauté over medium heat, sweating the vegetables, for 10 minutes. Add the fish and sauté for another 10 minutes. Pour in water to cover (approximately 5 cups) and season to taste. Bring to a boil, reduce heat, and cook slowly for 20 minutes. Strain.

SERVES 4

❦

The taste of lavender pairs perfectly with salmon, but its strong, distinctive flavor must be used judiciously.

FISH STOCK

2 pounds of bones and heads from non-oily fish, gills removed

6 cups water

½ cup *each* chopped leek, onion, and celery

3 or 4 sprigs each fresh parsley, chervil, and fennel leaves

1 cup dry white wine

Place the fish bones and water in a stock pot and bring to a boil over medium-high heat. Reduce heat to a simmer, skimming off any foam. Add the remaining ingredients and simmer gently, covered, for 20 minutes. Strain through dampened cheesecloth; discard solids.

MAKES 6 CUPS

ITALIAN CUISINE, CALIFORNIA STYLE

A deep love of Italian food started the friendship between Evan Kleiman and Viana La Place. Both had traveled in Italy and been impressed by the beauty, variety, and freshness of the produce in the colorful markets as well as the simple preparations that turned this glorious produce into delicious, satisfying dishes. By the time they met while working in the kitchen of Mangia, Los Angeles's first Tuscan restaurant, both were committed to nurturing others with their own interpretation of Italian food.

Evan and Viana wanted to bring the freshness and simplicity of the food they'd encountered in the Italian countryside to Los Angeles, lightening it to reflect today's tastes without losing any of the flavor. "You have to be true to the food," says Evan. "Respect the traditional ways, but adapt them to what you have and to your lifestyle."

This philosophy shaped their first cookbook, *Cucina Fresca*, which focused on recipes meant to be eaten cold or at room temperature. "Cooking this way avoids last-minute rushing about, so entertaining can be relaxing and fun," they point out. Although Evan is now chef-owner of Angeli, and Viana has left restaurant work to teach and write about food full time, they are collaborating on a second book about pasta.

In the restaurant and at home, Evan and Viana prefer fresh herbs because "you can use them abundantly and they don't become overpowering. Once you become familiar with herbs, your sense of taste will tell you how much to use," they advise. "We like to compare herbs to perfume," Viana says. "Their flavor goes right into the food itself. Sauces, on the other hand, are more like clothes, covering the food up."

❦

Serve these pickled vegetables, *left*, with crusty bread as an appetizer or a simple lunch. Pickled radicchio, *opposite*, is an interesting variation on the traditional pickled vegetables so popular in Italy. Serve it with boiled meats.

VERDURE ALL'OLIO E LIMONE

Any combination of vegetables such as carrots, cauliflower, onions, and peppers can be used instead of the artichokes, mushrooms, and onions here. If you prefer, you can substitute thyme for the rosemary.

1 pound small fresh mushrooms

2 pounds baby artichokes, trimmed

½ pound pearl onions, peeled

Coarse salt

3½ cups water

Juice of 2 to 3 lemons

½ cup extra-virgin olive oil

Few sprigs of fresh rosemary and Italian parsley

4 bay leaves

1 celery stalk, cut in half

8 to 10 black peppercorns

Small handful of black olives

Bring a large saucepan of salted water to a boil. Wipe the mushrooms with a damp towel and trim. Lightly cook the mushrooms, artichokes, and onions *separately* in the boiling water until tender-crisp.

Meanwhile, in a saucepan combine the water, lemon juice, olive oil, 1 sprig of rosemary and all the parsley, bay leaves, celery, and peppercorns. Bring to a boil, then reduce heat and simmer for about 20 minutes. Place the cooked vegetables, along with the olives and one or two sprigs of rosemary in a large glass jar. Pour the marinade over to cover the vegetables. Let cool, then refrigerate for several days or up to 2 weeks. Before serving, bring back to room temperature and remove vegetables from the marinade. Adjust seasonings, adding salt to taste.

SERVES 6

RADICCHIO SOTT'ACETO

12 heads radicchio, cut in half lengthwise

Coarse salt

2 tablespoons sugar

2 bay leaves

3 sprigs fresh rosemary

4 black peppercorns

¼ cup extra-virgin olive oil

1 quart white wine vinegar

Carefully wash the radicchio, discarding any loose, discolored, or limp outer leaves. Discard any heads that are soft and black in the center. Add salt, sugar, bay leaves, 1 sprig of rosemary, peppercorns, oil, and 1 cup of the vinegar to a stockpot full of water. Bring the water to a rolling boil, then blanch the radicchio in the boiling water for 1 minute. Quickly drain the vegetable and let it dry and cool on a clean dish towel; the red radicchio will have changed color to a silvery lavender.

When the blanched radicchio heads are completely cool, place them in a large sterilized glass jar or other glass container with a tight seal. Cover the radicchio with the remaining vinegar, and add the remaining rosemary sprigs for decoration. Let the radicchio mellow for at least 15 days before serving.

SERVES 12

The Southwest

Crunchy tacos and soft burritos, chunky guacamole and piquant salsas, pungent chiles and fresh green cilantro—the zesty flavors and textures of Tex-Mex cookery have typified Southwestern cooking for most of us over the years. But the authentic cooking of this rugged region is far more diverse, a complex mix influenced by the native Indians as well as the Spaniards and Mexicans who settled the land.

The Pueblo Indians, whose cuisine has changed little since prehistoric times, cultivated corn, squash, pumpkins, and beans. They roamed the mesas hunting deer, buffalo, rabbits, quail, and other small animals or foraged for wild herbs, seeds, fruits from the prickly pear cactus, and the nuts that nestled in the cones of the Piñon pine. Though

Kathy Kagel's chorizo burrito is served with both green and red chile sauces.

many of the herbs were used medicinally, wild oregano, wild mint, chamisa (a plant resembling sagebrush and also known as four-winged saltbush), and endless varieties of sage added flavor to their humble meals. It was common practice to burn the herbs, particularly juniper and chamisa, and add the mineral-filled ashes to food.

With the arrival of the Spanish and Mexicans, the indispensable chile peppers, tortillas, wheat, and rice, as well as beef, lamb, chicken, and pork were introduced to the

Southwest. Spanish missionaries planted orchards and vineyards. Slowly all these elements were blended into a single, indigenous regional cuisine.

Today many people are concerned with preserving authentic Southwestern cookery. Mark Miller of the Coyote Cafe is doing what he calls "culinary archeology"—researching foods, cooking methods, and their place in the culture of native Americans. "Unfortunately," he says, "male explorers weren't interested in the culinary tradition of the lands they explored." Miller is fascinated by the complexity and sophistication of this cuisine. The Indians were dependent on the seasons: wild foods had to be gathered when they were available; crops were harvested when they were ripe and preserved for the year ahead. And certain foods were important to religious ceremonies: blue cornmeal represented the sky, for example, and to keep it blue during cooking, a broth made from highly alkaline chamisa ashes was added to the pot.

Miller and others seek to protect the region's culinary heritage, using their knowledge as a starting point for a new level of Southwestern cooking. In their capable hands, indigenous ingredients appear in unexpected guises: grilled venison chops, recalling the smoky flavor of a spit-roasted deer, are served with a sauce of goat cheese and herb ashes; pasta is flavored with chile, then sauced with a cilantro pesto. The result is an exciting new chapter in Southwestern cooking that acknowledges its roots while exploring modern cooking methods and tastes.

At Santa Fe's Coyote Cafe, jalapeño-flavored tequila sits on the bar waiting for those brave enough to take a fiery sip.

Brad Brown transforms Spanish sangría and Mexican chocolate into cooling finales at Cafe Pasqual's.

A SONORAN LEGACY

In 1854, the United States acquired part of the northern Mexican state of Sonora through the Gadsden Purchase, including the area where Emojean Jordan Buechner's grandparents lived. When her grandfather found himself in U.S. territory, he moved south to Mexico, but Emojean's great-grandmother, grandmother, and mother—and their knowledge of Sonoran cooking—remained behind.

The cooking of old Sonora is simple and flavorful, based on inexpensive and easily prepared foods. Flour tortillas are often used in place of the corn variety because Sonora is Mexican wheat country. Produce was difficult to grow and the people were poor, so nothing was wasted. Wild plants like cactus and purslane were foraged to augment staples such as beans and corn, and foods were seasoned with cilantro, oregano, garlic, cumin, and mint. As chiles came to the United States from Mexico, they became part of the Sonoran cuisine, too.

Even though Emojean grew up in Arizona, her roots are in Sonora. "I learned about Sonoran cooking in my mother's kitchen," she recalls, and many of those recipes had been transmitted verbally from generation to generation. "Traditional Sonoran recipes are the inspiration for much Southwestern cooking, but they are relatively unknown because they were never written down," she says.

To ensure that this heritage wasn't lost, Emojean collected the recipes in a book called *Mexican Cooking Sonoran Style*. She started with recipes handed down from her great-grandmother and friends, then added more gathered on visits to longtime residents of Sonora. The recipe for shrimp cakes that follows is one she remembers from her childhood, and is a favorite of friends in New Orleans, where she now lives.

TORTA DE CAMERON CON CHILE COLORADO

(Shrimp Cakes in Red Chile Sauce)

The simplicity with which this dish is prepared and its unassuming look belie its delicious flavor and intriguing textures. Traditionally a fiery red chile sauce surrounds the shrimp cakes, but Emojean also often serves an alternative sauce made from milder green chiles (page 55).

- 12 to 14 medium raw shrimp, shelled and deveined
- 2 scallions (white and green parts), finely chopped
- 1 tablespoon finely chopped fresh cilantro

  Salt and pepper
- 3 eggs, separated
- 3 tablespoons flour
- 2 tablespoons vegetable oil
- 2½ cups Basic Red Chile Sauce (recipe follows)
- 2 garlic cloves, finely chopped
- ½ teaspoon cider or white wine vinegar

Process the shrimp very carefully in a food processor for 4 to 5 seconds, scraping down the sides of the bowl. When fairly smooth, transfer to a medium bowl and mix with scallions, cilantro, and salt and pepper to taste.

In a deep bowl, beat the egg whites until soft peaks form. One at a time, add the yolks, beating after each addition. Carefully fold in the flour, then the shrimp mixture.

In a small skillet, heat the oil over medium-high heat. When it is hot, drop spoonfuls of the batter into the skillet and brown slightly, about 3 minutes on each side. As they brown, remove cakes from skillet and drain on paper towels.

Meanwhile, warm the Basic Red Chile Sauce in a medium saucepan over low heat; season with garlic and vinegar. When the cakes are all browned, carefully place them in the hot chile sauce. Simmer over low heat for 12 to 15 minutes, then serve.

SERVES 4 GENEROUSLY

Mexican pottery reflects the rustic simplicity of Sonoran shrimp cakes, *left*. A cluster of Castilian roses, *right*, growing in front of an old Santa Fe bench.

BASIC RED CHILE SAUCE

For a spicy sauce, use 1 New Mexico and 7 California chiles. Eliminate the New Mexico chile for a milder sauce. The sauce will keep in the refrigerator, tightly covered, for about 5 days, or it can be frozen for 2 to 3 months.

- 8 dried red chiles
- 4 cups water
- 2 tablespoons flour
- 2 tablespoons vegetable oil
- 2 to 3 large garlic cloves, finely chopped

  Pinch of dried oregano or 1 teaspoon fresh
- 1 teaspoon cider or white wine vinegar

Wearing gloves, use a small knife to remove chile stems and seeds, then wash the chiles well. Place in a saucepan with the water and bring to a boil over high heat; boil for 5 minutes, then allow to sit for 10 to 15 minutes. Whirl the water and chiles in a food processor or blender, in batches if necessary, for 20 to 30 seconds, or until the skins are finely chopped. Pass through a strainer, pressing the chile pieces through with a wooden spoon.

In a medium skillet, make a roux by combining the flour and oil. Sauté over low heat for 2 minutes, then add the garlic, chile mixture, oregano, and vinegar. Stir well and simmer for 15 to 20 minutes.

MAKES APPROXIMATELY
4 CUPS

A VISUAL TREAT

"Cooking is a creative endeavor; it exercises the senses of smell, taste, and sight," says Nancy Bloch, a professional weaver whose Santa Fe shop is filled with clothes in a glorious mix of colors and patterns. Nancy's eye for color and form, developed at the loom, enables her to select serving dishes that complement the food she prepares. "Food has to look absolutely wonderful," she says. "I'm unhappy when the food and the plates are not visually harmonic."

Nancy wasn't allowed in the kitchen as a child, but decided to learn to cook when she married a man who liked to eat well. "You need an appreciative audience to become a good cook," she says. A native Easterner, Nancy honed her cooking skills in California before moving to Santa Fe about six years ago. Since then the tastes of the Southwest have seeped into her cooking. "The herbs and spices are great," she enthuses. "They go a long way in making food really interesting, even low-calorie cooking, and you need less salt."

Frequently Nancy doubles or triples the quantities of herbs called for in a recipe or substitutes one herb for another. "You need to experiment," she advises. "Herbs in a recipe can be interchanged for interest and excitement. When you grow your own, just use what's best at the moment as long as the tastes are compatible. Herbs look wonderful as garnish, too," she adds. "When you think visually, that's very important."

Lunch is served on the
flower-banked patio, with
its carved California redwood chairs.

SANTA FE CHICKEN ROLL

Have your butcher bone the chicken, keeping the skin intact.

- ½ pound chorizo in bulk
- ⅓ cup bread crumbs
- ¼ cup chopped fresh cilantro
- 2 tablespoons fresh oregano
  Salt and pepper
- 4 to 5 large mild canned chiles
- 4 to 5-pound roasting chicken, boned
- 10 pitted black olives, sliced
- 2 slices bacon

Preheat the oven to 350°F.

Sauté the chorizo gently for 10 minutes. Pour off the fat.

Mix the bread crumbs with the cilantro, oregano, and salt and pepper to taste. Slit the chiles; remove the seeds and veins.

Place the chicken, skin side down, on a work surface. Spread the chorizo over the chicken, leaving a 1-inch border down one side. Layer the chiles over the chorizo, then the herbed bread crumbs, and finally the sliced olives. Starting with the side away from the border, roll the chicken jelly-roll fashion toward the border. Tie the roll in as many places as necessary to keep the filling from coming out. Place the roll in a roasting pan with the bacon on top. Bake for 50 minutes, basting occasionally. Remove the bacon, increase oven temperature to 425°F. and bake 10 to 15 minutes longer, or until golden brown. Cool and refrigerate. To serve, remove the strings and slice carefully.

SERVES 4 TO 6

ENSALADA DE TRES FRIJOLES

- ¼ cup small dried lima beans
- ¼ cup dried black beans
- ¼ cup dried red lentils
- 2 onions, chopped
- 6 vegetable bouillon cubes
- ½ cup vinaigrette
- 1 red bell pepper, seeded and chopped
- ¼ cup chopped fresh tricolor sage
  Salt and freshly ground pepper

Keeping the beans separate, wash them well and discard any debris. Put each type of bean in a separate pot and add one-third of the chopped onions and 2 bouillon cubes to each pot. Add enough water to cover the beans by 2 inches; cook until tender but not mushy. The red lentils will cook in about 20 minutes; both the lima and black beans will take from 1½ to 2½ hours.

When the beans are done, drain and combine them with the red pepper in a large bowl. Stir in the vinaigrette while the beans are still warm, then allow to cool to room temperature. When cool, add the red pepper, chopped sage, and salt and pepper to taste; toss to blend.

SERVES 4 TO 6

A collection of majolica and an old painted cupboard enhance this simple buffet of white gazpacho and Old Pecos cornmeal muffins.

❧

GAZPACHO BLANCO

White Gazpacho

2 to 3 European seedless cucumbers, peeled and chopped

3 garlic cloves, minced

3 cups chicken stock

2 tablespoons mild vinegar or lime juice

2 cups buttermilk

¼ cup chopped scallions

¼ cup chopped fresh dill
   Chive flowers, for garnish

In a large bowl, combine the cucumbers, garlic, stock, vinegar or lime juice, buttermilk, scallions, and dill. Cover and chill in the refrigerator overnight to allow flavors to mellow. Stir the soup thoroughly and garnish with chive flowers before serving.

SERVES 4

OLD PECOS CORNMEAL MUFFINS

For more variety, stir 1 tablespoon of chopped black olives into half the batter in place of the chiles. The batter can also be cooked in an 8-inch tart pan to make a breakfast "tart." Nancy Bloch sprinkles the top with ground pepitas (pumpkin seeds) before baking. This recipe is for high altitudes such as Santa Fe. At lower altitudes, use ¼ cup less flour and cook about 5 minutes longer.

2 eggs, beaten

1 cup sour cream

½ cup (1 stick) butter, melted

1 cup canned creamed corn

1 tablespoon tequila

1 cup all-purpose flour

½ cup yellow cornmeal

2 teaspoons baking powder

½ teaspoon baking soda

1½ teaspoons salt

4 ounces cheddar cheese, grated

1 tablespoon chopped green chile

Preheat the oven to 400°F. Generously grease muffin tins.

In a large bowl, mix the beaten eggs, sour cream, melted butter, creamed corn, and tequila. In a separate bowl, mix the flour, cornmeal, baking powder, baking soda, and salt. Stir the dry mixture into the egg and cream mixture, mixing until just combined. Stir in the cheese and the chiles. Pour the batter into the prepared pans. Bake until the muffins spring back when you touch them and are golden, about 15 minutes.

MAKES 20 MUFFINS OR ONE 8-INCH TART PLUS 12 MUFFINS

CHOCOLATE MINT GLACÉ

The chocolate—mint leaf garnish in this recipe could also be used with ice cream, on cakes, or other desserts.

½ cup minced fresh mint leaves

1 cup heavy cream

4 egg whites

⅛ teaspoon cream of tartar

⅛ teaspoon salt

5 tablespoons sugar

1 tablespoon vanilla extract

2 tablespoons green crème de menthe

Few drops of green food coloring (optional)

3 ounces semisweet chocolate

Chocolate Mint Leaves, for garnish (recipe follows)

Combine ¼ cup of the mint leaves with the cream in a small bowl and refrigerate overnight. (If you are in a hurry, you can heat the cream, pour it over the leaves, and let stand, covered, until cool.) Chill and strain.

Beat the egg whites until foamy; add cream of tartar and salt, beating continually. As soft peaks form, add 4 tablespoons of the sugar, 1 tablespoon at a time. Beat until stiff and glossy.

In another bowl, beat together the mint-flavored cream, remaining tablespoon of sugar, vanilla, crème de menthe, and green coloring, if you are using it, until stiff. Fold the whipped cream into the egg-white mixture and place the bowl in the freezer for 2 to 3 hours or until ice crystals form.

Melt the chocolate over barely simmering water and quickly fold it into the partially frozen mixture. The chocolate will harden immediately. Fold in the remaining minced mint. Return the glacé to the freezer until serving time. If the glacé is frozen solid, remove it from the freezer 10 to 15 minutes before serving. Garnish with chocolate mint leaves.

SERVES 4 TO 6

CHOCOLATE MINT LEAVES

1 ounce semisweet chocolate

12 large fresh mint leaves

In a small, heavy pot, slowly melt the chocolate over low heat. Smooth the chocolate onto the face of the mint leaves with the flat side of a knife. Place the leaves on waxed paper, green side down, in the refrigerator. When the chocolate has hardened, carefully peel the chocolate leaves off the mint leaves and discard the mint leaves. Refrigerate the chocolate leaves until serving time.

Both fresh and chocolate mint leaves are used to garnish this refreshing frozen mint dessert.

THE FLAVOR OF NEW MEXICO

Mark Miller's approach to food is both intellectual and sensual. An anthropologist manqué, Mark's interest in ethnic cultures and cuisines finds an outlet in cooking. The intensity of tastes and unexpected mix of flavors of ethnic foods intrigue him, and once he's defined a culture's "flavor chords," he uses these basic tastes with other dishes and cooking methods. Intensity and complexity of flavor is also one of the reasons Mark Miller is so interested in herbs. "Mint, for example is both hot and sweet," he explains.

Before coming to Santa Fe, Mark had already explored the flavors of the Southwest at his Santa Fe Bar and Grill in Berkeley. He describes New Mexico's flavor as "a red bricky earthiness that comes from dried chiles and dry-roasted garlic; a hotness and sweetness from chiles; a hint of the desert from thyme, sage, and mesquite; a wild aridness from smoked herbs and wood grilling; and a smoky mellow sweetness and hotness from wild roasted oregano." Yet despite the intellectual curiosity behind his recipes, Mark Miller doesn't like pretentious food. "My requisite is that food be good enough and real enough to be enjoyed every day," he says.

Reed Hearon, a chef at Coyote Cafe, is a perfect match for Miller. A former student of philosophy and mathematics, Reed chose a food career because "both cooking and mathematics have the same harmonics, but more people can relate to and share those of food."

A Texan, Reed grew up with Southwestern food, but notes "there's a big difference between the cooking of New Mexico and Texas. Here in New Mexico there is much more cultural influence from the native American." In developing a recipe he works toward a combination of two to three readily perceived flavors. The very sweet flavor of scallops, for example, might play against the sweet, acid, hot herb flavor common to all salsas. Reed says "food should be real and honest but refreshing and intriguing, a mixture of new and old."

ᐱᐱ

Local fruits, vegetables, and herbs piled high on a platter welcome guests to the Coyote Cafe.

Pineapple, rather than the traditional tomato, is the base of this refreshing salsa that complements simply grilled scallops.

✁✁

GRILLED SCALLOPS WITH PINEAPPLE SALSA

If you do not have a grill, cook the scallops under the broiler for the same length of time. You will lose the taste subtleties of the wood smoke, but the scallops will still be delicious. Epazote is a favorite Mexican herb. It grows wild in many parts of the United States, can be grown from seed, and is found in markets specializing in Mexican foods. There is no substitute for its exotic taste, so if you cannot find any, omit it from the salsa.

PINEAPPLE SALSA

½ cup very ripe pineapple, cored and cut into ¼-inch dice

1 teaspoon lime juice, preferably Key lime

2 tablespoons minced red bell pepper

1 tablespoon minced fresh serrano chile

1 teaspoon minced fresh cilantro

½ teaspoon minced fresh mint

½ teaspoon minced fresh epazote, or a pinch of dried

¾ pound jumbo sea scallops, ¾ to 1 inch thick

1 tablespoon hazelnut oil

Prepare a fire in the grill using apple or pecan wood. While the coals are burning down, combine the salsa ingredients in a small bowl. When the flames in the grill have died down and the heat is medium low, brush the scallops with hazelnut oil and grill until medium rare, approximately 2 minutes per side.

To serve, place half the salsa in the center of each plate and arrange half the scallops in a circle around it.

SERVES 2

GRILLED VENISON CHOPS WITH GOAT CHEESE AND HERB ASH

Garlic chives can be substituted for the wild garlic tops.

3 sprigs wild garlic tops

3 fresh sage leaves

1 teaspoon fresh lavender buds

1 sprig fresh rosemary

2 sprigs fresh thyme

2 venison chops cut from a center loin, 2 inches thick (about 8 ounces each)

6 tablespoons heavy cream

2 tablespoons crème fraîche

4 ounces fresh goat cheese (chèvre)

Cracked black pepper

To make herb ashes, place the garlic tops, sage leaves, lavender buds, rosemary, and thyme in a dry, heavy saucepan with a tight-fitting lid. Cook over medium heat for 20 minutes without raising the lid. Still without lifting the lid, set saucepan aside to cool, about 30 minutes.

Meanwhile, light a mesquite fire or preheat the broiler, and grill the venison chops over medium-low heat until rare to medium rare, about 6 minutes per side. If possible, throw a juniper or cedar bough on the fire at the last minute and let it burn under the meat to impart a subtle flavoring.

Combine the cream and crème fraîche in a small saucepan and warm over low heat; whisk in goat cheese until smooth. Transfer the herb ashes to a spice mill or food processor (or use a mortar and pestle), and reduce to a powder. Whisk 1 tablespoon (or to taste) of ashes into the goat cheese crème.

To serve, place a venison chop on each plate, spoon half the crème around each chop, and finish with freshly cracked black pepper to taste.

SERVES 2

GRILLED HALIBUT WITH GREEN CHILE SALSA

2 pieces California halibut, approximately 1½ inches thick (7 to 8 ounces each)

2 tablespoons extra-virgin olive oil

GREEN CHILE SALSA

1 garlic clove

1 Anaheim chile, roasted, peeled, and seeded (page 46)

1 poblano chile, roasted, peeled, and seeded

1 red bell pepper, roasted, peeled, and seeded

1 yellow bell pepper, roasted, peeled, and seeded

2 tablespoons extra-virgin olive oil

1 teaspoon minced fresh marjoram

1 teaspoon minced fresh cilantro

1 teaspoon lime juice

1 teaspoon sherry vinegar

Salt

1 bunch fresh thyme (optional)

Preheat the oven to 350°F.

Brush the halibut pieces with the olive oil. Set aside.

Place the garlic in a small ovenproof pan and roast for 15 minutes, or until skin begins to

❧

The venison chops may be deboned and sliced before serving, then garnished with sage and edible cactus.

Adobe walls contribute to the restaurant's Southwestern atmosphere.

❧

color. Cool, peel, and mince. Chop the chiles and peppers into ¼-inch dice. In a bowl, combine the oil, chiles, peppers, garlic, herbs, lime juice, vinegar, and salt to taste. Set aside.

Build a fire in the grill using pecan wood or preheat the broiler. When the fire is medium hot, grill the halibut for about 3 minutes on each side, or until just cooked but still milky inside. One minute before removing the fish from the grill, add a large handful of thyme to the fire to add extra flavor. To serve, place each piece of halibut in the center of a plate and spoon half the sauce around it.

SERVES 2

A sophisticated, herb-laden version of the ordinary tamale is served with chile sauce and an icy glass of beer.

❦

Add the dried shrimp, roasted garlic, and toasted oregano. Simmer over very low heat for 30 minutes. Do not let the mixture brown. Strain through a fine sieve, reserving the butter and the shrimp mixture separately.

Clean and peel the fresh shrimp, reserving the shells. Set aside in a cool place.

In a small nonaluminum saucepan, combine the reserved shrimp from the shrimp butter, the reserved shrimp shells, the fish stock, and the bunch of cilantro. Cook over very low heat for 30 minutes. Strain through a fine sieve, pushing hard on ingredients to extract all the liquid. Reserve stock and keep warm; discard solids.

In a medium bowl, whip the cooled shrimp butter until fluffy. In a separate bowl, add the hot shrimp stock to the masa harina, stirring with a wooden spoon until it is smooth and slightly fluffy. Cool to room temperature. When cool, beat the masa, bit by bit, into the shrimp butter; continue beating until the mixture becomes very fluffy and aerated. Beat in the sea salt, ground chile, fresh herbs, and baking powder.

To make the green mole, grind the tomatillos, pine nuts, cilantro, chile, sorrel, and arugula into a paste or purée in a blender. Season with salt and anise seed.

SHRIMP TAMALE

Dried shrimp can be found in Mexican, Chinese, and Japanese groceries or gourmet shops. The ground mild chile should be available where Mexican foods are sold, or substitute paprika. If fish stock is unavailable, use a half-and-half mixture of clam juice and water.

SHRIMP BUTTER
2 teaspoons oregano, preferably Mexican

¾ cup (1½ sticks) unsalted butter

4 ounces dried Mexican shrimp

3 garlic cloves, roasted (page 39)

24 fresh large shrimp

1¼ cups shellfish or fish stock

1 bunch fresh cilantro

2 cups masa harina

½ teaspoon sea salt

2 teaspoons ground mild chimayo chile

6 tablespoons minced fresh cilantro

3 tablespoons minced fresh marjoram

2 tablespoons minced fresh mint

½ teaspoon baking powder

GREEN MOLE
4 fresh tomatillos, husked and cooked on a cast-iron griddle or skillet until blackened

3 tablespoons toasted pine nuts (page 50)

12 sprigs fresh cilantro

2 tablespoons roasted, peeled, and diced poblano chile (page 46)

2 sorrel leaves

2 arugula leaves

Pinch of salt

Pinch of ground toasted anise seed

12 large dried corn husks, soaked in hot water until pliable

24 leaves baby mustard or similar greens

Red Chile Sauce (page 31), optional

To make the shrimp butter, place the oregano in a small skillet over medium heat and cook, shaking the pan frequently, until it is lightly toasted, 2 to 3 minutes. Melt the butter in a small skillet over medium heat.

To assemble the tamales, place 1 corn husk on a work surface. Starting at the lower left-hand corner, spread approximately ⅓ cup of masa mixture over the corn husk to form a rectangle 4 inches at the base and 5 inches in height. (The top 2 inches should be left uncovered.) Place 2 leaves of baby mustard greens in the center of the rectangle; top with 1 teaspoon of green mole. Place 2 peeled shrimp on top of the mole and fold the corn husk over, rolling from left to right to form a cylinder. Fold the top of the husk over like an envelope flap toward the tamale. Repeat with remaining 11 corn husks.

Place the finished tamales in a single layer in a Chinese steamer. Steam over medium-high heat for 20 to 25 minutes. Turn the heat off; let tamales sit in the covered steamer for an additional 15 minutes before serving. Serve with Red Chile Sauce, if desired.

SERVES 12 AS AN APPETIZER

Underneath the crackling caramelized crust, a light touch of mint comes as a refreshing surprise in this rich crème brûlée.

MINT CRÈME BRÛLÉE

4 cups mint leaves, loosely packed

3 cups heavy cream

½ cup plus 6 tablespoons sugar

7 egg yolks

2 tablespoons green crème de menthe

Fresh mint leaves, for garnish

Place the mint leaves and cream in a food processor and pulse briefly until the leaves are just crushed. In a saucepan over medium heat, scald the cream mixture. Remove from the heat and let steep 30 minutes. Strain through a fine sieve, pressing well to extract all the liquid.

In a bowl, beat ½ cup of the sugar and the egg yolks together until they form a ribbon when dropped from the beater. Place the mint cream in the top of a double boiler and scald; whisk it into the egg-yolk mixture. Return the mixture to the double boiler and cook over hot water, whisking constantly, until the custard is thick. Strain into a bowl and cool slightly. Whisk in the crème de menthe. Divide the crème equally among six individual ramekins; refrigerate until cold and set, about 6 hours or overnight.

Just before serving, preheat the broiler. Dust the top of each crème brûlée with 1 tablespoon of sugar. Place under a hot broiler for 1 to 3 minutes, or until the sugar caramelizes. Let cool slightly and garnish before serving.

SERVES 6

PASTA, SANTA FE STYLE

Theo Raven's family history has been entwined with that of Santa Fe since 1928, when her mother came west as a governess for the granddaughter of Mabel Dodge, the well-known patron of the arts who married a Taos Indian. Theo's mother was soon joined by her parents, with whom she set up a homestead in Tesuque just north of the town.

It was in that kitchen, a family gathering spot, that Theo first learned about cooking and about chiles. Her mother and grandmother, originally from Germany, were influenced by the flavors of the Southwest, and Theo fondly remembers her grandmother putting red chiles in the turkey stuffing.

Since she loved to cook, it wasn't surprising that Theo's first job was waiting tables in a small Santa Fe restaurant. As she scurried from table to table, she noticed two young women who spent most of their day sitting in front of their shop reading. "I thought that was a glorious way to make a living," she confesses. When they offered to sell her the shop, she borrowed the money, made a fast trip to Mexico to stock the shop with wonderful folk art and handcrafts, and launched a new career. Now, thirty years later, the shop is so successful that Theo can't spend much time outside reading, but she still loves to cook. "I like to entertain, too," she says, but generally limits her guest list to two to four people.

She especially enjoys experimenting with various shapes and sizes of pasta, often finding ways to combine them with chiles, especially the milder green ones she particularly likes. One of her favorite recipes is this green chile-stuffed manicotti, which she likes to serve in front of a fire on a cool, starry Santa Fe night.

A blazing fire, old beams, the soft angles of adobe, and a chile-filled manicotti contribute to the welcoming warmth of Theo Raven's house.

MANICOTTI WITH GREEN CHILE AND CHEESE FILLING

Half of the manicotti can be tightly wrapped and frozen before cooking. It will keep in the freezer for up to 3 months.

SAUCE

5¼ pounds ripe tomatoes (seeded and peeled, if desired)

1 medium onion

2 tablespoons olive oil

2 tablespoons or more minced garlic

4 bay leaves

¾ cup chopped fresh basil, or ¼ cup dried

6 tablespoons chopped fresh oregano, or 2 tablespoons dried

Pinch of ground cinnamon

Pinch of sugar

½ cup frozen or canned chopped hot green chiles

Salt

2 cups chopped green bell peppers

½ cup minced fresh parsley, including stems

1 to 2 (6-ounce) cans tomato paste, as needed

1 pound dried manicotti

2 cups (8 ounces) shredded mozzarella cheese

2 cups ricotta cheese

¼ cup grated Parmesan cheese

1 bunch fresh parsley, finely chopped, including stems

½ teaspoon salt

½ teaspoon freshly ground black pepper

14 canned, peeled green chiles

To make the sauce, cut the tomatoes into chunks and purée in a food mill or food processor. Halve the onion. In a large saucepan, warm the oil over medium heat. Add the garlic and cook over low heat until the garlic becomes fragrant and translucent, about 5 minutes. Add the tomato purée, halved onion, bay leaves, dried basil and oregano if using, cinnamon, sugar, chiles, and salt. (If using fresh basil and oregano, do not add until later.) Simmer about 1½ hours, stirring from time to time to prevent the sauce from sticking to bottom of pan. Fifteen minutes before the sauce is done, add the green pepper and fresh herbs, if you are using them. Then thicken sauce with tomato paste to the consistency you prefer. Remove the bay leaves and the onion.

Cook the manicotti according to package directions; drain. Place in a single layer on foil to prevent the tubes from sticking together and set aside to cool.

Preheat the oven to 350°F.

In a large mixing bowl, combine the cheeses, parsley, salt, and pepper until well blended. Slice the chiles in half length-wise and place 1 strip of chile in each pasta shell. Spoon in enough of the cheese mixture to fill each tube.

Spread a thin layer of sauce on the bottoms of 2 pans large enough to hold 14 manicotti each. Arrange the stuffed manicotti in a single layer over the sauce and spoon the remaining sauce over the top. Cover with aluminum foil. Bake for a total of 55 minutes; after 40 minutes, remove the foil and bake 15 minutes uncovered.

SERVES 12

Theo Raven, a native of Santa Fe, still lives in the house where her grandparents homesteaded years ago.

AN ARTIST IN THE KITCHEN

Santa Fe, with its intense light, earthy architecture, vast countryside, and colorful Indian settlements nearby, is a mecca for artists. Mike Fennelly originally moved here from New York to concentrate on his painting, but the lure of the kitchen proved too strong; he is now a chef at Santacafé.

Mike collaborates on Santacafé's menus with owner Jim Bibo, a former architect. The food they serve reflects a California influence in its simple preparation and use of local ingredients. "I like dishes that require a minimum of time and fuss," Mike says. "I think it's very important to present food in its natural form so it looks like what it is." His background as a painter has inspired his presentation. "Mike is really creative," says Jim. "He treats the white space of the plate like an empty canvas."

Incorporating chiles, chamisa, wild sage, and pine nuts into the recipes gives the dishes a decided Southwestern slant. Mike also uses more familiar herbs and vegetables harvested from local gardens during Santa Fe's short growing season or flown in during the winter. Because herbs are used in everything from the brioche to the ice cream at Santacafé, Jim has planted an herb garden in the courtyard of the 160-year-old Spanish adobe building; more herbs grow in the garden behind Jim's house. "Whenever we can, we'll use our own herbs," says Mike. "Somehow, when you've grown them yourself and they come right from the garden to the kitchen, they seem to have more flavor."

**Grilled vegetables make a
light but delicious luncheon.**

GRILLED VEGETABLES WITH SAGE-CILANTRO SAUCE

Make sure the sweet potato and eggplant are sliced very thin so they will cook in the same amount of time as the other vegetables. Rice vinegar, sesame oil, and chili oil can be found in the oriental food section of a supermarket or in an oriental grocery. Extra sauce can be refrigerated for up to 2 weeks.

MARINADE
1 cup olive oil
2 garlic cloves, chopped
1 teaspoon crushed dried red pepper flakes
½ cup Japanese rice vinegar
1 tablespoon chopped fresh chives
1 tablespoon chopped fresh purple basil

2 red bell peppers, seeded and cut in 8 pieces
1 large carrot, peeled and sliced thinly on an angle
1 red onion, cut in 8 pieces
2 Anaheim chiles
2 ears corn, husks pulled back and silk removed
1 eggplant, very thinly sliced
1 bunch scallions, trimmed to about 6 inches long
1 sweet potato, very thinly sliced

SAGE-CILANTRO SAUCE
1 egg plus 2 egg yolks
2½ tablespoons rice vinegar
2½ tablespoons soy sauce
2½ tablespoons Dijon mustard
1 teaspoon finely chopped fresh sage
1 tablespoon finely chopped fresh cilantro
¼ cup sesame oil
1½ cups vegetable oil
⅓ cup olive oil
1 tablespoon chili oil
⅓ cup sesame seeds

2 radicchio leaves
Fresh herbs and flowers, for garnish

Combine the marinade ingredients in a small bowl. Pour over the raw vegetables and marinate for 2 hours.

While the vegetables are marinating, make the sauce. Combine the egg, yolks, vinegar, soy sauce, and mustard in a blender or processor and blend for 1 minute. Add the herbs. With the motor running, drizzle in the sesame oil, then the vegetable oil, and finally the olive oil. Add the chili oil. Process until the sauce has the consistency of mayonnaise. Stir in sesame seeds by hand and refrigerate.

Prepare a charcoal fire or preheat the broiler. When the coals are covered with a fine layer of white ash, grill or broil the vegetables until they are just tender, about 4 minutes per side.

To serve, spoon the sauce into radicchio-leaf cups and place on the side of each plate. Arrange the vegetables around them. Garnish with herbs and flowers if desired. Serve hot or at room temperature.

SERVES 2

CHILE RELLENOS WITH GOAT CHEESE AND SUN-DRIED TOMATOES

The sauce can be made a day ahead and kept in the refrigerator, tightly covered. Refrigerate any extra cheese mixture for future use.

8 poblano chiles
1¾ cups softened goat cheese (chèvre)
¼ cup softened cream cheese
½ teaspoon fresh lemon juice
8 to 10 sun-dried tomatoes packed in oil, drained, and cut into small pieces or strips

SWEET RED PEPPER SAUCE

8 red bell peppers
¼ cup olive oil
½ teaspoon salt
2 to 3 tablespoons sugar
1 tablespoon red wine vinegar

Sear the poblano chiles lightly on the grill or under the broiler until the skins begin to blister, about 5 minutes. The chiles should be tender but not soft. Plunge them into cold water. Carefully peel the chiles and slit them down one side. Remove the seeds. Dry the chiles inside and out with a paper towel, being careful not to tear them.

Mix the goat cheese, cream cheese, and lemon juice with an electric beater or processor until fluffy. Transfer the cheese mixture to a pastry bag and pipe a thick line of cheese down the center of each chile. With a dull knife, make a lengthwise groove in the center of the cheese mixture and fill it with pieces of sun-dried tomato. Close the chiles around the cheese and tomatoes and chill for at least 1 hour.

To make the sauce, grill, peel, and seed the red peppers the same way as the poblanos. Place the red bell peppers in a food processor or blender and process to a smooth purée. With the processor still running, slowly add the remaining ingredients. Pass the sauce through a food mill. If it seems too thick, add 1 or 2 tablespoons of water. Keep refrigerated until serving.

To serve, spoon some red pepper sauce on each plate. With a sharp knife, carefully cut the chiles crosswise into ¾-inch slices. Place on top of the sauce.

NOTE: Chiles contain an oil, particularly in the seeds and veins, that can irritate skin or eyes. Always wear gloves when working with hot chiles, and be sure to keep your hands away from your eyes and face. If you should accidentally touch your face or eyes, wash immediately with clear water.

SERVES 8

A sophisticated version of chiles rellenos is sauced with puréed peppers.

NEW MEXICO PHEASANT SALAD

1 to 1½ cups young arugula or other herbs and greens

4 radicchio leaves

1 smoked pheasant breast, thinly sliced

½ large grapefruit, sectioned

3 hard-cooked quail eggs in their shells

Chive blossoms and edible flowers, for garnish

Southwestern Vinaigrette (recipe follows)

Wash and dry the arugula and radicchio thoroughly. Make a nest of the arugula on one side of the plate; julienne the radicchio and sprinkle over the greens. On the other side of the plate arrange the pheasant slices and grapefruit sections alternately in a fan shape. Place the quail eggs in the center. Garnish the greens with the chive blossoms and flowers. Dress lightly with vinaigrette before serving.

SERVES 1

New Mexican pheasant breast is smoked for the salad.

SOUTHWESTERN VINAIGRETTE

Extra dressing can be refrigerated for future use.

5 tablespoons red wine vinegar

Juice of 1 large lemon

¼ cup sugar

1 cup olive oil

½ cup vegetable oil

8 whole cloves

6 bay leaves

¼ cup toasted pine nuts (page 50)

1 teaspoon dried red pepper flakes

¼ teaspoon powdered chili

Salt and freshly ground pepper

In a bowl, whisk together the vinegar, lemon juice, and sugar. Slowly whisk in the oils, then stir in the cloves, bay leaves, pine nuts, pepper flakes, and chili powder; season to taste. Let dressing sit for several hours or overnight. Remove the bay leaves and cloves before using.

MAKES APPROXIMATELY
2 CUPS

Mike and Jim occasionally cook for friends. *Above and opposite,* chile ravioli and lamb pizza prepared at Forrest Moses' beautiful old adobe house.

꧁

LAMB PIZZA WITH RED CHILE AND MINT

DOUGH
1 cup water

1½ tablespoons honey

2 tablespoons olive oil

1 tablespoon active dry yeast

1 teaspoon salt

3¼ cups all-purpose flour

4 red bell peppers, roasted, peeled, seeded, and chopped (page 46)

2 Anaheim chiles, roasted, peeled, and chopped

1 tablespoon chopped fresh cilantro

1 teaspoon medium-hot ground chile

1 teaspoon chopped fresh sage

1 cup toasted pine nuts (page 50)

½ cup grated Parmesan cheese

½ cup grated Monterey Jack or mozzarella cheese

1 pound grilled rare lamb from the leg, sliced

2 ears corn, husked, blanched, and sliced into ½-inch rings

24 fresh mint leaves

Place the dough ingredients in a food processor or the bowl of an electric mixer and combine for about 5 to 8 minutes, or until the dough is elastic and leaves the sides of the bowl. Form the dough into a ball and place in a greased bowl. Set aside, covered with a damp cloth, until dough has doubled in bulk, 1½ to 2 hours.

While the dough is rising, prepare the ingredients for the topping. Place the peppers, chiles, herbs, and nuts in a processor or blender and chop coarsely. Stir in the cheeses by hand. Set aside. Cut the corn rings in half and cut out the cob, leaving halfmoons of corn.

Preheat the oven to 500°F.

Turn the dough out onto a floured board and punch it down. Knead gently, then divide into 4 parts. Roll each piece of dough into a circle about 7 or 8 inches in diameter. Spoon a layer of the red pepper mixture on top of each pizza and top with the lamb slices and corn, divided equally among the pizzas. Place the pizzas on a pizza stone and bake for about 10 minutes, or until the crust is golden. Arrange 6 mint leaves on each pizza before serving.

MAKES 4 INDIVIDUAL PIZZAS

RED CHILE RAVIOLI FILLED WITH CHORIZO AND CILANTRO

Chorizos are spicy Mexican sausages sold in many supermarkets and ethnic shops. Any uncooked ravioli can be frozen on cookie sheets until firm, then stored in an airtight container. Cook the frozen ravioli, unthawed, for about 10 minutes.

PASTA

5 cups all-purpose flour

3 cups finely ground semolina flour

¾ cup finest ground Anaheim or pasilla chiles

8 eggs, lightly beaten

¼ cup olive oil

½ teaspoon salt

½ cup water

FILLING

10 chorizos

4 Italian sweet sausages

3 red bell peppers, roasted and chopped (page 46)

2 jalapeños, chopped

1 large red onion, chopped

1 bunch fresh cilantro, chopped

3 garlic cloves, chopped

¾ cup grated Monterey Jack cheese

Salt and pepper to taste

¼ cup bread crumbs

2 eggs

¾ cup virgin olive oil

Fresh herbs and edible flowers, for garnish

Place flours and ground chiles in a food processor or on a well-floured board. Add the eggs and begin to process or knead by hand. Add oil, salt, and enough water to produce a moist but not wet dough. Cover the dough and refrigerate for several hours.

Peel the chorizos and sweet sausages. Sauté over medium heat, breaking up the meat as it cooks, until cooked through, about 15 minutes. Drain on paper towels. Place the chorizo, sweet sausage, peppers, onion, cilantro, garlic, cheese, salt and pepper, bread crumbs, and eggs in the bowl of a food processor and combine just until they bind together; do not over-process. Set aside.

Roll the chilled dough through a pasta maker on number 6 setting two times; divide the dough into 4 parts. Roll one section of the dough through the machine again, keeping the remaining dough well wrapped so it does not dry out. Cut a piece of dough the size of a ravioli press, lay it over the press, and press it into the indentations. Fill the pockets with the filling. Cut another section of dough and place on top of the filling. With a rolling pin, roll over the press, sealing and cutting the ravioli. Set the ravioli aside, covered, and repeat with remaining dough and filling, using one section of dough before rolling out the next.

Bring a large pot of water to a boil. Cook the ravioli for about 5 minutes, until pasta is cooked but still firm. Drain and transfer to a warm serving platter. Drizzle with olive oil and garnish with cilantro and edible flowers, if desired.

SERVES 12 (APPROXIMATELY 144 RAVIOLI)

PINE NUT TORTE

To make this torte more decorative, powder the top with confectioners' sugar after it has cooled.

NUT TORTE PASTRY

⅔ cup butter

⅔ cup confectioners' sugar, sifted

1 egg

1⅔ cups all-purpose flour

⅛ teaspoon salt

⅔ cup pine nuts, ground

FILLING

2½ cups pine nuts

1 tablespoon crushed coriander seeds

1 cup confectioners' sugar

1 cup plus 1 tablespoon heavy cream

2 eggs, beaten

1 tablespoon vanilla extract

½ cup all-purpose flour

2 tablespoons Barbados or dark rum

Whipped cream sweetened to taste with honey

Preheat the oven to 350°F.

To make the torte shell, cream the butter in a medium mixer bowl. Beat in the sugar and then the egg. Stir in the flour, salt, and ground nuts; mix well. Form the dough into a ball and roll in waxed paper; refrigerate for 1 hour. When chilled, roll the dough on a floured surface into a circle large enough to fit into an 8-inch removable-bottom tart pan. Bake the torte shell for 5 minutes, then set aside, leaving the oven on.

Place the pine nuts on a baking sheet and roast in the oven, shaking occasionally, until they turn golden, about 15 minutes. Cool. Place the nuts in a food processor or blender and purée. You should have 1 cup of purée.

Transfer the purée to a bowl and stir in the coriander seeds. Mix in the sugar, cream, eggs, vanilla, flour, and rum. Pour the filling into the partially baked torte shell and bake until puffed in the center, about 40 minutes. Cool and serve at room temperature with honey-sweetened whipped cream.

SERVES 6 TO 8

Snake-shaped cookies in the green chile ice cream and a design reminiscent of Indian art on the pine nut torte add a Southwestern touch to the desserts.

GREEN CHILE ICE CREAM

This is a very rich ice cream. For a lighter version, substitute milk for 2 cups of the cream.

  4 cups heavy cream
  8 egg yolks
1½ vanilla beans, split
  1 cup sugar
  ½ teaspoon vanilla extract
  ½ cup diced roasted, peeled, and seeded Anaheim chiles (page 46), or canned green chiles, in ¼-inch pieces

Place 2 cups of the cream in a double boiler and scald; remove double boiler from the heat, keeping warm. In a large bowl, beat the yolks with an electric mixer until they are pale yellow. Slowly add the heated cream to the yolks, stirring as you pour. Scrape the insides of the vanilla beans into the egg-cream mixture and blend, then return to the double boiler and cook, stirring, until thick, about 20 minutes. Remove from heat and stir in remaining cream, sugar, vanilla, and chiles. Mix well and cool to room temperature. Place in an ice-cream maker and freeze according to the manufacturer's directions.

MAKES APPROXIMATELY
1 QUART

A chorizo quiche, framed by the adobe architecture and Indian blankets so typical of Santa Fe.

A RESPECT FOR TRADITION

As a young child, Kathy Kagel stood on a chair in front of the stove at the family's summer house in Maine to help the housekeeper cook. Now she stands at the stove of her own restaurant, the informal and lively Café Pasqual's, in Santa Fe.

Kathy first saw Santa Fe in 1969, as she drove across country, but she didn't return for good until ten years later. Her first endeavor was a catering business specializing in Chinese food, but when a small restaurant in the center of town became available, Kathy bought it. She named it Café Pasqual's, after the folk saint of cooks and kitchens—a monk who, according to legend, was so bad at prayer he was banished to the monastery kitchen, where he turned out to be a splendid cook.

Kathy was drawn immediately to Southwestern cooking. Natives working in Café Pasqual's kitchen became used to her lifting the lids of the pots or asking how their families made a particular dish. "I worry that with the chic and trendy interest in Southwestern cooking, tradition will be lost," she says. This traditional cooking style, developed by the hard-working poor, is based on simple ingredients such as red and green chiles, pinto beans, garlic, onions, blue and yellow cornmeal, and white cheese. "And they never use ground beef," she adds, "it's always shredded."

CHORIZO QUICHE WITH CORNMEAL CRUST

CRUST
1 cup yellow cornmeal
2 cups all-purpose flour
1 cup (2 sticks) butter
1 egg plus 1 yolk

3 eggs, beaten
1½ cups heavy cream
8 ounces chorizo sausage, crumbled
½ cup chopped scallions
½ cup chopped roasted green chiles, canned or fresh
1 cup shredded Monterey Jack cheese
Cayenne pepper

Put the cornmeal, flour, and butter in the bowl of a food processor. Process in short bursts until it is the consistency of oats. Add the egg and egg yolk, and process again for a moment. Turn the dough out onto a work surface and add just enough water, 1 tablespoon at a time, to work the dough into a firm ball. Roll the dough out on a floured surface into a circle large enough to fit a 9½-inch fluted quiche pan with 2½-inch sides and a removable bottom. Line the pan with the dough and crimp the edges. Refrigerate the crust for at least 20 minutes. Preheat the oven to 350°F.

Meanwhile, prepare the filling. In a bowl, whisk together the eggs and the cream. Add the crumbled chorizo, scallions,

Kathy Kagel greets guests at Cafe Pasqual's, her cheerful, informal restaurant.

and chiles, and stir to combine.

Prebake the crust for 5 minutes. Remove from the oven and sprinkle the bottom of the shell with half the cheese. Pour the egg and chorizo mixture over it and top with the rest of the cheese. Sprinkle the top with a fair amount of cayenne and bake until the custard is set and the top is a light golden color, about 40 minutes. Serve warm or at room temperature.

SERVES 6 TO 8

YELLOW AND BLUE-STRIPED POLENTA IN RED CHILE SAUCE

Any unused polenta may be covered with plastic wrap and stored in the refrigerator for a day or two.

14 cups water
2 cups yellow cornmeal
2 cups blue cornmeal
1 teaspoon salt
Butter
Red Chile Sauce (page 55)
Fresh cilantro leaves
Toasted pine nuts
Corn kernels and/or chorizo for garnish

Preheat the oven to 350°F.

Place 5 cups of water in each of two saucepans and bring to a boil over high heat.

While the water is coming to a boil, place the yellow cornmeal in one bowl and the blue cornmeal in another. Add ½ teaspoon salt and 2 cups of cold water to each bowl. Allow the cornmeal to sit for 5 minutes, then stir the contents of each bowl into a pot of boiling water.

Return to a boil, lower the heat, and simmer, stirring occasionally, for 20 minutes.

Grease 2 loaf pans with spray oil, then pour a layer of yellow cornmeal into the bottom of each pan, using approximately ¼ of the polenta in each. Layer half of the blue cornmeal into each pan, then top with another layer of yellow. Cover the pans tightly with foil.

Set the pans in a larger pan, adding enough water to come halfway up the sides of the loaf pans. Steam in the oven for 2½ hours, adding more water to the pan if necessary. When the loaves are done, remove the foil, and cool in their pans. Refrigerate, uncovered, overnight.

The following day, slice the cooled polenta into ½-inch-thick slices. Melt some butter on a griddle or in a frying pan and fry the polenta until it is heated through. To serve, flood a plate with Red Chile Sauce and top with two slices of polenta. Garnish as desired.

SERVES 18

Blue cornmeal, used here in polenta, represents the sky in Hopi Indian religious ceremonies.

The chorizo burrito is
hearty enough to satisfy two
hungry people.

CHORIZO BURRITO

2 teaspoons clarified butter

1 boiled potato, peeled and
diced

2 tablespoons chopped
scallions

1½ to 2 ounces ground
chorizo, or 1 chorizo
sausage, casing removed

2 eggs, beaten

1 large flour tortilla, about
10 inches

Green and/or Red Chile
Sauce (recipes follow)

½ cup or more grated
Monterey Jack cheese
Chopped scallions, for
garnish

Preheat the oven to 350°F.

Place the clarified butter in a
sauté pan over medium-high
heat. Add the diced potato and
cook, stirring, until browned on
all sides, about 5 minutes. Remove and set aside. In the same
pan, place the scallions and
chorizo, and cook over high
heat until the chorizo is completely cooked, about 5 minutes. Turn the heat down to me-

dium, add the beaten eggs, and
stir often until the egg is
cooked, about 5 minutes.

Warm the tortilla and place
on an ovenproof oval plate.
Place the egg-and-chorizo mixture and cooked potato down
the center, and fold the sides
over the filling. Roll the burrito
over, placing the seam on the
bottom. Cover with red chile
sauce or use half red, half green.
Sprinkle the cheese on top and
place in oven until the cheese
melts. Garnish with scallions.

SERVES 2

RED CHILE SAUCE CAFÉ PASQUAL'S

Chile sauce burns easily, so be very careful when reheating it, using a medium-low heat and stirring every few minutes. The red chiles used for this sauce are those sold in the Southwest in long bunches called ristras, *and are commonly known as California peppers.*

- 1 boneless pork butt, about 4½ pounds
- 12 to 16 dried red chiles, approximately 4 to 6 inches long
- 2 tablespoons all-purpose flour
- 2 teaspoons salt, or to taste

Place the pork butt in a heavy saucepan with water to cover. Bring to a boil over high heat, and continue to boil until the meat falls from the bone, about 2 to 3 hours. Remove pork to a plate, reserving the cooking liquid. When cool enough to handle, shred the meat. Set aside 1 cup for the sauce and freeze the rest for another use.

Meanwhile, in a bowl, soak the chiles in hot water for 1 hour; drain. Place the chiles in a saucepan with enough fresh water to cover and boil for 30 minutes. Remove chiles with a slotted spoon and place half in a blender bowl with enough pork stock to cover, plus 1 tablespoon flour. Blend until completely puréed. Put mixture through a fine strainer to get rid of seeds and unground chile pieces. Repeat with the remaining chiles and flour. Add salt.

Just before serving, stir the reserved pork into the sauce and place in a heavy saucepan. Heat the sauce over medium-low heat, stirring every few minutes.

MAKES 1 QUART

GREEN CHILE SAUCE CAFÉ PASQUAL'S

New Mexican green chiles are available canned, frozen, or fresh. If both hot and mild chiles are available, use 2 mild chiles for each hot chile.

- 4 cups diced and peeled New Mexican green chiles
- ¼ cup vegetable oil
- ¼ cup all-purpose flour
- 2 tablespoons chopped garlic, or to taste
- Salt to taste

Place the chiles in a saucepan with water to cover, 3 to 4 cups, and warm over a medium-low heat until very hot. Do not boil, and be careful not to burn the chiles.

In a small skillet, warm the oil over low heat. Make a roux by whisking the flour into the oil and cooking the mixture until it is thick and very slightly browned. Add the roux to the hot chiles; whisk thoroughly, and cook for 5 minutes. Add the garlic and salt. Reheat carefully before serving.

MAKES APPROXIMATELY 1 QUART

Chile fettuccine sits in front of the Castilian roses so abundant in Santa Fe.

NONA DORA'S RED CHILE FETTUCCINE WITH CILANTRO PESTO

The cilantro pesto can be stored in the freezer or topped with a thin film of olive oil and stored in the refrigerator.

PASTA
- 1½ cups semolina flour
- 1 cup all-purpose flour
- 3 heaping tablespoons ground red pasilla or Anaheim chile
- ⅓ cup olive oil
- 2 eggs
- 2 tablespoons water

CILANTRO PESTO
- 4 well-washed bunches cilantro (including stems but not roots)
- 6 garlic cloves
- ½ cup pine nuts
- ½ cup olive oil
- ½ cup grated Parmesan cheese
- Toasted pine nuts (page 50)
- Whole cilantro leaves

Sift the flours and ground chile into a mound. Make a well in the center and add the olive oil, eggs, and water. Work the flour and liquid into a dough and knead until it feels like your earlobe. (Add more water if dough needs to be softer, more flour to make it stiffer.) Gather into a ball, then let dough rest in a lightly floured bowl for 20 to 30 minutes.

While the dough is resting, combine the pesto ingredients in the bowl of a food processor fitted with a metal blade and purée. Set aside.

Roll the dough out by hand to a thickness of ¹⁄₁₆ inch, or put through a pasta maker; let rest another 10 minutes. Roll up jelly-roll style and cut into noodles or put through pasta maker on fettuccine setting. Cook the noodles in a large pot of boiling water until just tender, about 2 to 3 minutes. Drain.

Pour sauce over the pasta and toss thoroughly. Garnish with toasted pine nuts and fresh cilantro leaves, if desired.

SERVES 4 TO 6

Bunches of red peppers, known as *ristras*, drying in the sun, are a common sight in Santa Fe.

CORN CRÊPES

This is a versatile recipe. The vegetable filling can be made with any colorful combination of finely diced vegetables, and the sauce is also wonderful as a hot dip for tortilla chips.

CRÊPES
- ⅓ cup very finely diced red bell pepper
- 1 cup frozen corn kernels, cooked
- 3 large eggs
- ¾ cup milk
- ½ cup all-purpose flour
- ⅓ cup stone-ground yellow cornmeal
- 2 tablespoons (¼ stick) unsalted butter, melted and cooled
- 1 teaspoon salt
  Tabasco to taste
- ½ to 1 teaspoon cayenne pepper
- ¼ cup minced scallions
- ¼ cup chopped fresh cilantro
- 3 tablespoons freshly grated Parmesan cheese

QUESO BLANCO SAUCE
- 4 tablespoons (½ stick) unsalted butter
- 1 onion, finely chopped
- 5 tomatoes, peeled and chopped
- 4 mild green chiles, roasted, seeded, peeled, and chopped (page 45)
- 1 red bell pepper, diced
- 1 green bell pepper, diced
- ¼ teaspoon salt
- ¼ teaspoon pepper
- ½ cup half-and-half
- 8 ounces cream cheese, cut into small pieces
- ½ teaspoon cayenne pepper

FILLING
  Melted butter for pan
- 2 cups frozen corn kernels, thawed
- 2 cups diced red bell pepper
- 2 cups finely diced zucchini
  Melted unsalted butter for making crêpes

First, prepare the crêpe batter. Pat the diced red pepper dry with a paper towel. In a blender or food processor, blend the red pepper, corn, eggs, milk, flour, cornmeal, butter, and salt for 30 seconds. Stop, scrape down sides, and process 30 seconds more. Transfer to a bowl, add the Tabasco, cayenne, scallions, cilantro, and Parmesan. Cover and let stand 1 hour at room temperature. This is important!

While the batter is resting, prepare the sauce. In a skillet over medium heat, melt the butter, add the onion, and cook a few minutes, until it is transparent. Add the tomatoes, chiles, red and green peppers, salt, and pepper; cook uncovered for 15 minutes. Reduce the heat and add the half-and-half. When heated through, add the cream cheese. Cook until the cheese is melted and the mixture is thick, approximately 10 more minutes. Stir the mixture, as it burns easily. Stir in the cayenne pepper. Keep warm over warm water.

Brush a sauté pan with melted butter, add the filling ingredients, and cook over medium heat until heated through.

Heat a 6- or 7-inch iron crêpe pan over moderate heat until hot. Brush with melted butter. Ladle 3 or 4 tablespoons of batter into the center of the pan and quickly swirl to spread the batter over the bottom. Cook until lightly browned on the bottom, about 2 minutes; turn and cook the other side until brown, another 1 to 2 minutes. Place on a plate and cover with waxed paper. Continue cooking the crêpes until the batter is used up, stacking them on the plate as they are finished.

To assemble, place about ⅓ cup of filling on one half of each crêpe. Fold the crêpe over the filling. Place 2 or 3 crêpes on each plate and nap with the warm sauce.

SERVES 6 TO 9

Chive blossoms add color to a local garden.

BRAD BROWN'S SANGRIA SORBET

1½ cups dry red wine

1 (24-ounce) bottle lemon-lime soda

1 cantaloupe, peeled and cubed

⅓ cup fresh orange juice

Juice of 2 lemons

Juice of 2 limes

½ cup lavender or regular honey

8 mint leaves, finely chopped

Mint, orange, lemon, and lime slices, for garnish

Place all the ingredients except garnish in a food processor and blend thoroughly. Freeze the sorbet in an ice-cream maker or in ice trays in the freezer. If sorbet is frozen in ice trays, process the sorbet quickly before serving to improve the texture. Garnish with fruit slices before serving.

MAKES APPROXIMATELY
1 QUART

MEXICAN CHOCOLATE ICE CREAM

3 cups half-and-half

½ cup dark brown sugar

12 egg yolks, beaten

3 ounces unsweetened chocolate

7 ounces semisweet chocolate

2 tablespoons instant coffee powder

Fruity sangría sorbet and dense, rich Mexican chocolate ice cream.

3 tablespoons ground cinnamon

¾ cup confectioners' sugar

1 cup lightly toasted and ground blanched almonds

5 ounces semisweet chocolate, coarsely chopped

1 teaspoon chile piquin flakes

Preheat the oven to 350°F.

In a saucepan over medium heat, combine 2 cups of the half-and-half and the brown sugar; heat until the sugar dissolves. Remove from heat and whisk ⅓ cup of the half-and-half/sugar mixture into the egg yolks, then return the half-and-half to the stove and add the yolk mixture, stirring constantly. Cook, continuing to stir, until the custard coats a spoon or reaches 170°F. Remove from heat and strain into a bowl. Set aside.

Melt the chocolates and coffee together in a double boiler, being careful that the mixture does not burn. Scrape the melted-chocolate mixture into a food processor; add the remaining half-and-half, cinnamon, and confectioners' sugar. Process until smooth, then gradually whisk the chocolate mixture into the custard. Chill for 1 hour, then freeze in an ice-cream machine, according to the manufacturer's instructions. When frozen, the texture will be creamy rather than firm. Fold in the toasted almonds, ground chocolate, and chile flakes. Return to freezer until ready to serve.

MAKES APPROXIMATELY
1 QUART

The South

Southerners have always eaten well, and whether it's served in a stately mansion or a humble log cabin, food is an integral part of southern hospitality from Virginia to New Orleans.

The predominant culinary tradition of the South was based on the cuisine of Jamestown's English settlers on the southeast coast. Long before the Civil War, however, sailing ships began to bring exotic spices and ethnic influences to Southern seaports, enabling hostesses at the grand plantations and in the cities to serve more flavorful and diversified fare. Their menus were further augmented by corn and game from the Indians; an unlimited supply of fish from local waters; okra, yams, and spices from African slaves; and a touch of classicism from the French who settled in Louisiana.

❧

Kirk Moore's shop of garden antiques, fresh flowers, and herbs raised at the family farm.

Natchez caterers Anne Cayton and Mary Coleman Blackmon's Southern picnic includes pâté, pizza, and a grilled butterflied leg of lamb, all redolent of herbs.

In the economically troubled times that followed the Civil War, expensive herbs and spices disappeared from most Southern kitchens, and savory dishes were replaced by simpler, rather bland foods. The area around Louisiana was the exception. Here, the Creoles and Cajuns who had helped settle the Louisiana territory continued to use native herbs such as sassafras, bay leaves, and thyme to give their zesty cooking its distinctive flavor. Creole cooking is a lively melding of classic French cooking techniques and the spices of Spain: gumbo is undoubtedly a Creole version of bouillabaisse, and paella translates into jambalaya in Louisiana. To this aristocratic European base, Creole cooks added foods used by the Choctaws and other local Indians, along with vegetables like mirliton and tomatoes brought from the West Indies by slaves. German immigrants contributed fine sausages to the pot.

A Southerner's love of sweets would be satisfied by Gwen Griffen's lemon verbena cake.

While Creole cooking originated with the aristocracy, Cajun cooking was the creation of the Acadians (or Cajuns), French refugees from Nova Scotia who found a haven in the swamps and bayous of south Louisiana. They learned to live off the land, combining fish, seafood, wild game, wild vegetation, and herbs into an indigenous cuisine that betrayed little of their European heritage. With the help of the Indians and German neighbors, they devised ingenious ways of turning these ingredients into savory one-dish meals cooked in their traditional black iron pots.

A grilled iron gate leads to The Burn's enchanting garden, where boxwood and flowers share space with herbs.

Today, the sophistication of earlier days has returned to Southern kitchens. While cooks throughout the South cherish their culinary heritage, they are also reexamining these old recipes and looking at local foods with a fresh eye. The result is a new regional cuisine in which herbs enliven classic Southern foods such as biscuits, grits, crab cakes, and iced tea, and in which crayfish might be found as readily in a sauce for pasta as in a traditional jambalaya.

Serita's masterful flower arrangements, *above*. *Opposite*, dill-scented Creole tomato soup.

NEW WAVE SOUTHERN COOKING

After a brief but boring stint in the oil business, Margo Bouanchaud decided to put her culinary talents to use by opening a gourmet shop specializing in take-out foods and catering in Baton Rouge. The oldest of three girls, Margo has been cooking all her life, encouraged by her mother, Serita, who is a superb gardener as well as a cook. "I think the only way to cook is to experiment," she advises. "The creativity is what makes it fun. Just start; don't be afraid; and keep tasting." Margo gives her own interpretation to many traditional Southern foods and, once in the kitchen, "I do as I please," she says. For example, pecans, a Southern staple for pies and pralines, replace the conventional pine nuts in her pesto.

When her mother planted an herb garden, Margo had an opportunity to use fresh herbs in quantity. Among her favorites

are rosemary, dill, mint, and chives; and "parsley goes into everything." She might also heighten the flavor of boiled artichokes with lemon grass, perk up tomato sandwiches with lemon balm, or mix pesto, which she uses like an herb, with cream cheese and crab meat.

Serita also supplies flowers for the big parties Margo caters. "I've loved flowers all my life," admits Serita, "but about five years ago I wanted to try something different so I started growing herbs." Included in her herb garden are some "swamp flowers," plants native to southern Mississippi and Louisiana, such as apple mint, yarrow, and dill. The herbs add interest to her renowned flower arrangements, too. No rules govern her arrangements. "I just want it to look pretty, different, and eye appealing," says Serita. "That's what's important."

Margot gives such Southern staples as grits and okra an herbal update.

Even this birdhouse has a porch swing.

FRESH HERBED SHRIMP

Margo serves these herbed shrimp over herbed grits, but they would be delicious with rice as well.

- ½ cup (1 stick) unsalted butter
- 1½ pounds fresh jumbo shrimp, peeled with tails left on
- 1 tablespoon finely chopped fresh basil
- 1 tablespoon finely chopped fresh thyme
- 1 tablespoon finely chopped fresh chives
- 1 garlic clove, crushed
- 1 tablespoon cornstarch
- ½ cup dry white wine
- Salt and pepper
- Herbed Grits (recipe follows)
- Fresh rosemary, for garnish

In large saucepan over medium heat, melt the butter. Add the shrimp, basil, thyme, chives, and garlic; sauté for 2 to 3 minutes. Meanwhile, in a small bowl, mix the cornstarch with the wine. When the shrimp begin to turn pink, stir the wine mixture into the shrimp. Continue to cook until the shrimp are just done, another minute. Do not overcook. Season to taste with salt and pepper and serve immediately over grits. Garnish with rosemary.

SERVES 6

HERBED GRITS

- 4 cups water
- ½ teaspoon salt
- 1 cup quick-cooking grits
- ½ cup (1 stick) butter
- ¼ pound Boursin or other garlic-herb cheese
- ¼ cup chopped fresh parsley
- 2 tablespoons chopped fresh chives

In a large saucepan, bring water and salt to a boil. Slowly add the grits and cook for 10 minutes, stirring frequently. Add the butter and cheese. When they are melted, add the parsley and chives, and stir to blend thoroughly.

SERVES 6 TO 8

SQUASH ROCKEFELLER

Mirliton, a member of the squash family, is common in the South and can sometimes be found in ethnic markets or specialty food stores in other regions. Summer squash works equally well in this recipe, a variation on the traditional Oysters Rockefeller. If you are not preparing oysters at the same time or cannot get oyster liquor from your fishmonger, substitute clam juice.

6 to 8 large crookneck squash or mirliton

2 pounds fresh spinach

¼ cup oyster liquor or bottled clam juice

¼ cup Anisette liqueur

¾ cup grated Parmesan cheese

1 teaspoon chopped fresh tarragon

½ teaspoon chopped fresh basil

Salt

Coarsely ground black pepper

Cayenne pepper

1 to 2 cups seasoned bread crumbs

Preheat the oven to 350°F.

Bring a large pot of salted water to a boil. Cut the squash in half, remove seeds, and cook in boiling water until tender, about 5 minutes. Remove with a slotted spoon and set aside.

Wash the spinach thoroughly and remove the stems. Cook the spinach in boiling water until just tender, about 3 minutes. Drain and squeeze out as much water as possible with your hands. Finely chop the spinach and place in a mixing bowl. Add the oyster liquor, Anisette, ½ cup of Parmesan cheese, herbs, and salt and peppers to taste; mix thoroughly. Add the bread crumbs, ½ cup at a time, until the mixture has the consistency of a stuffing and is firm enough to hold its shape.

Divide the spinach stuffing equally among the squash halves. Top with the remaining Parmesan cheese. Transfer the stuffed squash to a baking sheet and bake until heated through, about 10 to 12 minutes.

SERVES 12 TO 16

Serita's flower arrangements follow no set rules but are done with a sure instinct for color and composition.

Pickling is a favorite way to prepare okra.

≪

Cheese-chive biscuits are cut in heart shapes for special occasions.

SPICY OKRA

2 pounds fresh okra

2 cups water

¼ cup fennel seeds

3 tablespoons dried rosemary

2 tablespoons dried tarragon

2 cups red wine vinegar

Dried red pepper flakes, black pepper, cayenne pepper, salt, and Tabasco to taste

Wash the okra under cold running water and trim the stems without cutting the pods.

In a saucepan, combine the water, fennel seeds, rosemary, and tarragon. Bring to a boil and cook for 15 minutes. Remove from heat and strain the liquid into a large bowl. Stir in the vinegar and seasonings. Mix well. Add the okra and let stand at room temperature, covered, for 8 to 10 hours. Serve at room temperature.

SERVES 8

CHEESE-CHIVE BISCUITS

2 cups all-purpose flour

1 tablespoon baking powder

1 teaspoon salt

¼ cup vegetable shortening

¾ cup grated cheddar or other sharp cheese

¼ cup chopped fresh chives

1 cup milk

2 tablespoons (¼ stick) butter, melted

Preheat the oven to 450°F.

In a large bowl, mix the flour, baking powder, and salt with a fork. With a pastry cutter, cut in the shortening until the mixture resembles coarse crumbs. Stir in the grated cheese and chives. Add the milk and stir just until the mixture forms a soft dough that pulls away from the side of the bowl.

Turn the dough out onto a lightly floured surface; knead quickly to mix the dough thoroughly. Roll the dough out until ½ inch thick. Cut out biscuits with a floured biscuit cutter and place on an ungreased cookie sheet. Brush tops with melted butter and bake until golden brown, 12 to 15 minutes.

MAKES ABOUT 2 DOZEN BISCUITS

CREOLE TOMATO DILL SOUP

This soup is made with Louisiana-grown Creole tomatoes. If they are not available where you live, substitute any sweet, ripe tomato.

4 tablespoons (½ stick) unsalted butter

½ cup chopped onion

¼ cup all-purpose flour

1 cup water

6 Creole tomatoes, peeled and coarsely chopped

1 tablespoon minced fresh dill

1 tablespoon sugar

1 teaspoon salt

½ teaspoon minced fresh
parsley

¼ teaspoon black pepper

1 bay leaf

Fresh dill sprigs, for
garnish

Sour cream, for garnish

In a large Dutch oven, melt
the butter. Add the onion and
sauté over medium heat until
tender, about 3 minutes. Reduce heat to low, add the flour,
and stir until smooth. Continue
to cook 1 minute longer, stirring
constantly. Gradually add the
water and cook over medium
heat, stirring constantly, until
thickened and bubbly, about 5
minutes.

Add the tomatoes and sea-
sonings, and bring to a boil.
Cover, reduce heat, and simmer
for 30 minutes.

Discard the bay leaf, then
transfer one-third of the mixture to a food processor and process until smooth. Pour into a
warmed serving tureen. Repeat
with the remaining soup mixture. Serve garnished with fresh
dill sprigs and sour cream, if desired.

SERVES 6

**An eclectic collection of
dried herbs, baskets, and
tropical plants nestles in a
corner of the back porch.**

PECAN PESTO

This pesto can be stored in the freezer, or refrigerated with a thin film of oil on top in a tightly covered jar.

2 cups fresh basil leaves, washed and dried

6 garlic cloves

1 cup shelled pecans

½ cup olive oil mixed with ½ cup vegetable oil

1 cup grated Parmesan cheese

¼ cup grated Romano cheese

Salt and pepper

Combine the basil, garlic, and pecans in the bowl of a food processor; chop coarsely. With the motor still running, add the combined oils in a slow, steady stream. Shut the motor off and add the cheeses and salt and pepper to taste. Process briefly to combine. Scrape the pesto into a bowl and cover until ready to use.

MAKES APPROXIMATELY 2½ CUPS

꙰

Refreshing blackberry mint sorbet and bourbon mint ice cream, *left,* **are served on the shaded porch to take advantage of any Southern breezes.** *Right,* **a basket of pansies.**

MINT JULEP ICE CREAM

Do not increase the amount of liquor in this recipe, since it will prevent the ice cream from hardening properly.

1 cup sugar

1 cup water

1 cup fresh mint leaves, tightly packed

2 (10-ounce) cans condensed milk

1 quart heavy cream

2 cups milk

1 teaspoon vanilla extract

Pinch of salt

½ cup Southern Comfort or bourbon

Green food coloring (optional)

Mint leaves, for garnish

In a saucepan, bring the sugar, water, and mint to a boil. Simmer over medium heat for 5 to 8 minutes to make a simple syrup. Cool and strain, discarding mint.

In a large bowl, combine the condensed milk, cream, milk, vanilla, salt and liquor. Stir in the mint syrup. Tint with a few drops of food coloring, if desired. Pour into an ice-cream maker and freeze according to manufacturer's instructions until firm. Garnish with additional mint sprigs.

MAKES APPROXIMATELY 2 QUARTS

BLACKBERRY MINT SORBET

1 cup sugar

1 cup water

1 cup fresh mint leaves, tightly packed

4 cups blackberries or dewberries

1 cup red Burgundy wine

Lemon juice (optional)

Additional berries, for garnish

In a medium saucepan, combine the sugar, water, and mint. Bring to a boil, then simmer over medium heat, stirring occasionally, for about 5 minutes to make a mint-flavored simple syrup. Strain, discarding mint leaves, and cool.

In a food processor, coarsely purée the berries. Turn into a bowl and stir in the wine and the mint syrup. Taste and add lemon juice if you prefer a tarter flavor.

Pour the liquid into an ice-cream maker and freeze according to manufacturer's directions until firm. Garnish with additional berries.

MAKES 1½ QUARTS

NATCHEZ HOSPITALITY

The Burn is one of Natchez's oldest and most historic houses. Built in 1832, it was a Federal troop headquarters and then a Union hospital during the Civil War. Today the lovely Greek Revival house and its glorious gardens have been restored to their former splendor as a charming inn and the home of Mayor and Mrs. Tony Byrne.

Loveta Byrne's innate graciousness and taste were augmented by the hands-on experience of running her own restaurant and a bed-and-breakfast before moving to The Burn. A self-taught cook who took advantage of whatever lessons were available, she concentrates on foods that are indigenous to the South. Meats and fish are generally grilled and herbs, rather than sauces, add pungent flavor.

Guests find such dishes as corn chowder and corn cakes, catfish baked with biscuit crumbs, and creamed potatoes on the menu, along with more modern additions like chocolate mousse cake. Loveta feels these foods complement the otherworldly atmosphere of the house, which is beautifully furnished to recall the days when the cream of Natchez society swirled through its rooms.

GREEN TOMATO PIE

When there are no ripe tomatoes available in the garden, try this green tomato pie: the thyme in the crust gives it a special zest. Serve the pie as an hors d'oeuvre, a light luncheon dish, or an accompaniment to grilled meats in place of potatoes.

CRUST

2 1/4 cups biscuit mix

  1/2 teaspoon dried thyme, or 2 teaspoons chopped fresh

  1/2 cup milk

FILLING

1 onion, thinly sliced

6 green tomatoes, peeled and sliced

1 teaspoon sugar

Salt and pepper

2 tablespoons chopped fresh basil

2 tablespoons chopped fresh chives

2 cups mayonnaise, preferably homemade

1 teaspoon fresh lemon juice

6 ounces sharp cheddar cheese, grated

Preheat the oven to 375°F.

To make the crust, place the biscuit mix and thyme in a large bowl. Quickly stir in the milk with a fork until just blended. Press the dough into a greased 10-inch pie pan.

Arrange the onion on top of the crust. Layer the tomatoes, sugar, salt, and pepper, and herbs on top. In a medium bowl, mix the mayonnaise, lemon juice, and cheese. Spread the mayonnaise mixture over the tomatoes and bake until it is golden and bubbly on top, about 30 to 40 minutes. Serve hot or at room temperature.

SERVES 6 TO 8

Warm Southern breezes caress diners as they enjoy a green tomato pie, *left and far left,* **on the upstairs porch. The imposing front door,** *above,* **greets guests.**

ENJOYING HERBS

"Herbs make life more fun," says Beverly Fennel. "My great-grandmother used herbs for dyeing, and my grandmother and mother were both good cooks. It seems I've been cooking with herbs forever."

For many years her husband's career kept Beverly's family moving around the United States, and she planted an herb garden wherever she lived. Now, settled at last in a charming old Louisiana farmhouse, Beverly has been able to fulfill her ambition of starting an herb business. Gardens all around the house and densely planted fields provide the herbs and flowers for seasoning blends and potpourris, herbal decorations, soaps, sleep pillows, and lingerie cases. Beverly also plans and plants gardens, lectures, and gives cooking classes to introduce others to the pleasure of herbs. "I teach theories, not recipes," she notes. "One thing I tell all my students," she adds, "is it's best to start small. Don't buy too many herb plants. You won't know what to do with the harvest."

Beverly gives roast chicken a faint lemony flavor by stuffing it with lemon balm.

MINTY YOGURT DESSERT CHEESE

Yogurt cheese is high in calcium and low in calories, fat, and sodium. It can be flavored with more savory herbs for predinner nibbling or be left unflavored to substitute for cream cheese, mayonnaise, or sour cream in many recipes.

32	ounces (4 cups) plain yogurt
⅓	cup chopped fresh mint
1	tablespoon grated orange zest
	Additional orange zest, for garnish

In a large bowl, combine the yogurt, mint, and orange zest. Line a colander with a double layer of cheesecloth and set over a bowl. Pour the yogurt mixture into the colander, then set in the refrigerator or a cool place to drain overnight. It will take 8 to 12 hours to make a very soft cheese, about 16 hours for one with the consistency of cream cheese. Turn the yogurt cheese out onto a plate and garnish with additional orange zest. Serve with fresh fruit.

MAKES 1 POUND

Fields of mint near Beverly's house provide the fresh flavor for yogurt cheese.

THE MAGIC OF HERBS

When Franklin Adams was 3½ years old, his pediatrician saw some of his drawings and predicted he would become an artist. He was right. Franklin designs buildings and does imaginative renovations and graphic design projects, but sculpture is his first love. "Each time I start a piece, it's an invitation to put together a lot of good things and get something brand new," he says. "I like to take very simple, commonplace materials and make magic out of them."

Franklin has the same approach to food. "I go to the store and see what's there. Tasso (smoked pork loin) or some crayfish, for example, will inspire me." There's also a definite Mediterranean influence in the Adams kitchen, where rosemary, pine nuts, and garlic are favorite seasonings. "I like heady flavors, hefty peppery tastes, and strong cheeses," he admits. Franklin found dried herbs quite satisfactory until he discovered fresh herbs on a trip in the Pyrenees with a friend. "We stopped for a picnic and the 'grass' was thyme," he recalls with delight. Now New Orleans markets provide the fresh herbs Franklin insists transform the simplest foods into the robust dishes he loves.

Above, a New Orleans doorway.

❦

BRAISED FENNEL WITH ROSEMARY

Fennel is frequently called anise in Louisiana, a reference to its licorice taste, but it bears no resemblance to the actual anise plant, which is grown primarily for its seeds.

- 12 garlic cloves, peeled
- 4 tablespoons extra-virgin olive oil
- 4 large or 8 small fennel bulbs, about 4 pounds
- ⅓ cup water
- 8 sprigs fresh rosemary
- 12 brine-cured black olives
- Salt and freshly ground pepper
- Lemon slices, for garnish

Bring 2 to 3 cups of water to a boil in a small pot and blanch the garlic cloves for 3 to 4 minutes; drain. Heat 1 tablespoon of the oil in a small skillet over medium heat and brown the garlic until golden all over.

Cut the leaf stalks and the hard butt ends from the fennel bulbs, leaving just the bulbous stem, a piece 2½ to 3½ inches long. Halve the small bulbs lengthwise; quarter the larger bulbs. In a large skillet, heat the remaining oil and the water over medium heat. Add the fennel in a single layer and the rosemary. (If you have more fennel than your skillet can accommodate in a single layer, save half the oil and rosemary to cook with half the fennel in a second batch.) Cover and cook the fen-

nel, turning once or twice, until the water cooks away and the fennel is tender and browning, about 15 minutes. If the fennel begins to brown before it feels tender, add a little more water; if it becomes tender before browning, raise the heat or take off the lid to speed browning.

When the fennel is tender and browned, add the garlic and olives to warm through. Season to taste with pepper and salt. Garnish with lemon slices.

SERVES 8

❦

The well-worn table in Franklin Adams's kitchen, *opposite*, doubles as a work area and serving space.

PAPPARDELLE WITH CRAYFISH

Crayfish (pronounced crawfish in Louisiana) can be purchased there live, boiled whole in their shells, or steamed and peeled. If you cannot find crayfish where you live, substitute medium shrimp. Dry vermouth can be used instead of Retsina.

- 1 cup white Retsina wine
- 2 cups heavy cream
- 2/3 cup coarsely chopped shallots
- 1 teaspoon cayenne pepper
- 3 teaspoons fresh thyme leaves
- 1 1/2 tablespoons tomato paste
- 1 teaspoon grated orange zest
- 2 red bell peppers
- Salt
- 1 1/2 pounds extra-wide egg noodles, preferably Italian pappardelle
- 1 pound steamed and shelled crayfish tails (5 to 6 pounds unshelled)
- 6 tablespoons (2/3 stick) unsalted butter, softened or cut into chunks
- Freshly ground black pepper
- 3 tablespoons chopped fresh basil leaves, for garnish
- Lemon slices, for garnish
- 1/2 pound whole boiled crayfish, for garnish

Whole crayfish decorate Franklin's pappardelle.

❧

In an enamel pot, reduce the Retsina over medium heat to about 1/3 cup. Add the cream, the shallots, cayenne, thyme, tomato paste, and orange zest; combine, then reduce again by one-third. Set aside.

Seed and vein the peppers. Cut lengthwise into 1/2-inch slices and steam until barely tender, about 3 or 4 minutes. Set aside.

In a very large pot, bring 6 to 8 quarts of salted water to a boil. Add the pasta and cook until al dente, 9 to 12 minutes. While the pasta is cooking, heat the sauce over low heat and stir in the crayfish tails. Cook until the crayfish is warmed through. When the pasta is done, drain it and transfer to a large serving bowl. Stir in the butter, the crayfish sauce, and a generous grinding of black pepper. Garnish with basil leaves, lemon slices, and whole crayfish.

SERVES 6

ORANGE, ONION, AND BASIL SALAD

Franklin Adams occasionally juliennes a small turnip and adds it to this salad. He says the flavor provides a nice surprise; the pink and white of the turnip a good color note.

- 3 large or 4 small navel oranges
- 2 large or 3 small red onions, sliced 1/8 inch thick
- 7 1/2 tablespoons extra-virgin olive oil
- 2 tablespoons balsamic vinegar
- Freshly ground pepper
- 2 rounded tablespoons pine nuts
- 2 to 3 cups unblemished fresh basil leaves
- Salt

Grate the zest from one of the oranges and place it in the bottom of a wide salad bowl. Without peeling, slice all the oranges about 1/4 to 3/8 inch thick. Squeeze the juice from the end slices into the bowl over the zest. Remove any seeds, then remove the peel from each slice by laying it flat and turning it as you take a series of straight downward cuts, leaving no white pulp. Place the peeled slices in the bowl. Separate the onion slices into rings and add to the bowl.

In a small bowl, whisk together 7 tablespoons of the oil, the vinegar, and some pepper. Pour this vinaigrette over the onion and orange slices. Toss gently, being careful not to break up the orange slices, until the oranges and onions are coated. Marinate for 30 minutes to 1 hour.

Heat the remaining 1/2 tablespoon of oil in a skillet and brown the pine nuts over medium heat until they are medium tan—don't allow them to blacken.

Wash and dry the basil. Chop the leaves if they are large; leave them whole if they are small. Just before serving, add the basil and pine nuts to the salad bowl, toss gently, and serve. Let guests add salt to taste.

SERVES 6

❧

Basil provides the greenery in a refreshing orange and onion salad.

HERBS FOR A LOUISIANA COOK

Ten years ago, when Bruce Zabov ordered a few plants to put in an old washtub at the foot of his back steps, he had no idea he would become hooked on herbs. He spent the following winter reading herb and garden books, drawing up plans for his garden, and bettering the soil by covering the garden area with waste by-products from cotton processing. In the spring he laid out the garden and planted culinary herbs like thyme, rosemary, basil, and dill. Bruce constantly battles the fungi that flourish in Louisiana's heat and humidity, but that doesn't detract from his enjoyment of his garden. "Gardening in the South is a love affair," he says. "It's work, but rewarding work."

A former social worker, Bruce now devotes full time to the antiques and restoration work that he loves. His home, an old Anglo architecture, center-hall house known as the Garrett-Drake House, is a good example of his work and is often the setting for the informal entertaining he prefers. "My mother admitted to being the world's worst cook and I love food, so I learned to cook in self-defense," he claims. Now that he has discovered the amazing difference fresh herbs can make, he relies on them whenever possible, using common sense as a guide for experimenting with what's available in the garden. "It's an aesthetic experience to use the herbs, and to relax in the garden after work and watch them grow."

A cool porch stretches across the front of the Garett-Drake House.

LOUISIANA MARINATED CATFISH

Bruce says there is no substitute for fresh basil leaves in this recipe, but in an emergency leaves that have been preserved in salt will do. Whole frozen leaves also have a near-fresh flavor but they will not stay green after defrosting.

2 large catfish fillets, 1 to 1¼ pounds total

MARINADE

3 large fresh basil leaves, coarsely chopped

1 sprig fresh lemon thyme (optional)

2 to 3 medium garlic cloves, coarsely chopped

1 small red cayenne pepper, coarsely chopped; or ¼ teaspoon dried red pepper flakes

Juice of 1 lime

2 tablespoons vegetable oil

Freshly ground pepper

Paprika

¼ cup chopped fresh parsley or to taste

Wash the fish fillets under cold running water, then place on a clean dish towel and roll the towel up. Refrigerate for 1 to 2 hours. Catfish is a very moist fish and this helps dry it so it absorbs rather than dilutes the marinade.

Combine the basil, lemon thyme if using, garlic, and red pepper in a mortar and grind with the pestle until they form a paste. Add the lime juice, oil, pepper, paprika to taste, and parsley; stir well.

Spoon half the marinade into the bottom of a glass dish large enough to hold the fillets in a single layer. Score the fillets on both sides and set in the marinade. Spoon the remaining marinade over the fish. Refrigerate, uncovered, for 1 hour.

Place an empty cast-iron griddle or skillet under the broiler and preheat the broiler. When the pan is very hot, carefully remove it. If the pan is unseasoned, add a little oil to the cooking surface, then add the fillets, skin side down. Broil the fish about 3 inches from the heat until fillets are browned and slightly crisped around the edges, about 7 to 10 minutes. Do not turn the fillets; the hot pan cooks the underside.

SERVES 2

The herb garden is a peaceful spot to relax and have an informal meal.

CHICKEN MARJORAM

This chicken will take on a more Mediterranean flavor if you scatter a few black olives over the casserole during the last 10 minutes of cooking.

¼ cup olive oil

2 garlic cloves, peeled

1 chicken (3 to 3⅓ pounds), cut into serving pieces

Flour for dredging

3 to 4 lemon slices

4 to 5 sprigs fresh marjoram

1 bay leaf

12 red new potatoes, cut in half

Freshly ground pepper

2 large onions, thickly sliced

1 cup chicken stock

½ pound green beans, trimmed

8 cherry tomatoes

Salt

Preheat the oven to 375°F.

In a large skillet, heat the oil over medium heat and sauté the garlic for 1 minute. Transfer the garlic to an ovenproof casserole with a slotted spoon. Wash and dry the chicken pieces, dredge

For easy entertaining, Bruce melds vegetables with chicken for a flavorful one-dish meal.

them in flour, and brown in the same skillet. With a slotted spoon, transfer the chicken pieces to the casserole; add the lemon slices, marjoram, bay leaf, potatoes, and pepper to taste.

In the same skillet, sauté the onion slices over medium heat until they are translucent and beginning to turn golden, about

15 minutes; add them to the casserole. Pour the chicken stock over the ingredients and bake, covered, for 30 minutes, basting occasionally. Uncover and bake an additional 20 minutes.

Meanwhile, cut the green beans into 1-inch pieces and blanch them in boiling water. Halve the cherry tomatoes.

When the chicken has baked for 50 minutes, add the beans and tomatoes; bake, uncovered, until the chicken and potatoes are tender, an additional 10 minutes. Adjust the seasoning; serve with rice.

SERVES 4

Wide steps lead from the back porch to the delightful fenced-in herb garden.

CATERING TO SOUTHERN TASTES

Sarah Gaede was in junior high school when Julia Child's *The Art of French Cooking* was published; reading it caused the first stirring of her interest in food. Years later Sarah was asked to put together a cookbook for the Pirate's House, one of Savannah's best-known restaurants, and pitching in in the restaurant's kitchen was a great hands-on way to learn about cooking. The experience inspired Sarah to start her own catering business.

"When you're a caterer, you've got to produce. Having a hysterical perfectionist personality helps," she laughs. "I've spent two days looking for asparagus that was just the right size." Sarah has updated preparations for traditional Southern foods such as biscuits and dishes made from the local seafood, but tries to change them as little as possible. "I do add herbs for flavor, like the dill in this crab salad," she says. "And I throw nasturtiums on everything. They really make plates of hors d'oeuvres look pretty." Basil is another of her favorites. It's a prime ingredient in her popular ricotta, walnut, and pesto turnovers, it flavors a crab and corn chowder, and is in the butter that sauces a beef tenderloin.

Sturdy fishing boats, *opposite*, ply the waters near Savannah in search of local crab, *left*, and shrimp.

DILLED CRAB SALAD IN TOMATOES

6   large ripe tomatoes
1   pound lump crab meat, picked over
½   cup Spicy Mayonnaise (recipe follows)
¼   cup chopped fresh dill
2   tablespoons chopped fresh chives
1   tablespoon fresh lemon juice
    Salt and freshly ground pepper
1   head Boston lettuce
    Additional sprigs of fresh dill, for garnish

Slice off the stem ends of the tomatoes, then hollow out, removing the seeds. Set upside down on paper towels to drain.

In a large bowl, place the crab, mayonnaise, dill, chives, lemon juice, and salt and pepper to taste. Mix lightly but thoroughly.

Stuff the tomatoes with the crab mixture, dividing it evenly among the tomatoes. To serve, place a few lettuce leaves on each plate and top with a stuffed tomato. Garnish with dill sprigs.

SERVES 6

SPICY MAYONNAISE

1   small sweet onion, preferably Vidalia, quartered
1   egg plus 2 egg yolks
1   teaspoon salt
1   teaspoon cayenne pepper
1   teaspoon celery seeds
1   tablespoon white wine vinegar
1   tablespoon fresh lemon juice
2   cups vegetable oil

Drop the quartered onion through the feed tube of a food processor while it is running; process until finely chopped. Add the egg and egg yolks, salt, cayenne, celery seeds, vinegar, and lemon juice; process 30 seconds longer. With the processor still running, add the oil in a slow, steady stream until it is thoroughly incorporated and mixture has the consistency of mayonnaise.

MAKES 2½ CUPS

A SAVANNAH SAVANT COOKS

Over the years, Esther Shaver built her bustling Louisville bookstore into one of the best in the South. But as she and her husband approached retirement, they decided to move to a more cosmopolitan city and devote more time to travel. Esther sold the shop without regret.

While on a trip to Savannah, the Shavers saw a spacious town house for sale and knew they'd found their new home. An empty corner shop was an unexpected bonus that has lured Esther out of her brief retirement, although it doesn't keep her from traveling. The store is a booklover's dream with every inch of space crammed with books on any subject you might want to explore. Esther herself finds inspiration for cooking in the wide selection of cookbooks.

Although Esther grew up eating nothing more exotic than steaks and chops, she loves to cook and entertain. "I finally discovered there were more interesting foods," she says. "Now I cook for relaxation." The large rooms of the Shavers' gracious home are often filled with people attending one of her big "bashy" cocktail parties or stand-up buffets.

Since Esther doesn't have a garden, fresh herbs are a relatively new addition to the Shaver kitchen. "I have to rely on what I can find at the store," she admits. Cilantro, discovered on a trip to Mexico, is a favorite and Esther particularly likes the way its exotic flavor complements the rather bland taste of turkey. "I like to use fresh herbs on vegetables, too," she adds. "I often put them on potatoes instead of butter."

When the Shavers entertain, *right,* **guests move easily from the gracious parlor to the formal dining room. A typical row of Savannah town houses,** *left.*

TURKEY WITH EMERALD SAUCE

Make the Emerald Sauce as close to serving time as possible. The sooner you use it, the brighter green the sauce will be.

- 2 to 2½ pounds turkey breast
- 1 tablespoon butter
- 1 tablespoon vegetable oil
  Salt
- ½ cup sour cream
  Chopped cilantro, for garnish

  EMERALD SAUCE
- ¼ cup vegetable oil
- 1 large onion, coarsely chopped
- 1 10-ounce package frozen chopped spinach, defrosted and drained
- 1 to 2 jalapeños, seeded and chopped (optional)
- ½ cup chopped cilantro
- ½ cup chicken stock
- ½ teaspoon salt

Preheat the oven to 350°F.

Place the turkey breast in a baking dish and cook in the oven for 1 to 1¼ hours. The turkey should be moist, not overcooked and dry. Set aside.

To make the sauce, heat the oil in a medium saucepan. Add the onion and sauté over low heat until soft but not brown, about 5 minutes. Add the spinach, chiles, cilantro, stock and salt. Increase heat to medium and simmer for 10 minutes. Transfer the sauce to a processor or blender, and purée until smooth. Add more salt if needed. Set aside.

Cut the turkey into 1-inch chunks, following the contours of the meat. In a large skillet, melt the butter and oil, and quickly sauté the turkey chunks over medium-high heat until lightly browned and warmed through. Season with salt. Quickly reheat the green sauce if necessary, and pour over turkey. Top with a dollop of sour cream and sprinkle with chopped cilantro.

SERVES 6

Esther adds cheese and chives to old-fashioned Southern biscuits.

AN ELEGANT APPROACH TO HERBS

Susan Mason likes to cook and especially to entertain. Dinners and parties at her house are always done with great flair, as were the gala events she used to organize for charity. Five years ago friends eager to avail themselves of her considerable talents persuaded her to start a catering business. "It is hectic but rewarding," she says, "and it certainly is creative." Susan's favorite affairs are cocktail parties, but "I've done everything, including a wedding for the governor's daughter. There were a thousand guests and my catering crew was made up of inmates convicted of armed robbery," she recalls with amusement.

Her Savannah catering business keeps growing. "I find there's more home entertaining today," Susan observes, "and people appreciate being invited to your home. There's a real return to elegance, too; everyone is pulling out their silver. Food has to look good and it has to look pretty." That's one reason Susan's so fond of herbs such as basil, which have both a decorative appearance and an appealing fragrance. "I love to decorate with herbs and edible flowers," she admits. The Flower Garden Brie is a perfect example of how a few flowers and a little imagination can transform a simple wheel of cheese into a spectacular offering.

Calla lillies and satin rib-
bons add enchantment to
the flower-bedecked brie.

FLOWER GARDEN BRIE

The flowers should be washed and carefully dried before using. If you are not using naturally flat flowers, carefully place flowers between two paper towels and set a heavy book on top of them for 15 to 30 minutes to flatten them.

2 cups dry white wine

1 package unflavored gelatin

1 large round brie

Edible flowers such as nasturtiums, johnny jump-ups, pinks, or violets, with stems and leaves if appropriate

In a saucepan, combine the white wine and gelatin and set aside for 5 minutes to allow the gelatin to soften. Set over medium heat and bring to a boil, stirring to dissolve the gelatin completely, then place the saucepan in a bowl of ice water to hasten cooling. Stir occasionally. The gelatin mixture should be clear, not cloudy.

While the gelatin cools, set the brie on a rack over waxed paper. When the gelatin mixture begins to thicken and is shaky when you shake the pot, spoon a thin layer of gelatin over the brie.

Hors d'oeuvres combining herbed cheese with endive or smoked salmon accompany the decorated brie.

Arrange the flowers on top, pressing them gently into the gelatin mixture. Place in the refrigerator for a few minutes to firm the gelatin, then spoon another layer of gelatin over the flowers. Repeat with the additional gelatin if necessary in order to cover the petals and leaves completely. Return to refrigerator to set. Remove just before serving.

SERVES 8 TO 10

A GARDENER IN THE KITCHEN

"I always loved to dig in the dirt as a small child," says garden designer Kirk Moore. Acting on the tenet you should enjoy what you're doing and make money, too, Kirk took a job as a garden curator and research assistant at Colonial Williamsburg, in Virginia. But he found himself drawn back to Savannah, his hometown, where with partner Frank Warthan, he is now proprietor of a delightful garden shop although he still plans and installs gardens.

"The only time I have to sit down and relax is over dinner," Kirk says. "I learned to cook from my mama, a good no-nonsense cook. But you know, in the South, people have a tendency to butcher vegetables. I had to find out for myself they're healthier and taste better steamed than boiled to death."

Mint is grown in most Southern gardens, and Kirk's is no exception. He still enjoys the minted cucumber sandwiches his mother has been serving ever since he can remember, and a few leaves from an unusual chocolate mint growing in the shop's garden give his juleps the faintest hint of chocolate.

One of Kirk's favorite garden plants is Southernwood. "It's pretty from an architectural viewpoint and for color," he notes, "and it's a good edging plant and very hardy. We keep some in the dog's bed to keep the fleas away," he adds, "and we tuck some in the closets to discourage moths." Finding ways to use it in the kitchen is harder. An adaptation of a cake from a nineteenth-century herbal filled with "lots of fabulous desserts with interesting tastes" is one of the best culinary uses he's discovered for this aromatic herb.

❦❦❦

Rambling roses grow on an old farm shed in the Georgia countryside.

CUCUMBER TEA SANDWICHES WITH MINT MAYONNAISE

MINT MAYONNAISE
2 large egg yolks
½ teaspoon Dijon mustard
2 tablespoons fresh lemon juice
¾ cup fresh mint leaves, loosely packed
1 cup vegetable oil
Salt and pepper

16 thin slices homemade white bread, crusts removed
1 cucumber, peeled and thinly sliced

In a blender or food processor, combine the egg yolks, mustard, lemon juice, and mint. With motor running, add the oil in a slow stream and blend until emulsified. Season to taste with salt and pepper and transfer to a bowl.

Spread each slice of bread generously on one side with the mayonnaise. On half the slices, arrange an even layer of cucumber slices. Top with remaining bread slices. Cut each sandwich into quarters before serving.

32 TEA SANDWICHES

SOUTHERNWOOD CAKE

1½ cups all purpose flour
½ cup self-rising flour
1 cup sugar
4 teaspoons finely chopped Southernwood leaves
4 eggs
¾ cup (1½ sticks) unsalted butter, melted and cooled
Whipped cream, lightly sweetened

Preheat the oven to 350°F. Grease and flour an 8-inch springform pan or 9-inch quiche pan.

Sift the flours into a large bowl. Stir in the sugar and chopped Southernwood. In another bowl, beat the eggs lightly, then stir in the cooled butter.

With a wooden spoon, stir the butter and egg mixture into the flour mixture. When the ingredients are blended, beat for 1 minute.

Pour the batter into the pan and bake for 30 minutes. Lower the temperature to 325°F. and bake an additional 45 minutes to 1 hour, or until a toothpick inserted in the cake comes out clean. Cool in the pan for 5 minutes, then turn out on a wire rack, right side up, to finish cooling. Serve with lightly sweetened whipped cream.

MAKES 1 9-INCH CAKE

Adding tarragon to deviled eggs is a Moore family tradition.

The Ellises enjoy their special meal in chairs John built from twigs gathered in the woods near their mountain home.

GOOD TASTE IN GEORGIA

Recognizing that he was probably a better chef than an artist, Gerry Klaskala left art school to attend the Culinary Institute of America. "I found I could still be very self-expressive in the kitchen," he says. His cooking style has evolved over the years. "When you cook all the time, your insecurities go, you have a steadier hand, and you keep getting better," he claims, "An innate sense takes over." His innovative creations at 45 South in Savannah earned him a loyal following, and on important occasions he was even persuaded to cater a dinner at home for special customers like Claire and John Ellis. These days he's in Atlanta launching a new restaurant, the Buckhorn Diner.

Gerry searches constantly for new ideas and presentations, delving into old cookbooks, traveling, and talking with other chefs for inspiration. "It's important to find a new way of looking at things, experiment just the way artists do," he explains. "Once you get an idea, build on it, imagine another way of handling it, change the ingredients."

Gerry enlisted a local grower to supply him with fresh herbs. "You have to *use* herbs to learn what they'll do," he says. He might put dill in the turkey stuffing instead of sage or serve crisp soft-shell crabs with a dill and shallot sauce. "Just think about what looks and tastes good together."

GRILLED QUAIL WITH CORN AND CHIVE SALAD

2 quail, with skin on

Olive oil

Salt and freshly ground black pepper

VINAIGRETTE

1 shallot, finely chopped

½ tablespoon extra-virgin olive oil

1 tablespoon sherry vinegar

¼ teaspoon Dijon mustard

Salt and freshly ground black pepper

1 ear corn

2 tablespoons finely diced fresh tomato

2 tablespoons minced fresh chives

½ head limestone lettuce

½ bunch arugula

½ bunch baby red-leaf lettuce

Few leaves of radicchio

Freshly ground pepper

Prepare a fire in the grill. Split the quail down the back so they will lie flat. When the coals are hot, lightly brush the quail with olive oil, season with salt and pepper, and grill, skin side down, until the skin is nicely browned, about 5 minutes. Turn and cook the other side about 2 minutes. The meat will still be pink.

While the quail is cooking, combine the first 4 vinaigrette ingredients in a small bowl and blend well. Season with salt and pepper and set aside.

Cut the kernels from the cob; blanch in boiling water for 1 minute. Drain. Place the corn in a small bowl with the tomato and 1 tablespoon of chives. Toss with ¼ cup vinaigrette. Set aside.

Wash and dry the lettuces. Toss with the remaining vinaigrette and chives; season with pepper. Arrange 1 small mound of lettuce and another small mound of corn and chive salad on each plate. Place a grilled quail on each plate and serve.

SERVES 2

RED SNAPPER WITH LEEKS AND CHIVES

1 liter red Burgundy wine

6 shallots, finely chopped

1 tablespoon red wine vinegar

6 tablespoons (¾ stick) unsalted butter, at room temperature

Salt and freshly ground pepper

2 red snapper fillets, 8 ounces each

3 leeks (white part only), julienned

2 tablespoons chopped fresh chives

2 chive blossoms, for garnish

In a noncorrosive saucepan, combine the wine, shallots, and vinegar. Reduce over high heat until only ¼ cup remains. Remove from heat; add butter, a small piece at a time, swirling the pan to combine. Do not stir. Season to taste with salt and pepper. Keep warm while fish cooks.

Season the fillets with salt and pepper. Place the fish in a steamer with the julienned leeks; cook just until the fish turns opaque, about 8 to 10 minutes. Place a cooked fillet on each plate and arrange the leeks on top, mounding them into a nice pile. Spoon half the Burgundy butter around each fillet and sprinkle generously with chives. Garnish with a chive blossom, if desired.

SERVES 2

The Ellises' columned double porch overlooks a sweep of lawn that ends at the river.

Grilled quail, *left*, and red snapper, *below*, are part of the special birthday dinner Claire Ellis ordered for husband John.

RESTORATIVE CUISINE IN VIRGINIA

For those seeking a respite from the hustle of "big" Washington, the Inn at Little Washington offers superb food in a luxurious setting amid the peace and fresh air of the Virginia countryside. The lush garden beyond the restaurant lures dinner guests outside for coffee and dessert. Designed to be just as beautiful when viewed from the upstairs rooms, the garden also serves the practical purpose of providing some of the herbs used in the kitchen. More herbs come from one of the inn's neighbors, a knowledgeable herbalist whose garden has for years been the source of herbal teas and remedies.

The inn's chef-owner, Patrick O'Connell, once a drama student, finds the restaurant a uniquely satisfying form of theater. "There's more participation," he says, "and being close to the growing of the food and the hands-on preparation balances the illusionary world of dining." Even while studying drama, Patrick worked in restaurants during summer vacations, but remembers "being a cook wasn't very highly thought of in America fifteen or twenty years ago." A trip to France made him see cooking in a different light. "I realized it could be an artistic pursuit and decided I could make cooking a career." He and partner Reinhardt Lynch still spend every off-season touring the great restaurants and hotels of Europe and the Orient, deriving inspiration from what they see in the kitchens, dining rooms, and markets.

As Patrick's cooking evolves, he sees himself moving more in the direction of a restorative cuisine that will help people feel better without feeling deprived. Herbs, with their healthful vitamins and minerals and their ability to enhance foods, play an important part in this kind of cooking. "I like to be able to give people food that's tantalizing to their taste buds and good for them without their knowing it," says Patrick. "When someone eats at the inn I want them to be refreshed, relaxed, and calmed," he says. "It should be like a little vacation."

The garden, inspired by L'Oasis in the south of France, invites guests to relax on a bench surrounded by silvery lamb's ears.

Herb-garnished green herb soup is both nourishing and sybaritic.

CREAM OF GREEN HERB SOUP

½ cup (1 stick) unsalted butter

1 cup chopped onions

½ cup chopped leeks (white part only)

¼ cup all-purpose flour

6 cups chicken stock, preferably homemade

4 cups mixed chopped green herbs, such as chives, dill, Italian parsley, watercress, spinach, sorrel, tarragon

⅔ cup heavy cream

Croûtons and edible flowers, for garnish

In a soup kettle, melt the butter over low heat. Add the onions and cook slowly until soft but not brown, about 5 minutes. Add the leeks and cook an additional 10 minutes. Add the flour and cook 5 minutes more, stirring occasionally. In a separate saucepan, bring the stock to a boil. Add hot stock to the onion mixture and simmer 15 minutes longer. Add the green herbs, return to a boil, then simmer for 5 minutes.

Transfer the soup to a blender or food processor, in batches if necessary, and purée. Strain the soup into a saucepan; stir in the cream and serve warm. Garnish with croûtons and flowers.

SERVES 6

SOFT-SHELL CRABS WITH GREMOLATA

Patrick O'Connell often serves his soft-shell crabs on a bed of shredded cabbage, tossed in a soy-flavored oriental dressing.

LEMON SAUCE

1 cup heavy cream

Juice of 6 lemons

3 tablespoons meat glaze

1½ pounds (6 sticks) unsalted butter

¼ cup finely chopped Italian parsley

¼ cup finely grated lemon zest

¼ cup minced garlic

12 large or 18 small soft-shell crabs

Flour for dredging

¾ cup (1½ sticks) unsalted butter

3 tablespoons vegetable oil

Salt and freshly ground pepper

12 to 18 thin lemon slices, peeled, for garnish

To make the sauce, heat the cream, lemon juice, and meat glaze separately in 3 small saucepans until each is reduced by half. Combine the reductions in a medium saucepan and, over low heat, whisk in the butter a tablespoon at a time. Set aside and keep warm.

For the gremolata, combine the parsley, lemon zest, and garlic in a small bowl. Set aside.

Dredge the crabs lightly in flour. Melt the butter and oil in a large skillet over medium-high heat and sauté the crabs until they are lightly browned on one side, about 3 minutes; turn and brown on the other side, 2 to 3 minutes longer. Season to taste. Spoon a pool of sauce onto each plate. Top with the sautéed crabs, add a lemon slice, and sprinkle with a ribbon of gremolata.

SERVES 6

FISH CAKES WITH SORREL CREAM SAUCE

Rather than just the usual crab cakes, Patrick O'Connell serves an elegant version, using salmon and sometimes tuna, too. Green mustard for the sauce is available in gourmet shops, or substitute Dijon mustard.

CRAB CAKES

1 pound fresh crab meat, picked over

3 tablespoons finely diced celery

2 tablespoons finely diced red bell pepper

1 teaspoon chopped fresh rosemary

1 teaspoon chopped fresh chives

2 teaspoons soy sauce

1 tablespoon lemon juice

Pinch of cayenne pepper

¼ teaspoon celery salt

1 teaspoon dry mustard

3 tablespoons mayonnaise

Flour

SALMON CAKES

1 pound fresh broiled or poached salmon

2 tablespoons chopped fresh chives

2 tablespoons chopped fresh tarragon

1 tablespoon minced garlic

1 tablespoon crushed green peppercorns

2 tablespoons Dijon mustard

2 tablespoons mayonnaise

1 tablespoon lemon juice

4 tablespoons olive oil

Sorrel Cream Sauce (recipe follows)

Fresh sorrel and red bell pepper, cut in chiffonade, for garnish

To make the crab cakes, combine the ingredients in a medium bowl. Season to taste with salt and pepper. Flour your hands, and then form mixture into 8 to 10 patties. Set on a plate, cover loosely with foil, and set aside.

To make the salmon cakes, flake the salmon into a medium bowl, discarding any small bones. Add the remaining ingredients and season to taste with salt and pepper. Flour your hands and form the mixture into 8 to 10 small cakes. Set aside on a plate loosely covered with foil.

Put 2 tablespoons of oil in each of 2 large skillets. Heat the oil over medium-high heat and place the 2 varieties of patties in the 2 skillets. Cook the patties, turning to brown both sides, until they are crisp and heated through, 3 to 4 minutes per side.

To serve, place the Sorrel Cream Sauce on a plate and put one of each variety of patty on top. Garnish, if desired, with chiffonnade of sorrel and strips of red pepper.

SERVES 8 TO 10

SORREL CREAM SAUCE

1 quart heavy cream

¼ cup lemon juice

¼ teaspoon grated nutmeg

3 tablespoons green mustard

1 tablespoon unsalted butter

1 pound fresh sorrel, cut in chiffonnade

Salt and pepper

Patrick O'Connell, *left,* **collects herbs from the garden where a quiet pond,** *above,* **adds a peaceful note.**

In a saucepan, reduce the cream, lemon juice, nutmeg, and mustard until bound and slightly thickened. In another pan, melt the butter, add the sorrel, and sweat for 2 minutes, until soft. Add the reduced cream and season to taste. Purée the sauce in a blender or food processor, and return to the pan to heat through before serving.

Fish cakes, *left,* **gain extra sophistication when served with a sorrel sauce.** *Far left,* **healthful and flavorful gremolata adds an Italian touch to soft-shell crabs.**

THE SOUTH 95

CAROLINA HOSPITALITY

Fearrington Village, in the Carolina countryside near Chapel Hill, is the creation of Jenny Fitch and her husband, R.B., who transformed an old farm into an idyllic country "village." The farmhouse has been remodeled into a charming restaurant known for its excellent food, and recently an inn has been added so travelers can enjoy the village, too.

A multitalented woman, Jenny is a skilled interior designer responsible for the interiors of the restaurant and the newly opened inn. She also arranges the masses of exuberant flowers that grace Fearrington House, sometimes mixing flowers from her garden with wildflowers from nearby fields. In addition to all this, Jenny is an accomplished cook and the author of the *Fearrington House Cookbook*, a compilation of recipes from the restaurant and favorite flower arrangements.

Jenny honed her kitchen talents with eight years of cooking lessons from renowned chef Judith Olney. "Judith started my interest in herbs," Jenny says, pointing out the herbs growing in the garden and in pots around Fearrington House. Fearrington chef Ben Barker uses herbs to add a creative twist to the indigenous Carolinian foods on the menu. "But don't mask the taste of the food with herbs," he cautions. "Use them to complement the flavors."

Lush roses from the garden decorate the table, *left*; croutons and chive blossoms garnish the soup, *right*.

CREAM OF VIDALIA ONION SOUP

If Vidalia onions are not available, substitute any sweet onion.

¼ pound sliced bacon, cut into ½-inch pieces

½ cup (1 stick) unsalted butter

3 pounds Vidalia onions, peeled and thinly sliced

8 garlic cloves, peeled

2 cups dry white wine

1 quart chicken stock

1 bay leaf

1 tablespoon fresh thyme, or 1 teaspoon dried

1 cup heavy cream

1 cup crème fraîche or sour cream

3 tablespoons lemon juice

½ teaspoon salt

Freshly ground white pepper

Tabasco

Nutmeg

1 cup sliced scallions, green and white parts

2 cups homemade croûtons

Chive, scallion, or society garlic blossoms, for garnish

In a large Dutch oven, cook the bacon slowly until crisp. Remove with a slotted spoon, drain on paper towels, and reserve. Add the butter, onions, and garlic cloves to the bacon renderings; cover and cook over low heat, stirring often, until onions are translucent and lightly caramelized, about 10 to 15 minutes. Add the wine,

Freshly picked edible flowers are often added to salads at Fearrington House.

⟜⟜

stock, bay leaf, and thyme; bring to a boil and simmer 30 minutes.

Strain the soup mixture, reserving both the liquid and solids. Discard the bay leaf and purée the remaining solids in a food processor or blender. Combine the purée with the reserved broth and chill.

Just before serving, whisk in the cream and crème fraîche or sour cream. Season with lemon juice, salt, pepper, Tabasco, and nutmeg. Serve in chilled bowls; garnish with the bacon pieces, scallions, croûtons, and chive blossoms.

SERVES 8

HERBAL DELIGHTS IN RURAL VIRGINIA

Chick Cove Manor was an abandoned chicken farm before Renée and Lee Chewning transformed it into a restaurant. Although not formally trained, Renée had learned the basics of cooking as a child. "And I always enjoyed eating," she says. "I spent ten years in New York, most of it in restaurants. I entertained and read a lot, too. When you're exposed to ideas," she says, "they spark ideas of your own."

Those ideas went far beyond the familiar fish fries and crab cakes served by other area restaurants. The Chewnings learned to smoke their own meats and fish, made rich pâtés, and baked breads and pastries in the restaurant's kitchen. Veal, poultry, or fresh Chesapeake Bay shellfish were served with generous helpings of fresh vegetables from the garden.

Since fresh herbs were hard to find in rural Virginia, the Chewnings planted a garden filled with herbs and salad greens behind the restaurant. And every dish, from crab meat strudel to luscious angel cake, became even more special when Renée's sure hand seasoned it with a few fresh herbs. This small garden was just the beginning—Lee now runs an herb farm that produces nearly 30,000 herb plants each year. With no professional gardening experience to fall back on, he read prodigiously and made many calls to Sal Gilbertie, seeking the advice of this well-known Connecticut herb grower. "I learned through trial and error and through my mistakes," he recalls.

Today, winters at Chick Cove are devoted to growing cuttings for the planting season. In the spring the farm sells herb plants, while during the summer, when the restaurant is at its busiest, cut herbs are sold. Falls were quiet until the Chewnings decided to take advantage of the harvest with a line of herbal vinegars, salad dressings, and jellies. The tantalizing flavors of their lavender and ginger vinegars or fragrant rose geranium marmalade reflect Renée's special talent for using herbs.

Renée's scented geranium garnish echoes the subtle lemon rose geranium flavor of the cake.

Chilled cucumber soup and a salad, spiced up with herbs and flowers from the garden, make a delightful warm weather lunch.

LEMON ROSE GERANIUM ANGEL CAKE

If you have time to plan ahead, the geranium flavor of this cake can be intensified by placing the sugar in a container with a tight-fitting lid and burying two or three geranium leaves in it for a week or so. This flavored sugar is also a wonderful treat with fruit, in other cakes, or served with tea.

1½ cups sugar
1 cup cake flour
12 egg whites
2 teaspoons cream of tartar
1 teaspoon vanilla extract
⅛ teaspoon salt

6 lemon rose geranium leaves
Additional lemon rose geranium leaves and blossoms, for garnish
Berries, for garnish

Preheat the oven to 350°F.

Sift ¾ cup of the sugar and the flour together; set aside. In a large mixing bowl, combine the egg whites with the cream of tartar, vanilla, and salt. Beat until soft peaks begin to form. Slowly add the remaining ¾ cup sugar, continuing to beat until stiff peaks begin to form. Do not overbeat; mixture should be stiff but not dry. Gently fold in the flour mixture, a small bit at a time.

Line the bottom of an ungreased 10-inch tube pan with the leaves. Pour the batter into the pan and bake until the cake is golden and springs back when gently touched, about 50 minutes. Invert the cake pan over the neck of a bottle and let the cake cool in the pan for 1 to 1½ hours. Gently run a sharp knife around the sides of the pan to release the cake. Garnish with geranium leaves and flowers and fresh berries, if desired.

MAKES 1 10-INCH CAKE

CHESAPEAKE BAY BLUEFIN CRAB STRUDEL

Herb butter can be made by creaming ½ pound (2 sticks) butter and then incorporating ¼ cup chopped herbs of your choice. One tablespoon of lemon juice can also be added. If you do not wish to make herb butter, add the chopped herbs to the butter as you melt it. A combination of chives and parsley would work well in this recipe.

¾ cup herb butter

½ cup chopped shallots

¼ cup chopped celery

1 cup Chardonnay wine

¾ pound backfin or lump crab meat

¼ pound cream cheese

1 tablespoon golden lemon thyme leaves

¼ cup chopped fresh parsley

4 egg yolks

¼ teaspoon ground white pepper

¼ pound phyllo dough

1 egg, beaten

❧

The lush green herb garden is visible from the restaurant's pleasant porch.

The flaky strudel is garnished with lemon thyme.

❧

Preheat the oven to 400°F.

In a large sauté pan, melt ½ cup of the herb butter; sauté the shallots and celery over medium heat until they are soft but not brown, about 5 to 8 minutes. Add the wine and reduce over high heat to ½ cup. Remove the pan from the heat and add the crab meat, cream cheese, thyme leaves, parsley, egg yolks, and pepper.

In a small pan, melt the remaining herb butter. Working quickly, place 1 sheet of phyllo dough on a clean work surface and brush it with herb butter. Top with another sheet and repeat until you have 8 layers. (Keep a slightly damp towel over the remaining sheets of phyllo as you work.) Spread half the crab mixture along one long edge of the buttered phyllo sheets and carefully roll it up. The finished roll should be about 2 inches in diameter. Repeat with another 8 sheets of phyllo and the remaining crab meat mixture. (Any leftover phyllo dough should be carefully wrapped and frozen.) Brush the rolls with beaten egg. Bake until golden, 12 to 15 minutes. To serve, use a serrated knife to cut the strudel in generous slices.

SERVES 12

CHILLED CUCUMBER DILL SOUP

2 tablespoons vegetable oil

10 cucumbers, peeled, seeded, and coarsely chopped

4 sweet onions (preferably Vidalia), coarsely chopped

5 garlic cloves

5 cups rich chicken stock

½ cup chopped fresh dill
Freshly ground white pepper to taste

2 cups heavy cream
Additional dill, for garnish

In a large saucepan, heat the vegetable oil over medium heat and sauté the cucumbers, onions, and garlic until the onions are transparent, about 5 minutes. Add the chicken stock and simmer until the cucumber is soft, about 15 to 20 minutes. Remove from heat and transfer the soup to a food processor, in batches if necessary. Blend until smooth. Strain the mixture through a fine sieve. While the mixture is still warm, stir in the chopped dill and season with pepper, then chill. Stir in the cream just before serving. Garnish with dill sprigs.

SERVES 10 TO 12

❧

The cucumber soup.

Eve coats hot, freshly boiled potatoes with butter, then sprinkles them with chopped dill before serving.

HERBS FROM A COTTAGE GARDEN

"Unless you've tasted good food, it's hard to know if what you're cooking is okay," says antiques dealer Eve Taylor. Lucky enough to grow up in a family of good cooks, she fondly remembers the long, food-laden table where everyone gathered for convivial meals. "I started learning about herbs then," she recalls. "My grandmother had an Eastern European background and always used dill. My stepfather, on the other hand, was Italian and loved basil."

When Eve began to cook for her husband and three sons, she continued to explore the possibilities of herbs, often finding inspiration in new recipes. "I still love to read cookbooks," she

admits. Now Eve harvests most of her herbs from her cottage garden, a charming mix of herbs and flowers. "I'd always wanted to have a garden," she explains. "I remembered the garden from my childhood and I've seen so many beautiful herb gardens traveling around antiquing."

As soon as she could supply her own fresh herbs, dried herbs were banished from her kitchen. "I use much more rosemary now that I have it growing outside," she says, but dill is still a favorite. When it's not in season, it's at the ready in the freezer, waiting to add its bittersweet flavor to simple potatoes or veal, just the way it did in her grandmother's kitchen.

CREAM OF CARROT SOUP

A touch of rosemary gives this soup its subtle but intriguing flavor.

- 4 tablespoons (½ stick) unsalted butter
- 1 large onion, preferably Spanish or Vidalia, chopped
- 12 carrots, sliced
- 1 potato, peeled and diced
- 4 cups chicken stock
- 2 tablespoons minced fresh ginger
- 2 teaspoons minced fresh rosemary
- ½ cup heavy cream
  Salt and pepper
  Additional rosemary sprigs, for garnish

Melt the butter in a heavy pot over low heat. Add the onion and let it cook slowly, covered, until it is soft but not browned, about 30 minutes. Add the carrots and potato, chicken stock, ginger, and rosemary; cook until the carrots and potatoes are soft, about 30 minutes longer. Mash with potato masher (or if you prefer a smoother texture, purée in a food processor). Stir in the cream and season to taste with salt and pepper. Garnish with rosemary, if desired.

SERVES 6

A small cottage garden lies just outside the front door.

AN EYE FOR HERBS

"Being in the antiques business is wonderful for someone who loves architecture and the arts," enthuses Marston Luce, a student of both. He and his partner, Julie Southwood, who studied decorative arts, find buying and selling antiques a great outlet for their combined talents. But the constant search for the distinctive country antiques that fill their charming Georgetown shop means they're away most weekends. As a result, most of their entertaining is done midweek, after a busy day at the shop.

"We eat out a lot" says Julie, "and when we eat at home, it has to be easy." Tasty pasta salads that include herbs and vegetables from the garden are typical. "I love to cook with anything I can get out of the garden," says Julie. "It's so much fun to use something you've grown yourself." Tomatoes, lettuce, and herbs such as sage and basil thrive in the beds around the house. More herbs grow in pots on the terrace and in a small herb garden at the shop. Julie, who has a collection of old herb books and likes to read about nineteenth-century American gardens, also enjoys gathering food in the wild.

Julie and Marston prefer to entertain on a small scale, inviting two other couples for dinner and enjoying some pleasant conversation. Sometimes they share the cooking chores with guests such as Pat Ridgeway, a dealer who got her start "picking" yellowware and majolica for Marston. "Simplicity in foods is wonderful," she says. "That's why I like this chicken recipe. There's too much emphasis on the exotic today. I like to work with what's on hand."

With all this visual talent, meals are as appealing to the eye as to the tongue. "How things look is very important," says Marston. "Since that's my primary sense, I tend to put more emphasis on appearance and I think it makes food taste better."

❦

When Julie and Marston can eat outdoors, entertaining seems even easier, and guests are often invited on the spur of the moment.

HERBED CHICKEN

1 chicken, about 3 pounds

1 ½ tablespoons unsalted butter

1 ½ tablespoons olive oil

Salt and freshly ground black pepper

1 tablespoon chopped fresh basil

1 tablespoon chopped fresh thyme

1 cup chicken stock

1 tablespoon each chopped fresh basil, thyme, and parsley, for garnish

1 lemon, thinly sliced

Wash and dry the chicken. Cut into serving pieces.

In a large, heavy skillet, melt the butter in the oil over medium-high heat. Add the legs and thighs, sautéing for about 5 minutes. Add the wings and breasts to the pan, continuing to sauté until all the pieces are evenly browned, about 15 minutes more. Reduce the heat to medium-low, season chicken to taste, and sprinkle with the herbs. Cover the skillet and continue to cook slowly for 30 to 35 minutes, basting occasionally with the pan juices.

When the chicken is done, place on a serving platter. Skim any excess fat from the pan. Pour the chicken stock into the pan and cook over medium heat, stirring vigorously, until the sauce is reduced to about ½ cup. To serve, pour the sauce over the chicken pieces and garnish with the chopped herbs and lemon slices, if desired.

SERVES 4

COLD PASTA SALAD WITH FRESH HERBS

8 ounces whole-wheat wagon wheel pasta or rigatoni

2 tablespoons mayonnaise

Juice of 1 lemon

4 to 6 scallions, chopped, white and green parts

1 (7-ounce) can artichoke hearts, drained and sliced

¼ cup basil leaves, torn into small pieces

Fresh oregano to taste

¼ teaspoon salt

¼ cup grated Parmesan cheese

1 head Boston or Romaine lettuce

Fresh parsley, for garnish

Cook the pasta according to directions on the package until just tender. Drain and transfer to a medium mixing bowl. Stir in the mayonnaise and lemon juice. Add the scallions, sliced artichoke hearts, herbs, salt, and cheese; stir until well mixed. If the salad seems too dry, add a little more mayonnaise and lemon juice. Cool to room temperature and serve on lettuce leaves. Garnish with parsley.

SERVES 4

A SENSE OF BALANCE

Nancy Lendved and Lisa Cherkasky met while working on a cookbook for Time-Life Books. Lisa, a graduate of the Culinary Institute of America, was working up new recipes and preparing the food for photography. Nancy, a student of decorative arts and architecture, contributed her keen sense of style to selecting dishes and settings to enhance the food. Now friends, the two frequently merge their talents to entertain.

Whether cooking for a dinner or party for friends or working for a client, Lisa aims for simplicity. "Food should taste good and not be overly complicated. It's important to think about what foods go well together," she advises. "Not every dish can make a statement; you need balance." When Lisa serves a heavy dish, she will prepare a light one to offset it. A creamy recipe will be played against something with bite. "Outspoken foods need to be eaten by themselves," she adds.

Herbs can help adjust the balance. The refreshing taste of mint makes a creamy dessert seem lighter; the pungency of a sage stuffing offsets the rich fattiness of a pork chop; and the sweetness of beets is modified by the sharpness of dill. "Herbs can make all the difference in plain food, too," she notes. "Take a simple potato. Adding just one herb makes it." "And the right setting helps," adds Nancy.

A homespun cloth and pottery are in keeping with the informality of this main course soup and bread sticks.

COLD BEET SOUP WITH SHRIMP

1 pound cooked beets

1 red onion, quartered

2 large garlic cloves

2 cups water

1 (46-ounce) can tomato juice

1 cup beef stock

2 tablespoons lemon juice

2 ½ cups buttermilk

Salt and freshly ground pepper

½ pound small shrimp, peeled, cleaned, and cooked

¼ cup snipped fresh dill

1 bunch fresh chives, minced

GARNISHES

4 hard-cooked eggs, chopped

2 cucumbers, peeled, seeded, and finely sliced

1 small red onion, diced

½ cup sour cream or crème fraîche

In a food processor or blender, purée the beets, onion, and garlic with some of the water until very smooth. Combine the purée, remaining water, tomato juice, beef stock, lemon juice, and buttermilk. Season to taste with salt and pepper, cover, and refrigerate until very cold, at least 1 hour. Stir in the shrimp, dill, and chives before serving.

Serve the garnishes on the side to be added to each bowl individually.

SERVES 8 AS A MAIN COURSE

HERBED BREAD STICKS

3 cups all-purpose flour

1 package rapid-rise dry yeast

1 tablespoon salt

¼ cup chopped fresh parsley

1 bunch fresh chives, chopped

2 tablespoons chopped fresh dill

7 tablespoons olive oil

6 tablespoons very warm water (130°F.)

Cornmeal

In a large bowl, mix the flour, yeast, salt, and herbs. Add the olive oil and water, and mix until a dough is formed. On a floured surface, knead the dough until smooth and elastic, about 5 minutes. Place the dough in an oiled bowl, cover with a towel, and set in a warm place to rise. When the dough has doubled in size, about 30 minutes, punch it down and divide it into 16 pieces. Roll each piece into a 12-inch "snake."

Sprinkle 2 sheet pans with cornmeal. Transfer the bread sticks to the sheet pans, cover with dish towels, and leave in a warm place to rise for about 20 minutes. Preheat the oven to 400°F.

When the bread sticks have completed the second rising, bake until lightly browned, about 15 to 20 minutes.

MAKES 16 BREAD STICKS

The Midwest

The Midwest is the country's heartland, supplying much of our wheat and cattle, corn and hogs, as well as a bountiful supply of vegetables and fruits. Not settled until the mid 1800s, long after the East and South, there were times when weather or economics forced the pioneers of this ever-advancing frontier to subsist on little more than potatoes, salt pork, fried mush, and corncake. But generally the munificence of the land provided a varied larder. Wild ducks, prairie chickens, and venison roamed the woods and fields; cranberries and other berries and plums and grapes flourished in the wild; the Indians harvested wild rice; and a plentiful supply of fish swam in the lakes and rivers. The settlers' skill in preserving, salting, drying, canning, smoking, and pickling made it possible to keep fruits, vegetables,

Masses of Robin Hood roses climb the fence behind Linda Veffer's country lunch.

and fish on their tables throughout the long and often treacherous Midwestern winters.

Meals, designed to satisfy the appetites of hard-working farmers, were hearty rather than elegant, and potluck suppers, to which each cook contributed her favorite dish, were as common then as they are now. Today's Midwestern cooks still draw on their rural roots and often incorporate the rich cream and eggs of their farm heritage and flavorful fresh chicken into simple regional dishes.

The heavy influx of Scandinavian and German settlers left its mark on Midwestern cooking as did the community of Shakers in Ohio and the flavors of the neighboring Southern states. Nevertheless, the accent in Midwestern kitchens has always been on corn, meat, and vegetables of such superb quality they need no adornment, and on a wide variety of breads made from the region's wheat.

Early homemakers grew a few herbs to flavor pickles, chutneys, catsups, canned vegetables, and vinegars, or to add zest to sausages and stuffings. But today in the Midwest, as in other areas of the country, a wide variety of herbs are used to season everything from grilled spare ribs to old-fashioned pound cake. As Karen Kloster, a native of rural Illinois, notes, "You'll find a lot of plain country folk do a lot of herb growing. And everyone uses herbs to try and reproduce the foods they eat in restaurants."

Sue Ellen Lawton's dessert buffet features old candlesticks and a "bouquet" of feathers.

Park Studebaker follows family tradition by serving German onions, an appetizing mixture of onions, cream, salt and pepper, and a little vinegar, over baked potatoes.

Jean True adds mint to her mother's shortcake recipe.

MEMORIES OF FOOD

An avid collector, one of Karen Kloster's greatest pleasures is using her quilts, pottery, and china with the delicious foods she prepares for family and friends. "I have another collection that's not so tangible," she says, "my food memories. My husband and I love to travel and collect memories of eating in different places around the world."

Born and bred in rural Illinois, Karen loved to cook even as a child. After earning a home economics degree, she worked with the Swift meat company, then began doing free-lance recipe development and photo styling. But even when she's not working, she's apt to be in the kitchen cooking for her husband and any visiting family members. "I'm definitely not a gardener," Karen admits, "but I always have some herbs growing close to the kitchen door for cooking. I love to use them as garnish, too, to indicate what a dish is going to taste like."

She enjoys taking simple, fresh foods and doing something interesting with them. For instance, the stoneground cornmeal from the nearby Graue Mill, an old-time grist mill turned museum, inspired her variations on basic corn bread, and farm-fresh chicken and vegetables might be turned into a sophisticated tarragon-flavored pot pie under a parsley crust. "You'll discover that everyone in the Midwest has their own way of cutting a vent in a pie crust even though they may not be aware of it," notes Karen. "They'll always use their own special design that's probably come down through the family."

Karen flavors white wine, *right*, with woodruff from her backyard. Peonies and lamb's ears are mixed into a casual bouquet for lunch in the eat-in kitchen, *far right*.

TARRAGON CHICKEN POT PIE

PARSLEY PASTRY
- 2 cups all-purpose flour
- 2 tablespoons chopped fresh parsley
- 1 teaspoon salt
- ⅔ cup shortening
- ½ cup cold water

- 1 3-pound frying chicken
- 3 tablespoons chopped fresh tarragon
- ¼ cup chopped celery leaves
- 1 bay leaf
- 2½ teaspoons salt
- ½ teaspoon freshly ground pepper
- 4 tablespoons chicken fat or butter
- 1 onion, chopped
- ⅓ cup all-purpose flour
- 1 cup heavy cream or milk
- 1 cup diced cooked carrots
- 1 cup cooked peas
- 1 cup diced cooked potatoes
- 1 egg yolk beaten with a little cold water

To make the pastry, combine the flour, parsley, and salt in a bowl. With a pastry blender or fork, cut in the shortening until it is the size of small peas. Add the water, a tablespoon at a time, tossing with a fork until the mixture can be gathered into a ball; you may not need all the water. Wrap the dough in waxed paper and chill for at least 30 minutes.

Preheat the oven to 375°F.

Place the chicken in a large saucepan with cold water to cover and add the tarragon, celery leaves, bay leaf, 2 teaspoons of the salt and ¼ teaspoon of the pepper. Bring to a boil over high heat, then reduce heat and simmer, covered, for about 1 hour, or until the chicken is tender. Remove the chicken, strain the broth and reserve it. When the chicken is cool enough to handle, discard the skin and remove the meat from the bones and cut it into chunks. Skim the fat from the reserved broth.

In a medium saucepan, melt the chicken fat or butter; add the onion and sauté until it is transparent, about 5 minutes. Stir in the flour, the remaining ½ teaspoon salt and ¼ teaspoon pepper, then blend in 2 cups of the reserved broth and the cream or milk. Cook, stirring, over medium heat until the mixture comes to a boil and thickens, about 15 minutes. Place the chicken, carrots, peas, and potatoes in a 3-quart casserole and top with enough sauce to cover them and almost fill the casserole.

On a lightly floured surface, roll out the chilled dough to fit the top of the casserole. Place the dough on top of the casserole, folding the edges under and moistening the edge of the casserole to make the pastry adhere. Cut vents in the crust and brush it with the egg wash. Bake for about 40 minutes, or until the crust is golden and the sauce is bubbling.

SERVES 6

GRILLED SPARERIBS WITH SPICED ROSEMARY MARINADE

MARINADE
2 tablespoons paprika

2 tablespoons chili powder

2 tablespoons fresh rosemary leaves, crushed

2 tablespoons garlic powder or 2 garlic cloves, minced

1 teaspoon salt

2 teaspoons dry mustard

½ teaspoon freshly ground pepper

2 tablespoons vegetable oil

3½ to 4 pounds pork baby back spareribs

In a bowl, mix the dry marinade ingredients with the oil until well combined. Rub the meaty side of the ribs with the mixture, cover with plastic wrap, and marinate (or refrigerate) for four hours or overnight.

Prepare a fire in a grill with a lid. When the coals are medium hot (covered with a coating of white ash), add the ribs, meaty side up. Cover and cook for about 45 minutes, or until the ribs are well browned and cooked through.

SERVES 4

❧

A country picnic in the shadow of the old Graue Mill includes herb butter for the dilly-bacon cornsticks.

MINTED PEA SALAD

4 cups fresh peas or 1 16-ounce package frozen peas

3 to 4 sprigs fresh mint leaves

½ cup sliced celery

½ cup sliced scallions, green and white parts

2 tablespoons chopped fresh chives

1 teaspoon salt

3 tablespoons white wine vinegar

1 tablespoon chopped fresh mint

¼ cup olive oil

Mint sprigs for garnish

Place the peas and mint sprigs in a covered saucepan with a small amount of water. If using fresh peas, cook over medium heat until just tender, about 10 to 12 minutes; cook frozen peas just until heated through. Drain peas and discard mint. In a bowl, combine the peas, celery, scallions, chives, and salt. In a small bowl, combine the vinegar, chopped mint, and oil and mix well; pour over the pea mixture and toss until it is evenly coated. Cover and chill for several hours. Garnish with additional mint sprigs before serving.

SERVES 8

DILLY-BACON CORN BREAD

1 cup all-purpose flour

1 cup stoneground yellow cornmeal

⅓ cup sugar

1 tablespoon baking powder

1 teaspoon salt

8 slices bacon, cooked crisp

2 tablespoons finely chopped fresh dill or 2 teaspoons dried

1 cup milk

¼ cup vegetable oil

1 egg

Preheat oven to 425°F.

In a bowl, combine the flour, cornmeal, sugar, baking powder, and salt. Crumble the bacon and add it to the cornmeal mixture along with the dill. In a small bowl, mix the milk, oil, and egg until they are well blended, then stir the liquid into the cornmeal mixture until just combined. Spoon the batter into a greased 8 × 8-inch pan or a cornstick mold. Bake for about 20 minutes or until golden brown and firm.

MAKES 1 8 × 8-INCH CAKE OR
1 DOZEN CORNSTICKS

A TOUCH OF SWEDEN

Twelve years ago Martha Geffen, who had found herself becoming more and more interested in cooking, finally decided to trade in her career in social work for a catering business. When the opportunity to work in one of the first wave of women-owned restaurants came along, Martha leapt at the chance to enlarge her knowledge of cooking, because the chef-owner was serving a menu filled with culinary innovations.

Now Martha and her partners, Samantha Peterson and Anne Buchanan, run the restaurants at the Minneapolis Institute of Art and the Walker Art Center. "We try to serve very good food at reasonable prices," she says, "so we even make all our breads and desserts." In addition, the trio caters private and corporate parties and special openings at the museums. "People here want basic food with a creative touch," she notes. Herbs often provide that extra distinction. "Ten years ago, when pesto first struck my fancy, I had to grow the basil myself," says Martha. These days fresh herbs are available at the local farmer's market.

Like many Minnesotans, Martha has a Swedish heritage, but she seldom serves traditional Swedish dishes to clients. "They tend to be very basic," she says, "very brown and white looking. Although we might offer a casserole of Swedish brown beans among many other dishes in a smorgasbord, we generally adapt the traditional recipes to make them lighter, and to give them more color and flavor to appeal to American tastes."

The Swedish-inspired dinner, *right*, is set in front of an old ceramic stove at the Swedish Institute.

POACHED SALMON WITH DILL AND MUSTARD SAUCE

POACHING LIQUID
- ½ cup dry white wine
- 2 slices lemon
- ½ teaspoon peppercorns
- 1 sprig fresh dill
- 1 teaspoon salt

- 6 salmon steaks, 8 ounces each

DILL AND MUSTARD SAUCE
- 2 tablespoons (¼ stick) butter
- 2 tablespoons all-purpose flour
- 2 cups half-and-half
- 1 tablespoon sugar
- 2 tablespoons white wine vinegar
- 1 tablespoon dry mustard
- Salt and pepper
- 1 egg yolk
- ¼ cup chopped fresh dill

Fresh dill for garnish

Place the ingredients for the poaching liquid in a large pot with 2 quarts of water. Bring to a boil over high heat, then reduce the heat to low and simmer for 15 minutes. Add the

❧

Aquavit encased in a flower-laden block of ice is served on a delicately painted Gustavian table from the eighteenth century in the drawing room of the Swedish Institute.

salmon steaks to the barely simmering liquid and poach for 5 to 8 minutes, or until they turn opaque and are firm to the touch. Remove from the liquid and keep warm.

To make the sauce, melt the butter in a saucepan over low heat. Stir in the flour with a whisk and cook, stirring occasionally, for 2 to 3 minutes. Gradually stir in the half-and-half and whisk until it is thick, about 5 minutes. Add in the sugar, vinegar, mustard, and salt and pepper to taste and remove from the heat.

Place the egg yolk in a medium bowl and beat lightly. Stir a little of the hot sauce into the yolk, then pour in the remaining sauce, stirring with the whisk. Mix in the chopped dill. Serve the sauce over the salmon steaks or in a separate bowl. Garnish with fresh dill.

SERVES 6

STEAMED VEGETABLES WITH CHIVE-CARDAMOM BUTTER

Cauliflower and root vegetables are popular with Scandinavians because they can be easily stored for use during the cold northern winters.

- 1 head cauliflower
- 1 small rutabaga, peeled and diced
- 12 new potatoes, with a strip of skin removed around the middle
- 2 cups frozen peas
- 12 small carrots, peeled
- 6 small scallions with their tops

CHIVE-CARDAMOM BUTTER

- ½ pound clarified butter
- ¼ teaspoon ground cardamom
- ¼ cup chopped fresh chives

Each of the vegetables should be steamed separately. Remove the outer leaves from the cauliflower and steam the whole head for 8 to 10 minutes, or until just crisp-tender. The potatoes will need 15 to 18 minutes; the rutabaga 12 to 15 minutes; the peas 2 minutes; the carrots 10 to 12 minutes; and the scallions 8 to 10 minutes.

While the vegetables are steaming, melt the butter and stir in the cardamom and chives. To serve, place the cauliflower in the middle of a round platter and arrange the remaining vegetables around it. Spoon the herb butter over the vegetables just before serving.

SERVES 6

The sauce for this poached salmon, *left*, was inspired by the sweet mustard-dill sauce traditionally served with gravlax, the dill-marinated salmon so popular in Scandinavia.

᭯᭯᭯

Vegetables, steamed and served with an herb butter flavored with cardamom, a favorite Swedish seasoning, make a simple but festive presentation.

BAKING WITH HERBS

Most of Sue Hodder's herbs grow in a collection of clay pots at the family's lakeside cottage in northern Minnesota, but she makes sure there are enough plants in her suburban garden to provide fresh herbs during Minneapolis's short growing season. When fall comes, both crops are harvested and dried for use throughout the long Minnesota winter, or to be turned into fragrant potpourris.

An exuberant cook, Sue enjoys preparing meals for family and friends, but likes baking best. Both her mother and grandmother were superb bakers, and Sue carries on the tradition, using old family recipes along with those she gets from friends. Fennel seed and dill are often called for in her family recipes; in others, Sue adds herbs as she sees fit. "I like to experiment with flavors," she says. "Doing the same thing over and over is boring." Among Sue's favorite breads are her mother's Swedish rye recipe and one of her grandmother's Swedish recipes that can be baked in a shape called a triple crown, which represents the symbol of Swedish royalty.

Each family member has a favorite bread that Sue likes to bake for them on special occasions. "Baking is another way of saying 'I love you,'" says Sue. "And when anyone new moves into the neighborhood, I take them a loaf of bread. It's a sign of friendship."

Sue might take a selection of rolls, bread, and a potted chicken to a potluck supper.

JENNY'S ROLLS

This recipe produces a rather sweet, dense roll that would be particularly good with tea or coffee or with a light dish like fruit or chicken salad. Although traditionally made in the shape of a knot, Sue likes to cut her dough into heart shapes with a deep cookie cutter. Alternately, the dough can be baked in a tube pan to make a triple crown.

1 package active dry yeast

¼ cup warm water

1 cup milk

⅓ cup sugar

⅓ cup (⅔ stick) butter or margarine

1 egg, lightly beaten

½ teaspoon ground coriander or cardamom seeds

½ teaspoon salt

4 or more cups unbleached flour

½ cup (1 stick) margarine, melted

¾ cup sugar

Soften the yeast in the warm water and set aside until it dissolves and begins to bubble.

While the yeast is proofing, place the milk, sugar, and butter or margarine in a saucepan and heat gently until the butter has melted. Remove from the heat, cool slightly, then stir in the egg. Mix in the coriander or cardamom, the salt, and the yeast mixture. Stir well. Gradually add flour, mixing it in with a large wooden spoon, until the dough is so stiff it can no longer be stirred. Turn the dough out onto a floured work surface and knead until smooth and elastic, about 10 minutes. Place the dough in a greased bowl, lightly grease the top, cover with a damp towel and allow to rise for 2 to 2½ hours or until doubled in bulk.

When the dough is ready, punch it down, turn onto a floured surface, and roll it out about ½" thick. With a heart-shaped cookie cutter, cut out 24 rolls; dip the tops in the melted margarine, then the sugar. Place the rolls on a greased cookie sheet. Mix any remaining butter and sugar together and sprinkle over the tops. Allow them to rise again until doubled in size, about 1 hour. Preheat the oven to 375°F.

Bake for 30 minutes or until the sugar is melted and the rolls are done.

Variation: To make the triple crown, grease two fluted tube pans. Once the dough has been punched down, cut off a piece of dough a little smaller than a tennis ball, dip one side in margarine and sugar, then place in the ring with the sugared side on top; continue around the ring, placing the balls rather close together. Repeat with the second pan. Mix any remaining sugar and margarine together and sprinkle over the top. Allow to rise until doubled in size, about 1 to 1½ hours. Bake for 20 to 25 minutes, or until golden brown on top and a cake tester in the middle comes out clean.

MAKES 2 DOZEN ROLLS OR
2 8-INCH RINGS

SAVORY FROSTED FRENCH BREAD

Sue generally uses a loaf of home-made French bread for this, but you can substitute a good crusty version from the bakery. Serve it with simple grilled meats and poultry, soups, or salads.

SAVORY FROSTING

1 cup mayonnaise, preferably homemade

½ cup grated Parmesan cheese

½ cup chopped onions

1 teaspoon Worcestershire sauce

3 dashes Tabasco sauce

1 tablespoon chopped fresh chives

1 tablespoon chopped fresh oregano or 1 teaspoon dried

1 loaf French bread, split in half lengthwise

Paprika

Preheat oven to 350°F.

Place the frosting ingredients in the bowl of a food processor and blend with three or four on-and-off motions, or mix by hand in a small bowl.

Spread half of the frosting mixture evenly over each loaf half, then sprinkle with paprika to taste. Place the bread, frosted side up, on the oven rack and bake for 15 to 20 minutes, or until bubbly and golden. Slice with a serrated knife or pizza cutter before serving.

SERVES 6

POTTED CHICKEN

This tasty, low-calorie chicken dish should be cooked in a special unglazed terra-cotta pot that is soaked in water for 30 minutes before using. If you do not have a clay pot, use a heavy, covered casserole. Vegetables, such as carrots, green beans, or scallions, can be added to the pot 30 minutes before serving.

1 4-pound chicken

1 to 2 tablespoons olive or vegetable oil

1 large sprig fresh rosemary

3 sprigs fresh sage

1 sprig fresh lemon thyme
Lemon pepper to taste

1 cup white wine or dry vermouth

The potted chicken, *above*. Hot and pungent, herb-frosted bread, *opposite*, is easy to make and delicious with simple grilled meats and fish.

Preheat the oven to 400°F.

Wash and dry the chicken, discarding the heart, liver, and gizzards. Rub the skin with oil.

Place the rosemary, 1 sprig of sage, and the lemon thyme in the cavity of the chicken, then place it, breast side up, in the presoaked pot. Sprinkle the chicken with lemon pepper, pour the wine into the pot, and place a sprig of sage on the breast. Cover and bake for 1½ to 2 hours, or until the chicken is nicely browned and the juices run clear when the thigh joint is pierced with a fork. Place the remaining sprig of sage on the breast before serving warm or at room temperature.

SERVES 4

OLD-FASHIONED SWEDISH RYE

This dough can be baked as loaves or rolls. Additional seeds can be pressed into the tops of the loaves or the rolls before baking if desired.

1 teaspoon anise or fennel seeds

1½ cups scalded milk

1½ cups cool water

½ cup dark brown sugar

½ cup vegetable oil

½ cup molasses

2 packages active dry yeast

2 teaspoons salt

2½ cups rye flour

6 to 7 cups unbleached all-purpose white flour
Melted butter

Combine the seeds, milk, water, brown sugar, oil, and molasses in a large bowl, stirring just until mixed. Add the yeast and salt and let stand until the yeast and brown sugar have dissolved and the mixture begins to bubble.

Gradually stir in the rye flour, then beat in the unbleached flour a cup at a time. When the dough becomes too stiff to beat, turn it out onto a floured board and knead in more flour until the dough is smooth and no longer sticky. Continue to knead until smooth and elastic, about 5 to 10 minutes.

Place the dough in a greased bowl, cover with a damp towel, and let rise until doubled in bulk, about 1 to 1½ hours.

For loaves, divide the dough into 4 equal parts, shape each into a loaf and place in an oiled 9 × 5 × 3-inch loaf pan. Allow the bread to rise again for 1 to 1½ hours, or until doubled in bulk. Preheat oven to 350°F.

Bake for 40 to 45 minutes, or until the bottom sounds hollow when tapped. Brush the tops with butter; cool on a rack.

For rolls, pull off a piece of dough slightly larger than a golf ball, shape it into a ball, and place on an oiled baking sheet, pressing the top lightly with the palm of your hand to flatten it a bit. Repeat until all the dough has been used. Cover the rolls with a damp towel and let rise for about 1 hour, or until doubled in bulk. Bake for 15 to 20 minutes, brush the tops with butter, and cool on a rack.

MAKES 4 LOAVES OR 3 DOZEN ROLLS

Sue Ellen's antique furniture and accessories mix well with contemporary wicker in her light-filled dining room.

AN ANTIQUES LOVER'S HERBS

Sue Ellen Lawton never cooked until she got married, and only became involved with herbs because she was in the antiques business. "We moved into an eighteenth-century reproduction house," she says, "and I had an antiques shop there. I started an herb garden to complete the picture." Reading ensured that the herbs she planted were historically correct. Once she had them, she decided she might as well learn to use them.

With memories of her mother's good cooking to guide her, she soon became an accomplished cook as well as an avid gardener. "I really like herbs, particularly parsley, chives, and tarragon," says Sue Ellen, "because they're so hardy. They're up early in the spring and useable throughout the season with all the fresh summer produce." Now, even though she no longer lives in an historic house, Sue Ellen still has a few herbs in her garden. They add their pungent taste to the foods she cooks, show up as garnishes to make the simplest dish special, and even find their way into the charming bouquets scattered throughout the house.

The casserole, *above,* **and the fruit loaf,** *below right.*

❦

SPINACH AND ARTICHOKE CASSEROLE

Serve this as a first course, a light luncheon dish, or as an accompaniment to simply cooked meat or poultry.

- ½ cup (1 stick) butter
- ½ cup chopped onion
- 2 10-ounce packages frozen spinach, cooked and drained
- 1 16-ounce can artichoke hearts, drained and diced
- 1 pint sour cream
- ½ cup grated Parmesan cheese
- 3 sprigs fresh parsley, chopped
- 2 sage leaves, chopped
  Salt
  Grated Parmesan cheese

Preheat oven to 350°F.
Melt the butter in a small skillet over medium heat. Add the onions and sauté until they become transparent but not brown, about 3 to 4 minutes.

Combine the spinach, artichoke hearts, sour cream, and cheese in a 1½-quart casserole. Stir in the herbs and the sautéed onions. Salt to taste. Sprinkle the top with Parmesan and bake for 20 to 30 minutes, or until golden brown and bubbly.

SERVES 6 TO 8

CHICKEN LOAF WITH MUSHROOM SAUCE

Reserve the liquid used to poach the chicken for the sauce.

- 1 3½-pound chicken, poached and cooled
- 1 cup cooked rice
- 1½ cups soft bread crumbs
- ½ cup half-and-half
- 1½ cups milk or chicken stock
- 3 eggs, beaten
- ½ teaspoon dried sage
- ½ teaspoon dried marjoram
- ½ teaspoon dried thyme
- 1 tablespoon chicken bouillon powder
- 1 small jar pimientos, drained and diced
  Salt, pepper, and cayenne pepper to taste
- 1 clove garlic, mashed
- 3 scallions, white and green parts, chopped
- ½ to 1 cup herbed stuffing mix
- 2 tablespoons (¼ stick) butter

MUSHROOM SAUCE
- ¼ cup (½ stick) butter
- ½ pound mushrooms, sliced
- ⅓ cup flour
- 1 cup chicken stock
- 1 cup milk
- 1 cup light cream or half-and-half
- 1 tablespoon chopped fresh parsley
- ¼ teaspoon paprika
- 1 teaspoon finely chopped onion
  Salt and pepper to taste

Preheat oven to 350°F.
Remove the chicken meat from the bones, discarding the skin, and dice. Combine the chicken, rice, and bread crumbs in a bowl. Stir in the cream, milk or chicken stock, and the eggs. Add the herbs, bouillon powder, pimientos, seasonings, garlic, and scallions, stirring until well blended.
Pour the chicken mixture into a lightly oiled 9 × 5 × 3-inch loaf pan. Top with the stuffing mix and dot with butter. Bake for 1 hour, or until the top is golden brown and the loaf is set.
While the loaf is baking, make the mushroom sauce. In a small skillet, melt 2 tablespoons of the butter over medium heat, add the sliced mushrooms, and sauté until they have changed color and the juices have evaporated. Melt the remaining butter in a saucepan over medium heat, then stir in the flour and cook, stirring for 2 to 3 minutes. Gradually add the stock, milk, and cream and cook, stirring constantly, until the sauce is thick and smooth. Stir in the

mushrooms, parsley, paprika, onion, and salt and pepper. Keep warm. Then transfer the chicken loaf to a platter, crumb side up, and serve with the mushroom sauce on the side.

SERVES 6 TO 8

FRUIT LOAF

- 1 cup all-purpose flour
- 1 cup sugar
- ½ teaspoon salt
- ½ teaspoon baking soda
- 1 teaspoon ground coriander
- 1 egg, beaten
- 1 cup canned fruit cocktail, undrained
  Whipped cream

Preheat oven to 350°F.
Combine the dry ingredients and coriander in a bowl. In a separate bowl, mix the egg with the fruit cocktail. Add the dry ingredients to the fruit mixture, stirring until just mixed. Pour the batter into a greased loaf or 8 × 8-inch square pan and bake for 50 minutes, or until the top is golden brown and the cake feels firm in the center. When cool, slice and serve with whipped cream.

SERVES 8

COUNTRY COOKING

"When we moved here from Columbus ten years ago, this old house inspired me to grow herbs," says Linda Veffer. "An herb garden just seemed like a natural extension of the house." Linda's garden started with six or so culinary herbs given to her by a friend, but the formation of a local herb group served as inspiration to expand her plantings. Soon the original plants were augmented by fragrant herbs and a greater variety of those used in the kitchen. Thyme became such a favorite, Linda is planting a separate thyme garden. "I like the way thyme grows, all the different textures and foliage," she says.

Although she's always loved to cook, Linda finds that having fresh herbs just outside the door adds to her enjoyment in the kitchen. "There's something about being able to walk out and sniff and cut the herbs that gives you a feeling of doing something special," she says. A vegetable garden and orchard also offer up their bounty to the Veffers' kitchen and the abundant crops are canned or frozen for winter consumption.

"I always think of Midwest food as winter food, hearty dishes like rich soups, casseroles, and stews," she notes. But summer or winter, everything cooked in the Veffer kitchen is well seasoned with homegrown herbs that have been freshly picked or carefully dried.

A picket fence encloses the herb garden, *right*. Brick walks separate the beds where culinary herbs grow alongside fragrant herbs such as lavender. The delicious vegetable chowder, *opposite*, was adapted from the local herb group's cookbook.

VEGETABLE CHOWDER

Although this chowder is hearty enough for a winter day, Linda likes to serve it when she can get the vegetables fresh from her own garden.

- 1 cup (2 sticks) butter
- 1 cup diced onion
- 1 cup diced celery
- 10 tablespoons flour
- 4 cups chicken broth
- 1 cup broccoli flowerets
- 1 cup sliced carrots, cut ¼-inch thick
- 1 cup sliced zucchini, cut ⅜-inch thick and halved
- 1 cup diced tomatoes
- 1 cup whole kernel corn
- 4 cups half-and-half
- 1 tablespoon salt or to taste
- 1 teaspoon pepper
- 3 tablespoons fresh thyme
  Thyme for garnish

Melt the butter in a large saucepan over medium heat. Add the onion and celery and sauté until transparent, about 4 to 5 minutes. Mix in the flour and cook, stirring, for 2 minutes. Set aside.

In a large saucepan, bring the chicken stock to a boil over high heat. Add the broccoli and carrots, lower heat to medium, and cook for 3 minutes; then add the zucchini, tomatoes, and corn and continue to cook another 3 minutes, or until the vegetables are just crisp-tender. Strain, reserving both the vegetables and the stock.

Return the onion mixture to medium heat and stir in the stock. Cook, stirring, until the soup thickens, about 15 minutes. Stir in the vegetables, half-and-half, salt, pepper, and thyme, and serve very hot. Garnish with fresh thyme sprigs if desired.

SERVES 8

POTATOES, GREEN BEANS, AND HAM WITH MINT

This is a one-dish meal that's a cross between a soup and a stew. The tasty pot liquor should be served with the vegetables and ham, to be enjoyed with a bit of bread.

 2 tablespoons (¼ stick) butter
1 ½-pound ham steak, ¼-inch thick, cut in ¼ × 2-inch strips
 1 cup chopped onion
2 ½ pounds new potatoes, peeled
1 ½ pounds fresh green beans
 2 tablespoons fresh chopped mint
  Salt and freshly ground pepper
  Fresh mint for garnish

Melt the butter in a large, heavy pot over medium heat. Add the ham and onion and brown lightly. Pour 1½ quarts of cold water into the pot and bring to a boil over high heat. Add the potatoes, whole beans, mint, and salt and pepper to taste. Lower the heat to medium and cook 20 to 25 minutes or until the potatoes are done. Serve with the pan liquid and garnish with fresh mint.

SERVES 6

Linda enjoys serving from her collection of Blue Willow china.

APPLE BUTTER STREUSEL CAKE

 ½ cup (1 stick) butter
 1 cup apple butter
 1 egg, beaten
 1 teaspoon vanilla extract
1 ½ cups all-purpose flour
 1 teaspoon baking soda
 1 teaspoon ground coriander
 ½ teaspoon salt
 ½ cup raisins

  STREUSEL
 ⅓ cup (⅔ stick) butter, softened
 ⅓ cup granulated sugar
 ⅓ cup dark brown sugar
 ⅓ cup all-purpose flour
 1 teaspoon ground coriander
 ¾ cup chopped walnuts or pecans

  Whipped cream

Preheat oven to 350°F.

In a large saucepan, melt the butter over low heat. Remove from the heat; stir in the apple butter, egg, and vanilla. Combine the dry ingredients and gradually beat them into the egg mixture. Stir in the raisins. Pour the batter into a greased and floured 9 × 9-inch pan.

Place the streusel ingredients in a bowl and cut together until thoroughly combined. Sprinkle the streusel over the top of the batter. Bake for 40 to 45 minutes or until the top springs back when lightly touched. Serve with whipped cream.

SERVES 9 TO 12

A thick layer of coriander-flavored streusel makes this apple butter cake doubly appealing.

COTTAGE HERBS

Although Denise Adams has always grown a few herbs, she didn't have a proper herb garden until she and her husband moved into their present home. "It was a natural addition to this old house," says Denise. The design for the garden evolved from studying pictures and visiting as many gardens as possible; the pattern for the small knot in its center was taken from an old carved English chest in the living room. "It helps to create the feeling that house and garden flow together," she says.

"I cook with herbs every day," notes Denise, "but it's really pretty traditional—tossing some herbs on the chicken or into the vegetables. Lavender is one herb she delights in using. Since her husband adores this fragrant plant, the path to the front door is bordered on both sides by bushy lavenders and seven or eight different species grow in the garden. The fragrant blossoms flavor cookies, cakes, jellies, and teas. And she recently added a separate fragrance garden because there was no room in the original garden for the old roses she wanted to grow.

For the past nine years, Denise has been sharing her knowledge of herbs, giving classes in wreathmaking and other herbal crafts in her home, and serving herbal luncheons. With a newly won degree in landscape horticulture, she has now expanded her business to include selling plants in the spring and is also researching and growing old flowers, particularly those indigenous to Ohio. But whether she's lecturing at Ohio State or at home in her garden, Denise inspires her students with her knowledge, enthusiasm, and a sampling of the herbal specialities from her kitchen.

Denise gathers fresh lavender to use in her pound cake and cookies as well as in a bouquet. The small building on the right houses her shop.

SALMON TART

Serve this tart as a first course or a light luncheon or supper dish. It is equally good hot or at room temperature.

PASTRY
1½ cups all-purpose flour

1 tablespoon sesame seeds

½ cup vegetable oil

2 tablespoons cold milk

FILLING
2 tablespoons (¼ stick) unsalted butter

¼ cup chopped scallions, green and white parts

½ cup chopped mushrooms

1 pound canned red salmon, drained, liquid reserved

2 tablespoons minced fresh parsley

1 teaspoon chopped fresh dill

1 teaspoon chopped fresh tarragon

1 to 1½ cups half-and-half

4 eggs, beaten

Fresh dill for garnish

Preheat oven to 425°F.

Place the flour and sesame seeds in a 9-inch quiche or pie pan, making a well in the center. Mix the oil and milk together and pour it into the well. Blend the flour into the liquid with a fork until it is well mixed; then, with your fingers, gently press the dough evenly into the pan and up the sides. Flute the edges and refrigerate briefly.

In a small skillet, melt the butter over medium heat. Add the scallions and mushrooms and sauté until soft but not brown, about 5 minutes. Finely flake the salmon and spread it over the bottom of the pastry shell. Distribute the mushroom mixture evenly over the salmon and sprinkle with the herbs. Measure the reserved salmon liquid and add enough half-and-half to make 1½ cups. Combine the cream with the eggs and pour into the pastry shell. Bake for 10 minutes; lower oven heat to 350°F. and bake another 40 minutes or until the custard is set. Garnish with fresh dill if desired.

SERVES 6 TO 8

Herbs from the garden outside flavor the simple but savory meal laid out on the antique pine table in the dining room, *right and far right.*

CHICKEN WITH ROSEMARY AND LEMON

Denise generally serves this chicken with steamed new pota-toes, broccoli spears, and tiny car-rots dressed with melted butter to which she's added chopped rose-mary and parsley.

1　4-pound chicken

6　to 8 sprigs of rosemary, 2 to 3-inches long

½　lemon, thinly sliced

½　cup (1 stick) butter, melted

　　Sprig of rosemary for basting

Preheat oven to 450°F.

Rinse the chicken with cool water and pat dry with paper towels. Place the rosemary and lemon slices in the cavity and set the chicken on a rack in a roasting pan. Brush well with the melted butter, using a sprig of rosemary as a brush. Place in the oven and immediately lower the heat to 350°F. Cook for about 1 hour and 20 minutes (20 minutes per pound), basting frequently with pan drippings and/or melted butter. The chicken is done when it is well browned and the joints move easily.

SERVES 4 TO 6

LAVENDER POUND CAKE

This cake tastes faintly of lavender. For a more pronounced flavor, double the quantity of lavender flowers.

2　cups (4 sticks) butter

3 ½　cups all-purpose flour

2　teaspoons baking powder

12　large eggs, separated

2 ½　cups sugar

2　tablespoons sweet sherry

1　tablespoon dried lavender flowers

Preheat oven to 325°F.

In a large bowl, cream the butter until it is light and fluffy. Combine the flour and baking powder and gradually add to the butter, beating until the mixture is a smooth paste. In a separate bowl, combine the egg yolks and sugar; beat until thick and light. Add the sherry and lavender, then gradually beat in the butter and flour mixture.

In a separate bowl with clean beaters, beat the egg whites un-til they form stiff peaks but are not dry. Quickly and gently fold the whites into the flour mix-ture. Turn the batter into a well-greased and floured 10-inch tube or bundt pan. Bake for 1 hour and 15 minutes or until a straw inserted in the center comes out clean.

MAKES 1 10-INCH CAKE

LAVENDER COOKIES

½　cup (1 stick) unsalted butter

1　cup sugar

2　eggs

½　teaspoon vanilla extract

1　teaspoon dried lavender flowers, finely chopped

1 ½　cups all-purpose flour

2　teaspoons baking powder

Preheat oven to 375°F.

In a medium bowl, cream the butter and sugar until light and fluffy. Beat in the eggs, vanilla, and lavender, and mix well. Combine the flour and baking powder and add to the lavender mixture, stirring until well blended. Drop by teaspoonfuls onto an ungreased baking sheet. Bake 8 to 10 minutes, or until lightly browned on the edges. Cool on baking sheet for a min-ute or two, then transfer to a rack to finish cooling.

MAKES ABOUT 4 DOZEN COOKIES

The Northeast

The scope of Northeastern cooking has always gone far beyond the stereotype of a bland boiled New England dinner. Perhaps nowhere else in the country have people been so open to new ideas and new tastes: ethnic restaurants and food shops proliferate in the big cities, and exotic foods arrive at the markets daily from all around the world. This diversity of flavors and culinary influences in the hands of creative cooks has inspired a wealth of exciting cooking and helped enliven traditional American fare.

Since the days of the first English settlers, when the seeds of such herbs as chives, burnet, marjoram, parsley, and mint were carefully stowed in the precious cargo brought to America, those living here have welcomed new foods and

The glowing dining room of Diane Madden's Cape Cod house welcomes guests to dinner.

135

Nasturtium sandwiches and iced herb tea make a lovely offering for afternoon tea.

❦

Part of the extensive majolica collection at Lord Jefferd's Inn, *below. Opposite,* basil tea is served in front of scented geraniums in C. Z. Guest's Long Island garden.

flavors into their kitchens. The Indians taught the settlers to make tea from native herbs such as bergamot and American pennyroyal; later, waves of immigrants converged on the Northeast, incorporating the seasonings of their homelands into the culture: basil and oregano from Italy; dill from Germany; cilantro and garlic chives from China.

The Northeast was also the birthplace of Shaker cooking, one of America's true native cuisines. The first commercial herb growers in this country, the Shakers embraced a philosophy of cooking not unlike the New American Cuisine. Since cooking was done in the service of God, care and attention were lavished on the ingredients and their preparation. Vegetables were cooked until just crisp-tender; herbs were used with a sure hand; and flowers garnished the desserts. This sophisticated approach makes Shaker recipes as tempting and timely today as they were in the 1800s.

In recent years, Northeastern palates have been broadened further by influences from Japan, Thailand, Mexico, India, Greece, and the Middle East, exposing those interested in food to herbs such as perilla and lemon grass—and teaching them new ways of using more familiar seasonings. You'll find a Long Island chef flavoring grilled Rock Cornish game hens with cilantro and jalapeños to give them a Mexican flavor; a Cape Cod cook using marjoram in an Italian osso buco; and a garden writer adding extra zest to a baked apple with cinnamon basil from Thailand. The result is an eclectic, exciting cuisine that gains much of its character from a skillful handling of herbs.

Ethel has learned to cook both chicken and vegetables in her large open hearth.

HEARTHSIDE COOKING

Ethel Wilson prepares meals in the hearth of her 1744 Connec-ticut farmhouse much the same way Ezekiel Phelps and his family might have done when it was first built. She began by cooking stews in the hearth to feed her children and their friends after a long day of skiing. Later, when she found an 1820 reflector oven, she became more adventuresome, experimenting with whole beef filets, pork roasts, and boned legs of lamb as well as chickens and ducks. "When members of the Herb Society showed an interest," she recalls, "I began preparing entire meals in the hearth for small groups of people."

Once she mastered the tricky skills of controlling the heat, Ethel found cooking in the hearth didn't differ dramatically from cooking on an ordinary stove. She learned to judge how hot the coals were and how and when to add wood for more coals without causing the embers to burst into flame. For most dishes, pots are set on trivets over hot coals or hung directly over the flame; burying a pot in hot coals gives the effect of a Dutch oven; while the reflector oven works like a rotisserie (although the meat must be turned by hand), with the added advantage of the heat reflecting onto the back side of the meat.

Mrs. Wilson has always enjoyed using herbs, even in des-serts. "I have to have an herb garden," she confesses. "In my pre-vious house it was a small one. Here I have three small beds border-ing the terrace outside the kitchen and a whole hillside, too."

SAGE CHICKEN STUFFING

Ethel makes this flavorful dressing for her hearth-roasted chicken, but it will taste just as good with an oven-roasted chicken. And extra stuffing can be baked separately in a 350°F. oven.

1 (11-ounce) can mandarin orange sections

6 tablespoons (¾ stick) unsalted butter

1 cup diced onions

1 cup diced tart apple

3 tablespoons applejack

Juice of ½ lemon

1 cup cooked wild rice

2½ cups toasted fresh bread crumbs

½ cup fresh sage leaves

¼ cup chicken stock, approximately

Salt and freshly ground pepper

Cut the orange sections in half. Set aside.

In a large skillet, melt the butter. Add the onions and cook over medium heat until the onions start to become translucent, about 5 minutes. Add the apple and continue to cook for a few minutes. Remove from heat. Add the applejack and lemon juice, then stir in the wild rice, bread crumbs, orange pieces, and sage; mix well. If the stuffing seems too stiff, add a bit of chicken stock. Season to taste. Refrigerate, covered, until using.

MAKES 5 CUPS

The vegetable purée cooks over hot coals, *above*. Rose geranium cake and sage cheese with pears, *below*, are offered after the hearth-cooked meal.

※

PURÉE OF YELLOW VEGETABLES

To prepare this vegetable purée in the hearth, place the casserole on a trivet over hot coals.

1 sweet potato, peeled and diced

2 carrots, diced

1 yellow turnip, diced

¼ cup chopped fresh dill

½ cup heavy cream

3 tablespoons butter

Salt and freshly ground pepper

Preheat the oven to 350°F.

In a large saucepan, cook the sweet potato, carrots, and turnip in boiling water until tender, about 15 minutes; drain. Transfer the vegetables to a blender or food processor and purée. Stir in the dill, cream, and butter, and season to taste. Put the purée in an ovenproof casserole and bake, uncovered, until the casserole is heated through, about 10 to 15 minutes.

SERVES 6

ROSE GERANIUM CAKE

The butter for this cake must rest, wrapped in geranium leaves, overnight.

12 rose geranium leaves

1 cup (2 sticks) butter

1¾ cups granulated sugar

6 egg whites

3 cups sifted cake flour

4 teaspoons baking powder

½ teaspoon salt

¾ cup milk

½ cup water

ROSE FROSTING

⅔ cup unsalted butter

1 egg yolk

2 cups confectioners' sugar

1 teaspoon vanilla extract

6 rose geranium leaves

Rinse and dry the geranium leaves. Wrap 6 leaves around each stick of butter. Cover with foil or plastic wrap and chill overnight.

The next day, unwrap the butter and remove the leaves. Place the butter in a mixing bowl; rinse the leaves and set aside.

Preheat the oven to 350°F. Grease and flour two 9-inch round cake pans.

Add the sugar to the butter and cream until light. Add the egg whites, 2 at a time, beating well after each addition. Sift the flour, baking powder, and salt together. In a separate bowl, mix the milk and water. Alternately add the flour and milk mixtures to the butter mixture, beginning and ending with the flour. Beat until smooth after each addition.

Arrange 6 of the geranium leaves on the bottom of each cake pan. Spoon the batter over leaves. Bake until the cake springs back when touched in the center and has begun to pull away from the sides of the pan, about 30 to 35 minutes. Cool in the pan for 10 minutes, then turn out onto wire racks to finish cooling. Gently remove the leaves from the bottoms of the cakes and discard.

Meanwhile, prepare the frosting. In a bowl, cream the butter well. Beat in the egg yolk, then gradually add the sugar, beating constantly. Stir in the vanilla. Chop the geranium leaves very fine by hand or in a food processor and stir into the frosting.

When the cake layers have cooled completely, fill and frost.

MAKES 1 9-INCH LAYER CAKE

A COLLECTOR'S KITCHEN

Collecting comes naturally to antiques dealer Paul Madden and his wife, Diane, who shares his love of beautiful things and his enthusiasm for finding them. With a background in art history and a great talent for cooking, Diane loves to collect kitchen and serving pieces that add to the pleasure of cooking and eating. "When we go on trips I always look around the markets, thinking about what I would like to have for the table," she says. "Everything that surrounds us goes back to food."

The Maddens' Cape Cod house, furnished with their splendid collection of antique furniture and accessories, is a perfect backdrop for entertaining friends and family. "The nature of the house makes it equally good for casual or formal entertaining," says Diane. "When you entertain, the object is to please other people, to make them feel comfortable and at home. The food you serve is part of that."

An intelligent and inquiring cook, Diane feels strongly about eating fresh foods. "Because we try to eat fresh foods, we eat very seasonally," she notes. Herbs enhance the taste of everything. "Diane seems to have an innate feeling for what a dish needs," adds Paul.

"Ever since my mother took me to Caprilands as a young child, I've been fascinated with herbs," says Diane. "Not just the taste, but with their decorative nature, too. I've been mixing herbs in with the flowers in my bouquets for years."

Diane has planted an herb garden, *left,* **to ensure a basic supply of her favorites.**

RATATOUILLE ON A CLOUD

2 eggplants

1 large green bell pepper

1 large red bell pepper

1 large yellow bell pepper

1 large onion

2 yellow summer squash

2 zucchini

1 pound fresh mushrooms

¼ cup olive oil

4 garlic cloves, minced

3 large tomatoes, cut in eighths

3 tablespoons chopped fresh oregano or to taste

½ teaspoon dried red pepper flakes (optional)

1 rectangle of baked puff pastry, about 8 × 12 inches, or 8 individual squares approximately 3 × 4 inches

1 (10-ounce) log Montrachet or other goat cheese (chèvre)

Fresh oregano or parsley, for garnish

Cut the eggplants, peppers, onion, yellow squash, zucchini, and mushrooms into random-size cubes. Heat the olive oil in a large saucepan, then add the eggplant and garlic. Cook over medium heat, stirring, for 5 minutes. Add the peppers and onion, and cook, stirring, for another 5 minutes. Add the squash, zucchini, and mushrooms, and cook, still stirring, for 5 minutes more. Add the tomatoes, oregano, and pepper flakes, if you are using them, to the pot; stir and cover loosely. Simmer for 20 minutes, removing the cover for the last 5 minutes. The vegetables should be tender but not mushy.

Put the puff pastry on an ovenproof platter and spoon the ratatouille over the top. Slice the cheese into 8 pieces, then cut each piece in half and scatter over the ratatouille. Run the ratatouille under the broiler until the cheese starts to melt, about 3 minutes. Garnish with some fresh oregano or parsley.

SERVES 8 FOR LUNCH

᪴᪴

Occasionally the Maddens serve dinner in front of the living room fireplace, *left*. Diane's collections of Canton china and brass candlesticks make the meal even more inviting. The charming Cape Cod house, *above*, sits behind a traditional picket fence.

Diane serves her osso buco
with rice timbales.

OSSO BUCO
MILANESE

½ cup all-purpose flour

Salt and freshly ground
pepper

6 thick slices of veal shank,
½ to ¾ pound each

⅓ cup virgin olive oil

3 tablespoons unsalted
butter

2 large carrots, peeled and
diced

1 large onion, diced

2 celery stalks, diced

1 tablespoon freshly
chopped garlic

2 bay leaves, crushed

3 tablespoons chopped
fresh marjoram, or 1
tablespoon dried

3 tablespoons chopped
fresh basil, or 1
tablespoon dried

1 cup chopped fresh Italian
parsley

Grated zest of 1 lemon

1½ cups dry white wine

1½ cups Italian plum
tomatoes, either fresh or
canned, peeled

1½ cups veal stock or
chicken stock

Gremolata, for garnish
(page 94), optional

Put the flour in a plastic bag
and season to taste with salt
and pepper. Tie a piece of string
around each shank, then place
each in the bag with the flour
mixture; shake well to coat
each. In a large skillet, heat the
oil over high heat, add the
shanks, and brown on all sides.
Transfer shanks to a plate.

Preheat the oven to 325°F.

Reduce the heat under the
skillet to medium, add the butter to the oil, and let it melt.
Add the carrots, onion, celery,
garlic, bay leaves, marjoram,
basil, parsley, and lemon zest;
and sauté for 5 minutes. Pour in
the wine and sauté an additional 5 minutes. Stir in the to-

matoes and stock. Place half the sauce in a large Dutch oven, add the shanks, and cover with the remaining sauce. Bake, covered, for 2½ to 3 hours, turning and basting the shanks twice during cooking. When the shanks are tender, remove the strings and arrange the shanks in the center of a large platter. Spoon the sauce over them and garnish with gremolata, if desired.

SERVES 6

SAUTÉED SUMMER SQUASH WITH WOODRUFF

5   yellow summer squash
4   tablespoons (½ stick) butter
8   whorls woodruff, cut into individual leaves
    Salt and freshly cracked white pepper
    Sour cream (optional)

Score the squash in a star shape to resemble the whorls of woodruff, then slice. Melt the butter in a large skillet with a cover. When the butter is melted, add the sliced squash, the woodruff, and salt and pepper to taste. Stir, cover, and cook over medium heat for 5 minutes, stirring once. Remove the cover, stir again, recover, and turn the heat off. Let the squash sit until done but not mushy, about 10 minutes. Serve with sour cream, if desired.

SERVES 4 TO 6

PUNGENT WHEATBERRY RICE

Wheatberries, the whole grains of wheat before they have been cracked, have a wonderful nutty flavor and crunchy texture. Both hard and soft wheatberries are available in health food stores. You can use either, but the hard berries have more crunch.

6   tablespoons (¾ stick) butter
3   large carrots, peeled and finely chopped
3   large leeks (white part only), finely chopped
3   large celery stalks, finely chopped
1   garlic clove, minced
1½ cups long-grain white rice
½   cup wheatberries
    Leaves of 6 sprigs fresh thyme, or 2 teaspoons dried
2   cracked white peppercorns
4   cups chicken stock
½   cup chopped fresh parsley

In a deep pot, melt the butter over medium heat. Add the carrots, leeks, celery, and garlic; sauté until slightly tender, about 8 minutes. Add the rice and wheatberries and cook, stirring, for another few minutes. Add the thyme and peppercorns. Stir in the chicken stock and bring to a boil. Turn the heat down and simmer, covered, for 20 minutes. Remove the cover and cook for another 5 minutes. Just before serving, stir in the chopped fresh parsley.

SERVES 8 TO 10

A collection of exquisitely engraved eighteenth-century wine glasses adds a special feeling to the simplest dinner.

❦

❦

Woodruff is an unexpected but delicious addition to summer squash.

WEEKEND COOKING

Pat and Bryan Webb have been skiing in Vermont for years, and recently they've taken to spending part of their summers, traditionally spent on Long Island's beaches, here as well. "It's so peaceful and friendly, really wonderful for a family," says Pat. "And it's such fun to shop. You tend to talk a lot in the stores."

In New York or Vermont, the Webbs consider summer a time for local produce, prepared quickly and simply. "On the Island you can get everything, including lots of fresh fish, so the choices are endless," says Pat. "In Vermont, it's simpler because less is available." Wherever they are, herbs play an important role in their menus. The Webbs planted an herb garden in Amagansett and one is planned for Vermont, too. "Since I've had the garden, I find I use more herbs," Pat notes. "They really do give food a lot of flavor with less salt."

During Vermont's colorful falls and white winters, more time is spent in the kitchen. Bryan may spend the morning baking a loaf of bread while Pat stirs up a hearty chowder or stew. "You should be relaxed about cooking," they agree. "It's a time you should enjoy."

HERBED CORN CHOWDER

5 tablespoons butter

1½ cups minced onions

⅓ cup all-purpose flour

3 cups chicken stock

½ cup dry white wine

2 cups heavy cream

1 teaspoon chopped fresh sage, or ⅓ teaspoon dried

1 tablespoon chopped fresh marjoram, or 1 teaspoon dried

The historic house, *above*, built in 1836, was moved from Brookfield, Vermont. *Left and opposite*, lunch in the beautifully restored dining room.

3 tablespoons chopped fresh parsley

1 green bell pepper, seeded, deveined, and chopped

2½ cups fresh corn kernels, about 4 to 5 ears

6 ounces cheddar cheese, grated

Tabasco and/or Worchestershire sauce

3 tablespoons chopped fresh dill, for garnish

In a large saucepan, melt the butter over medium heat. Add the onions and sauté until transparent, about 5 minutes. Add the flour and cook, stirring, for 3 minutes. Whisk in the chicken stock and wine, and continue to whisk until the soup thickens slightly. Add the remaining ingredients; simmer for 15 minutes.

Coarsely purée the soup, then return to the saucepan and reheat. Remove from the heat and stir in the cheese until it melts. Season to taste and garnish with the fresh dill.

SERVES 6 TO 8

IRISH WHOLE-WHEAT SODA BREAD

½ cup (1 stick) butter

3 tablespoons sugar

1 egg

1¼ cups all-purpose flour

1 teaspoon salt

1 teaspoon baking soda

2¼ cups whole-wheat flour

1¼ cups buttermilk

2 teaspoons fennel seeds

2 teaspoons sesame seeds

Preheat the oven to 400°F.

In a food processor fitted with a steel blade, cream the butter and sugar. Add the egg and blend quickly. In a large bowl, sift together the flour, salt, and baking soda. Stir in the whole-wheat flour. Add half the flour mixture to the egg mixture and blend quickly, turning the processor on and off. Then add the balance of the flour and blend quickly again while slowly pouring the buttermilk through the feed tube. When the machine slows down, turn the dough out onto a floured surface.

Scatter the seeds over the dough and knead for 1 minute. Form the dough into a round loaf and set on a lightly greased baking sheet. Cut a cross on top of the loaf with a sharp knife. Bake until the loaf sounds hollow when tapped on the bottom, about 45 minutes. Cool on a rack.

MAKES 1 LOAF

A KNOWLEDGEABLE COOK

Twenty-six years ago, when Jackie Rose moved to a farm perched on a mountain near Waitsfield, Vermont, the town bore little resemblance to the sophisticated village of tempting shops that exists today. "It was difficult," admits Jackie. "Waitsfield had no market, so when we went to Canada to have our hair done or to Burlington, we'd bring back bread and vegetables; in winter that meant root vegetables and squash. My husband and I were part of a small group of nonnatives in Waitsfield who entertained one another, and we had to try and make something out of what was available."

Jackie couldn't find a source for any of the good kitchen equipment she needed to do all this cooking, so she decided to open a cookware shop on Sugarbush Mountain. The Store recently moved down to the village and shifted its emphasis to tabletop accessories. "You eat with your eyes, too," she notes.

Jackie, always an enthusiastic and experimental cook, regularly held ethnic nights while her children were growing up to introduce them to different foods. She also planted herbs in the garden of her hilltop farm. "Years ago if you wanted fresh herbs, you had to grow them yourself," says Jackie. "But I only planted what grows well here." That includes parsley, thyme, basil, sage, sweet fennel, and mint, so adaptable to this climate that it's found wild all over the state.

≈≈

Friendly cows, *right*, admire the picnic lunch set out in the field. Farms and woods intermingle at the foot of the mountains, *left*.

END OF HARVEST CASSEROLE

Any vegetables in this recipe can be replaced by an equal amount of whatever vegetable you may have growing in the garden.

Salt and freshly ground pepper to taste

½ cup chopped fresh parsley

2 tablespoons chopped fresh thyme

1 tablespoon chopped fresh rosemary

1 cup thinly sliced potatoes

1 cup broccoli or cauliflower flowerets

1 cup thinly sliced celery

1 cup thinly sliced onion

1 cup thinly sliced zucchini or summer squash

1 cup shredded cabbage

2 to 3 tomatoes, sliced

½ cup chicken stock

2 garlic cloves, finely minced

½ cup grated Vermont cheddar cheese

Vermont cheddar adds flavor to this vegetable casserole, *left*. Turkey birds, *right*, are cooked ahead, served at room temperature.

Preheat the oven to 350°F.

In a small bowl, mix the salt and pepper, parsley, thyme, and rosemary. In a 3-quart casserole, arrange a layer of each vegetable, starting with the potatoes, broccoli, celery, onions, or other slow-cooking vegetables and ending with the tomatoes, sprinkling mixture between each layer and over the tomatoes. Pour the chicken stock over the casserole and scatter the garlic and cheese on top. Cook, covered, until the vegetables are tender and the cheese melts, about 45 minutes to 1 hour. Serve at room temperature.

SERVES 8 TO 10

VERMONT TURKEY BIRDS

1 fresh Vermont turkey breast, about 2 to 2½ pounds

2 tablespoons (¼ stick) unsalted butter

2 tablespoons olive oil, approximately

1 pound Vermont turkey sage sausage (see note)

½ cup chopped fresh sage
Cracked pepper to taste

½ cup all-purpose flour

1 cup turkey or chicken stock

½ cup dry vermouth or white wine

3 fresh sage leaves, chopped

½ cup chopped fresh parsley
Sage leaves, for garnish

Cut the fillets from the breast and reserve for another use. Cut the breast in thin, even slices, then pound the slices between 2 pieces of waxed paper until they are very thin and flexible.

In a large sauté pan, melt the butter with the olive oil. Remove the sausage from its casing and add to the pan. Heat through for 4 to 5 minutes, breaking up the sausage with the back of a wooden spoon. Transfer the sausage to a bowl with a slotted spoon and stir in the chopped sage and pepper. Place a tablespoon of stuffing in the center of each pounded turkey slice and roll it up, tucking the sides in. Secure the birds with string or toothpicks. Dust them with flour; brown lightly in the same sauté pan used to cook the sausage, about 4 minutes, adding more oil if necessary. Do not overcook.

Remove the birds from the pan and keep warm. Add the stock and wine, and reduce by half over high heat. Season with additional pepper, the sage, and half the parsley. Return the birds to the pan, reduce the heat, cover, and simmer for 10 to 15 minutes. Cool in the sauce.

When ready to serve, drain the birds and remove the toothpicks or strings. Serve at room temperature, garnished with the remaining chopped parsley and a few sage leaves.

NOTE: If you can't find turkey sausage, make your own by grinding the reserved turkey fillets and the turkey scraps in a processor with 1 cup chopped fresh sage, 2 tablespoons finely chopped fresh parsley, and 2 tablespoons finely chopped fresh thyme.

SERVES 8 TO 10

By varying the fruits, this refreshing dessert can be served year round.

SKEWERED FRUIT

½ cup vodka or white wine

1 cup chopped fresh mint
Juice of 1 lemon

3 cups mixed seasonal fruits in bite-size pieces: strawberries, peaches, pineapple, bananas, etc.
Fresh mint, for garnish

Mix the vodka, mint, and lemon juice in a large bowl. Marinate the fruit in the vodka mixture for several hours or overnight. Divide the fruit evenly among 6 skewers, starting and ending each skewer with a strawberry if possible. Garnish with fresh mint.

SERVES 6

THE MANY TASTES OF BASIL

Before the Burpee Seed Company introduced its Purple and Green Ruffles basil varieties, they asked prominent gardeners such as C. Z. Guest and Elvin McDonald to test-grow the plants. In one corner of her gracious Long Island estate, Mrs. Guest has a working garden where she and Elvin grow herbs and vegetables for the kitchen and flowers for bouquets, and where they work with new plants. When they were asked to test the Ruffles basils, they decided to investigate other basil species at the same time, checking on their appearance in the garden as well as the different flavors they might bring to the kitchen. "Since we both write syndicated columns about gardening, we're constantly experimenting," says Elvin.

One section of the working garden was set aside for the basil plants, most of which were grown in pots, as are many of the plants that winter over in the greenhouse. Since potted plants require more watering during hot weather, the garden's watering system was designed for easy accessibility. In the beds, wood chips help keep moisture while discouraging weeds.

Globe basil, a favorite edging plant; curly basil, a beautiful garnish as well as a tasty seasoning; aromatic lemon basil; and spicy cinnamon basil were among those grown and harvested for use in the kitchen. "Both C. Z. and I like simple foods," Elvin says, "so I love to experiment with new flavors in old standbys like baked apples or bread."

The basil-flavored lunch on the patio, *opposite*. A variety of basils growing in the working garden, *left*.

Lemon basil adds its zest to avocado salad, *above*, while cinnamon basil contributes its spiciness to a baked apple, *below.*

AVOCADO SALAD WITH LEMON BASIL

2 avocados
Juice of 2 lemons
1 large tomato, peeled and diced
¼ cup minced fresh lemon basil
2 tablespoons olive oil
Salt and pepper
4 cups Purple Ruffles or Green Ruffles basil

Peel, pit, and dice the avocados. Place in a bowl and toss gently with the lemon juice to make sure the pieces are coated so the avocado doesn't discolor. Add the tomato and chopped basil, splash with the olive oil, and toss lightly. Season to taste. Place a bed of Ruffles basil on each plate and top with the avocado salad, dividing it equally among the plates.

SERVES 4

CINNAMON BASIL BAKED APPLES

1 cup water
½ to 1 cup honey, or to taste
8 sprigs fresh cinnamon basil
4 large baking apples

Preheat the oven to 350°F.
In a 2-quart saucepan, combine the water, honey, and 4 sprigs of cinnamon basil. Bring to a boil and simmer over medium heat for about 5 minutes. Meanwhile, core the apples and place in a baking dish.
When the syrup is done, remove from the heat, strain out the basil, and pour the hot liquid in the apples, filling the cavities. Reserve remaining syrup. Bake apples for 30 to 45 minutes, depending on how soft you want them, basting occasionally with the reserved syrup. Serve warm with a sprig of cinnamon basil as garnish.

SERVES 4

A hearty loaf of basil-scented bread.

❦

BASIL BEER BREAD

This quick and easy bread may not have the fine texture of a yeast bread, but it is nourishing and entirely satisfactory for a busy and hungry gardener. It is especially good toasted. Elvin McDonald got the recipe from Linda Steele of Fox Hill Farms in Michigan.

3 cups self-rising flour
3 tablespoons sugar
½ chopped fresh basil leaves
1½ cups warm beer

Preheat the oven to 350°F.
In a large bowl, mix the flour and sugar. Stir in the basil, then the beer. Mix until thoroughly blended, then pour into a well-greased 9 × 5 × 3-inch loaf pan. Bake until a straw inserted in the center comes out clean, about 50 minutes. Turn the bread out of the pan and cool on a rack. Slice the bread thinly.

MAKES 1 LOAF

❦

Basil mixed with roses in a charming arrangement, *opposite.*

INNKEEPING IN MAINE

Looking at the Captain Jefferd's Inn, surrounded by inviting gardens and a handsome picket fence, it's not hard to imagine a rich New England sea captain returning to the house after a long trip at sea. Don Kelly and Warren Fitzsimmons bought the inn almost ten years ago, leaving Long Island's Hamptons and careers in antiques and real estate to become innkeepers. "We'd always had the notion of innkeeping," says Warren, "and we felt Kennebunkport was the perfect spot. It's cosmopolitan, yet not too close to a city; it's country, but not isolated."

Warren, who has been cooking since he was a child, inherited the role of chef for the splendid breakfasts and afternoon teas enjoyed by the inn's guests and the parties he and Don host around the holidays. "I used to watch my mother and grandmother; it just came easily," he says.

Although Warren prefers fresh herbs most of the time, Fauchon's Herbes de Provence are a standby in his kitchen, used in dishes as diverse as grilled fish and, with a bit of extra tarragon, Bearnaise sauce. The most-used herbs, such as thyme, parsley, mint, basil, and summer savory, grow in the garden, but with Maine's short growing season they must rely on local suppliers, too. "And we always buy lots of parsley," says Warren. "I'm nuts about all the different varieties. We eat it as a vegetable, sautéed lightly with a little oil, and we can't grow enough."

The inn's gracious entry hall, *top*. Kennebunkport's harbor, *above*.

A gleaming copper pot holds mulled wine for a party in the dining room, *opposite*.

HOT MULLED WINE WITH LEMON THYME

10 cinnamon sticks

24 whole cloves

12 whole allspice

12 sprigs fresh lemon thyme

2 (1½-liter) bottles dry red wine (preferably claret)

1 cup sugar

2 lemons, sliced thin

Lemon thyme and lemon slices, for garnish

Place the cinnamon sticks, cloves, allspice, and the lemon thyme in an 8-inch square of cheesecloth, gather the corners, and tie with string to form a bag. Pour the claret into a large pot suitable for serving. Add the sugar and bring to a boil. Reduce the heat, add the seasoning bag, and float the lemon slices on top. Simmer for 30 minutes. Remove the cheesecloth bag. Garnish with fresh lemon slices topped with lemon thyme, if desired.

SERVES 12

Lemon thyme and lemon slices garnish the mulled wine, *below.* Don and Warren serve lobster bouillon in their private dining room, *right.*

LOBSTER BOUILLON

This bouillon gets its rich flavor from boiling whole lobsters in a seasoned broth. The lobster meat can be saved for another meal, or made into a salad.

- 2 Spanish onions, chopped
- 4 carrots, peeled and diced
- 2 turnips, peeled and diced
- 1 celery root, peeled and chopped
- ¼ cup chopped fresh parsley
- 2 bay leaves, crushed
- 1 teaspoon caraway seeds
- 1 sprig fresh wild marjoram
- 1 teaspoon whole allspice
- 1 tablespoon salt
- 2 live lobsters, 1½ pounds each
- ¼ cup sour cream

In a large stockpot, combine 3 quarts of water with onions, carrots, turnips, celery root, herbs, allspice, and salt. Bring to a boil and boil gently, uncovered, for 2 hours; the stock should be reduced to 1½ quarts.

Strain the stock, discarding the solids, and return to the pot. Add the lobsters, return to a boil, and continue boiling for 15 minutes. When done, split the lobsters, remove the meat from the shells, and reserve for another use. Break up the lobster shells and return them to the bouillon. Bring to a boil again and cook for a few more minutes. Strain the bouillon and serve immediately, topped with sour cream.

SERVES 4

Whole fresh basil leaves garnish the frittata.

ZUCCHINI FRITTATA WITH SWEET BASIL

- ⅔ cup olive oil
- 2 garlic cloves, minced
- 6 zucchini, in ¾″ cubes
- 20 eggs
- ¾ cup milk
- 1 tablespoon salt
- 1 teaspoon freshly ground black pepper
- ½ cup chopped fresh basil
- ½ cup grated Parmesan cheese
    Paprika
- 10 fresh basil leaves, for garnish

Heat 1 tablespoon of the oil in a saucepan and sauté the minced garlic for about 3 minutes over medium heat. Add the zucchini and sauté until almost soft, about 10 minutes.

In a large bowl, beat the eggs well; stir in the milk, salt, pepper, and chopped basil.

Put the remaining olive oil in a 12-inch sauté pan suitable for serving. Add the egg mixture and cook over moderate heat, folding as you would an omelet. When the eggs are fluffy, stir in the reserved zucchini and garlic. Continue to cook, without stirring, until semifirm. Top with Parmesan and sprinkle with paprika. Run the frittata under the broiler for a few minutes until it is slightly brown on top. Before serving, arrange fresh basil leaves in a circle around the edge. To serve, cut in pie-shape wedges.

SERVES 10

POOLSIDE ENTERTAINING

For most of the year Joan Burstein is in London watching over Browns, the high-fashion stores she owns there; or in Paris, Milan, or New York searching for the newest fashions. But summer is Joan's time to relax, and she retreats to her spacious house on Long Island. During long sunny days, she gardens, swims, walks on the beach, and entertains friends and family, storing up energy for the months ahead.

Much of her entertaining centers around the pool. A gracious hostess, Joan seems to pamper guests and serve delicious meals with no apparent effort. Because she prefers healthful foods, guests are always offered lots of salads and simple grilled veal, chicken, or fish. For dessert, they can choose between a bowl of fresh fruits or indulge in raspberry pie from a nearby farmstand or the delectable cheesecake that is the house-keeper's specialty.

Although healthful, the meals are far from dull. Joan is frequently inspired by the food encountered in her travels, and her dishes are always superbly seasoned with the herbs she grows in big terra-cotta pots around the pool. Before she returns to England in the fall, whatever herbs remain are harvested and made into vinegars to be saved for the following summer or shared with friends.

ROSEMARY POTATOES

2 pounds large red potatoes

½ cup olive oil

3 tablespoons chopped fresh rosemary, or 1 tablespoon dried

   Salt and pepper

Cut the unpeeled potatoes in ¼-inch slices. In a skillet, heat the oil over medium heat. When the oil is hot, add the potatoes, sprinkle with the rosemary, and cook, turning occasionally, until the potatoes are browned on both sides and tender, about 20 to 25 minutes. Season to taste with salt and pepper before serving.

Alternately, you can cook the potato slices in a 350°F. oven. Pour the oil over the potatoes in a bowl and stir carefully until slices are well coated. Spread the slices in a single layer on a baking sheet; sprinkle with rosemary, salt, and pepper. Bake, covered with foil, for 30 minutes. Remove the foil and bake until brown and tender, an additional 20 minutes.

SERVES 6

An old quilt serves as a tablecloth for a poolside luncheon, *opposite*. Simple grilled chops and potatoes, *right*, are enhanced with garlic and rosemary.

ROSEMARY VEAL CHOPS

4 veal chops, 1½ inches thick

¼ cup olive oil

   Freshly ground pepper

12 shallots, chopped

4 garlic cloves, minced

¼ cup chopped fresh rosemary, or more to taste

Preheat the oven to 400°F.

Cut 4 squares of heavy-duty foil, each large enough to enclose 1 chop. Place a chop in the center of each square and brush each with 1 tablespoon of olive oil. Season to taste with pepper. Mix the shallots, garlic, and rosemary together and divide the mixture equally among the packages. Gather 2 sides of the foil together and fold over several times to make a seal. Seal each end in the same way.

Place the foil packages on a baking sheet and bake for 20 minutes. Turn the oven to Broil, open the tops of the packages, and brown the chops for 3 minutes on each side.

SERVES 4

Part of the potted herb garden.

SHAKER HERBS

In 1774 Mother Ann Lee and eight of her followers left England, settled near Albany, New York, and founded the Shaker movement. The members of this sect eventually came to be as well known for their agricultural skills, superb craftsmanship, and well-cooked meals as they were for their unconventional religious beliefs. By the mid 1800s the movement, which advocated separation from the world, common property, celibacy, and equality of the sexes, had established eighteen settlements from Maine to Kentucky.

At Hancock Village in Massachusetts, as at many of the settlements, the Shakers devoted their agricultural expertise to growing herbs as well as food crops. First to package and sell dried herbs and seeds for both culinary and medicinal use, the Shakers built the cultivation of herbs into one of their most profitable businesses. They also made good use of them in their own kitchens, where the sisters showed great sophistication in the way they seasoned nearly every dish. Visitors from the "world" who ate with the brethren wrote complimentary accounts of the plentiful and delicious food, whose fine quality and simplicity of preparation shared much with present-day American cuisine. When celibacy and a declining rate of converts depleted Shaker ranks, Amy Bess Miller was the leading force in transforming Hancock into a museum. Over the years she gathered the sisters' recipes into a book, *The Best of Shaker Cooking*, that clearly illustrates their modern approach to food.

A simple Shaker meal, *left*, is set out on the sparsely laid table in the dining room where the Hancock ministry once took their meals. Jars of Shaker pickles, *right*, with dill from the herb garden.

SISTER MARY'S ZESTY CARROTS

6 carrots
Salt
2 tablespoons grated onion
2 tablespoons prepared horseradish
½ cup mayonnaise
¼ teaspoon white pepper
¼ cup water
¼ cup buttered bread crumbs

Preheat the oven to 375°F.

Cut the carrots into thin strips, and cook in salted water until tender, about 8 minutes. Drain the carrots and place in a 6 × 10-inch baking dish. In a small bowl, mix together the grated onion, horseradish, mayonnaise, 1 teaspoon salt, pepper, and water. Pour over the carrots and sprinkle with the buttered crumbs. Bake, uncovered, until well heated, about 15 minutes.

SERVES 4 TO 6

❧

Rosemary-flavored spinach and horseradish-flavored carrots, *right*, are examples of the Shakers' innovative way with vegetables. The herb garden, *above*.

SPINACH RING WITH CREAMED RADISHES

This spinach ring could also be filled with creamed mushrooms, eggs, or chicken.

2 pounds fresh spinach
1 teaspoon minced dried rosemary
1 tablespoon chopped fresh parsley
1 tablespoon chopped scallions
2 tablespoons (¼ stick) butter
Salt and freshly ground pepper
CREAMED RADISHES
4 cups thinly sliced spring radishes

2 tablespoons (¼ stick) butter
2 tablespoons flour
½ teaspoon salt
¼ teaspoon white pepper
Milk (optional)
½ cup heavy cream

Chopped fresh parsley

Preheat the oven to 350°F.

Wash the spinach well. Discard the tough stems and chop leaves rather fine. Place the spinach in a heavy pot with the rosemary, parsley, scallions and butter. Cover and simmer over medium-low heat until tender, about 15 minutes. Season to taste with salt and pepper. Squeeze out all juice and pack the spinach firmly into a greased 1-quart ring mold.

In a saucepan, simmer the sliced radishes in water to cover. When tender but not mushy, about 6 minutes, drain the radishes, reserving the stock for the sauce. In another small pan, melt the butter. Stir in the flour, salt, and pepper, and cook 2 minutes over medium heat. Pour in the radish stock, adding milk to make 1 cup if necessary. Simmer, stirring, until the sauce is smooth. Add the radishes and heat well. Remove from the heat and stir in the cream.

When ready to serve, place the spinach mold in a pan of hot water, cover, and place in the oven until heated through, about 15 minutes. Unmold onto a large platter and fill the center with creamed radishes. Sprinkle with parsley if desired.

SERVES 4 AS A MAIN DISH

HERB BREAD

If you would like to vary the taste of this bread, two teaspoons of celery seeds is a nice addition.

- 2 cups milk
- ¼ cup sugar
- ¼ teaspoon salt
- 2 envelopes active dry yeast
- 2 eggs, well beaten
- 1 teaspoon grated nutmeg or ground cloves
- 2 teaspoons crumbled dried sage
- 4 teaspoons caraway seeds
- 1 teaspoon dried rosemary
- 1 teaspoon dried dill
- 7½ to 8 cups all-purpose flour
- 4 tablespoons (½ stick) butter, melted

Scald the milk and place in a large bowl. Stir in the sugar and salt. Cool to lukewarm, then add the yeast and stir until completely dissolved. Beat in the eggs, nutmeg, herbs, and 4 cups of the flour, mixing until the dough is smooth. Add the butter and enough of the remaining flour to make a soft dough that is easy to handle. Turn out onto a lightly floured board and knead until smooth and elastic,

about 8 to 10 minutes. Place the dough in a greased bowl, cover, and let rise in a warm, draft-free place until doubled in bulk, about 2 hours.

When the dough has risen, punch it down and divide into 2 loaves. Place each in a greased 9 × 5 × 3-inch loaf pan and let rise, covered, until doubled, about 1 hour.

Preheat the oven to 425°F.

When the second rising is complete, bake for 15 minutes, then reduce heat to 375°F and bake for an additional 35 minutes. The bread should be golden brown and sound hollow when tapped on the bottom. Cool on racks.

MAKES 2 LOAVES

Large stoves and special ovens, *above right*, aided the sisters in their preparation of the daily meals for the settlement. One of the community's classic buildings, *above*.

SHAKER JAM PIE

- 4 tablespoons (½ stick) butter, at room temperature
- ⅓ cup sugar
- 2 eggs, beaten
- 3 tablespoons ginger or rosehip jam
- 1 unbaked 8-inch pastry shell

  Candied mint leaves and borage flowers for decoration

  Heavy cream (optional)

Preheat the oven to 350°F.

In a bowl, cream the butter and sugar well, beating until light and fluffy. Add the eggs and jam, and mix well. Pile the mixture into the pastry shell and bake for 30 minutes. Cool and decorate the top with candied herbs. Serve with cream, if desired.

SERVES 6

SEASONAL HERBS

Although Anna Pump grew up in Germany, her home was just a few kilometers from the Danish border, and traditional Danish cuisine strongly influenced her family's kitchen. "We always ate lots of goose and chicken; pork loin; fish like herring, eel, and salmon; lettuce; and always red cabbage for the holidays. And in the summer we were never without cucumbers," she says. At eighteen, Anna went off to cooking school. "Actually it was kind of a finishing school," she remembers. "We were taught to set the table, greet guests, fold napkins, and serve."

Anna and her husband came to America almost thirty years ago, and after her children were grown, she decided to learn more about cooking. Classes with James Beard, Anna Marie Huste, and Maurice Moore-Betty gave her the confidence to buy a small Long Island gourmet take-out shop and establish a large catering business, called Loaves and Fishes. Anna's daughter, Sybille, a professional cook, has also joined the business and both enjoy developing new dishes.

"Cooking should be fun, not something that gets you uptight. If you don't have one ingredient, substitute something else. If you don't like the herb that's called for in a recipe, change it," advises Anna. "I couldn't cook without fresh herbs and freshly made chicken stock," she adds. "We used to grow herbs indoors on the windowsill. Now we grow some herbs and vegetables behind the store, but in the busy season we use three *cases* of dill a week so we have to buy it."

ROAST GOOSE WITH PRUNE AND APPLE STUFFING

The goose can be baked 1 hour ahead, covered, and kept warm in the oven.

1 goose, about 11 pounds
  Salt and pepper
2 cups chicken stock
2 cups dry white wine
  STUFFING
2 onions, coarsely chopped
2 McIntosh apples, coarsely chopped
3 tablespoons fresh thyme, or 1 tablespoon dried
1 tablespoon chopped fresh sage, or 1 teaspoon ground dried
1 teaspoon salt
1 teaspoon ground black pepper
12 pitted prunes, halved

Preheat the oven to 450°F.

Rinse and dry the goose well. Rub it inside and out with salt and pepper. Place the goose on a rack in a roasting pan.

For the stuffing, combine the onions, apples, herbs, salt, pepper, and prunes in a bowl. Toss to blend. Fill the cavity of the goose with the stuffing, then tie the legs together with string. Roast the goose, uncovered, for 30 minutes.

A hearty winter dinner is set out before the wonderful old fireplace in Anna's large family kitchen.

Meanwhile, heat the stock and wine in a saucepan. Add it to the roasting pan, lower the oven to 375°F. and bake, uncovered, for an additional 1½ hours. Allow the goose to rest for 10 to 15 minutes before carving and serving. Serve the goose while still hot.

SERVES 6

Anna Pump, with a variety of the home-baked breads she offers in her shop.

More-formal dinners are served in the handsome dining room, *above*. Sage and apples, *below*, combine to make an appealing centerpiece.

BRAISED RED CABBAGE

1 large head red cabbage
1 large onion, coarsely chopped
6 tablespoons olive oil
½ cup red wine vinegar
½ cup water
2 teaspoons salt
1 teaspoon black pepper
  HERB BAG
1 tablespoon mustard seeds
1 tablespoon coriander seeds
2 teaspoons cardamom seeds
1 bay leaf, crumbled
1 teaspoon fennel seeds
1 teaspoon dried red pepper flakes

Shred the cabbage in a food processor or by hand. Place the cabbage, onion, oil, vinegar, water, salt, and pepper in a medium saucepan with a lid. Toss the ingredients to mix well.

Cut an 8-inch square of cheesecloth. Place the herb bag ingredients in the center, gather the edges, and tie with a string. Bury the herb bag in the center of the red cabbage mixture.

Braise, covered, over low heat for about 45 minutes, stirring occasionally. Remove the herb bag before serving.

SERVES 6 TO 8

BLACK BEAN SALAD WITH CILANTRO

2 pounds dried black beans

3 jalapeños, seeded and minced

2 red onions, coarsely chopped

1 bunch fresh cilantro, stems and leaves coarsely chopped

1½ tablespoons salt

1 tablespoon black pepper

DRESSING

1 tablespoon ground cumin

2 garlic cloves, minced

½ cup red wine vinegar

1 cup olive oil

Place the dried beans in a saucepan and cover with cold water. Bring to a boil, then reduce the heat and simmer until the beans are al dente, about 35 to 40 minutes. Be careful not to overcook them or they will be too soft and lose their shape. Drain and cool the beans.

Transfer the cooked black beans to a medium mixing bowl. Add the jalapeños, onions, cilantro, salt, and pepper.

For the dressing, combine the cumin, garlic, vinegar, and oil in a jar with a tight-fitting lid. Shake to blend. Pour the dressing over the bean mixture. Mix the salad thoroughly with your hands before serving.

SERVES 10 TO 12

BLUEFISH SALAD

3 quarts court bouillon (page 19) or fish stock (page 23)

8 pounds very fresh bluefish fillets

1 large onion, coarsely chopped

4 celery stalks, coarsely chopped

1 bunch fresh dill, chopped

½ cup drained capers

½ cup distilled white vinegar

1 tablespoon salt

2 teaspoons black pepper

1¾ cups mayonnaise

Place the court bouillon or fish stock in a large pot over medium heat. Bring to a boil, then reduce the heat, add the fillets, and simmer gently for about 8 minutes. The fish should be cooked through but still firm. Allow the fish to cool slightly, then remove and discard the skin and dark center meat. Chill the fillets several hours or overnight.

When the fillets are cool, remove any bones and place the fish in a bowl. Add the onion, celery, dill, capers, vinegar, salt, pepper, and mayonnaise.

Mix the salad with your hands, being careful not to break up the fish too much.

SERVES 10 TO 12

The wicker-filled porch, *above,* is an inviting spot to enjoy a luncheon of tasty bluefish and black bean salads, *below.*

A garlic lover's feast is laid out in the kitchen of the historic Stevens Coolidge house in Andover.

HIGH FEASTING IN MASSACHUSETTS

It was fairy tales that led Betsy Williams to herbs. "When my children were young I read them my favorites. I'd always wondered what all the plants looked like," she says, "so I decided to grow some of those we were reading about." Soon, the chamomile Peter Rabbit loved so much for tea, the lavender Mrs. Rabbit sold as rabbit tobacco, and a bed of thyme for Shakespeare's fairies filled Betsy's garden.

As the children grew, the Williamses bought a big old house where Betsy had enough garden space to plant vegetables and herbs, which she raised organically and sold to local grocers. "It was a wonderful way to make spending money without having to leave the children," she remembers. Before long Betsy found dried flowers more profitable than vegetables, especially

when she combined them with fragrant herbs in beautiful wreaths and dried arrangements. The demand for these decorative items was so great, she opened a shop.

A natural cook, Betsy inherited a love of food from her father, an agricultural writer and historian. "It was always high feasting time around my father," she recalls. Since she especially enjoys ethnic foods, herbs are indispensable to her cooking. "I think 90 percent of my customers became interested in herbs through the culinary route," says Betsy. With so much interest in using herbs in the kitchen, she's added cooking classes, including one focusing on garlic, to the craft classes she teaches. "Food and herbs go hand in hand," says Betsy. "You can't have one without the other."

SKORDALIA

Skordalia is a Greek dish, traditionally served with fried fish, fried eggplant or fried zucchini, but it is equally good as a dip for crudités.

6 garlic cloves

1 teaspoon salt

3 large potatoes, peeled, boiled, and mashed (about 2 cups)

½ cup olive oil

¼ cup white wine vinegar

Peel the garlic cloves and mash them with the salt in a mortar until you have a smooth paste. Beat the paste into the mashed potatoes, mixing well to distribute the garlic evenly. Add the olive oil and vinegar alternately, in small amounts, continuing to beat until the liquids are absorbed and the skordalia is stiff enough to hold its shape. Serve warm or at room temperature.

SERVES 6

Roasting mellows garlic's robust flavor to a sweet nuttiness that makes garlic lovers of most who taste it.

AÏOLI

This heady garlic mayonnaise is a favorite in the south of France, where it is served as an accompaniment to steamed vegetables and fish. It is a good dip for crudités.

8 to 10 large garlic cloves, peeled

2 tablespoons lemon juice

3 egg yolks

2 cups olive oil
Salt

Combine the garlic, lemon juice, and egg yolks in a blender or food processor, and purée until the mixture is smooth, about 1 minute. With the blender or processor still running, slowly add the oil in a thin, steady stream. All the oil should be incorporated as it is added. The finished sauce should have the consistency of mayonnaise. If it gets too thick, add water or more lemon juice, a teaspoonful at a time. Salt to taste. Aïoli will keep in the refrigerator for about 4 days.

MAKES ABOUT 3 CUPS

ROASTED GARLIC

Long, slow cooking of garlic gives it a sweet, nutty flavor. These roasted cloves are delicious served as an appetizer with toasted bread that's been sprinkled with a little olive oil; or as an accompaniment to roasted meats, especially lamb and veal.

2 tablespoons (¼ stick) butter

1 tablespoon peanut oil

1 tablespoon olive oil

12 large garlic cloves, peeled
Salt and white pepper

Preheat the oven to 350°F.
In a small flame-proof casserole, melt the butter, peanut oil, and olive oil over medium heat. Place the garlic cloves in the casserole in a single layer, stirring to coat them with the oil mixture. Bake, uncovered, for 20 to 30 minutes, basting occasionally, until the cloves are well browned and soft. Season to taste with salt and pepper, if desired.

SERVES 4

HARMONIOUS FLAVORS ON LONG ISLAND

"Cook simply and present it well," says Mark Sanné, a caterer with clients in Long Island and New York. "Making food look beautiful is more than half the battle. If food looks terrible, people are turned off before they even taste it."

Mark prefers to cater for small groups. A favorite assignment is preparing farm-fresh foods for a small informal dinner party for city dwellers weekending in the country, like New York realtor Jonathan McCann and his guests. "It's nice to be able to work in an area where people have come to relax and have time to enjoy the food instead of rushing off somewhere else," says Mark. "You get spoiled by the produce out here, too. My favorite farm stand has such quality; a wonderful selection, things no other greengrocer has; and unusual herbs, too."

Thyme is Mark's favorite herb; he uses it with everything, especially roasted meats and vegetables. "But I like to try new combinations," he says. "Food needs herbs to enliven it. You just have to harmonize the flavors." He relies on his sense of smell to help him create that harmony. "If it smells right to me, then I know it works."

French doors and large windows bring the outdoors into this gracious dining room, *right*. Herbs and roses, *left*, are massed in a bowl to decorate the table.

Mild yellow tomatoes add both color and flavor to the salsa for the cornish hens, *left,* as opal basil does to the salad. Zinnias are just for decoration. *Below,* the lawn sweeps down to water behind the house.

SPICY RICE

¼ cup olive oil

2 large garlic cloves, lightly crushed

2 cups long-grain rice

4 cups chicken stock

1 cup chopped scallions, white and green parts

¼ cup chopped fresh parsley

¼ teaspoon cayenne pepper

In a heavy 3-quart saucepan, heat the oil. Add the garlic and sauté over medium heat until it is soft, about 3 to 5 minutes. Add the rice and continue sautéing for 3 to 4 minutes. Pour in the stock and bring to a full boil. Reduce the heat to very low, cover, and cook, without lifting the lid, for 25 minutes.

Turn off the heat and let sit for 10 minutes. Spoon the rice into a large bowl, sprinkle with scallions, parsley, and cayenne, and toss well.

SERVES 10

MEXICAN GRILLED HENS WITH YELLOW TOMATO SALSA

4 fresh Rock Cornish game hens, split lengthwise

MARINADE

½ cup extra-virgin olive oil

½ cup fresh lime juice

8 large garlic cloves, coarsely chopped

¼ cup chopped fresh cilantro

2 fresh jalapeños, seeded and chopped

2 teaspoons salt

2 teaspoons freshly ground black pepper

SALSA

2 pounds yellow cherry tomatoes

¼ cup lime juice

2 tablespoons grated lime zest

¼ cup chopped scallions

¼ cup chopped fresh cilantro

2 (4-ounce) cans chopped green chiles

Salt and pepper

Spicy Rice

Fresh cilantro, for garnish

Arrange the hens, skin side up, in a single layer in a non-aluminum pan. Combine the marinade ingredients in a bowl and pour over the hen halves. Marinate for at least 6 hours or overnight.

About 4 hours before serving the hens, prepare the salsa.

Chop the tomatoes coarsely, put them in a bowl, and add the lime juice and zest, scallions, cilantro, and chiles. Season to taste. Cover and let sit for at least 2 hours.

Prepare a charcoal fire. When the coals are covered with a fine white ash, place an oiled grill on top and let it heat for a few minutes. Grill the hens, skin side up, for about 10 minutes, making sure the coals do not flame too much. Turn the hens over and continue cooking until the juices run clear when a thigh is pricked, about another 10 minutes. Remove from the fire and let the hens rest for 15 minutes before serving.

Serve the hens on a bed of Spicy Rice, napped with the salsa and garnished with fresh cilantro.

SERVES 6 TO 8

PEACH RASPBERRY COBBLER WITH CINNAMON GERANIUM LEAVES

If you cannot get cinnamon geranium leaves, substitute rose or lemon geranium leaves and omit the ground cinnamon.

FILLING

- 8 cups peeled, pitted, and sliced fresh peaches
- 2 cups fresh raspberries
- ¾ cup sugar
- 2 to 3 tablespoons cornstarch, depending on juiciness of peaches
- 2 tablespoons lemon juice
- 10 cinnamon geranium leaves
- 1 teaspoon ground cinnamon

DOUGH

- 2 cups all-purpose flour
- 1 teaspoon salt
- 1 tablespoon baking powder
- 3 tablespoons sugar
- 6 tablespoons (¾ stick) unsalted butter, very cold
- ⅔ cup half-and-half

Milk

Sugar

Sweetened whipped cream

Cinnamon geranium leaves, for garnish

Preheat the oven to 375°F. Butter a deep 4-quart terrine or casserole.

In a large bowl, combine the peaches, raspberries, sugar, cornstarch, lemon juice, geranium leaves, and cinnamon; mix well. Pour into the buttered dish and bake for 20 minutes.

While the fruit mixture is baking, prepare the dough. Place the flour, salt, baking powder, and sugar in a food processor; combine. Cut the butter into 6 pieces and add to the flour mixture. Combine by turning the processor on and off 10 times. Add the half-and-half and continue to process until the dough starts to come together. Do not overprocess or the dough will be tough. Turn the dough out onto a floured work surface and knead it into a ball. Flatten the dough and roll it ½ inch thick.

Remove the dish from the oven and carefully place the dough on top of the fruit, patting it into place and trimming the dough with a knife. Make sure the dough meets the edge of the dish. Brush the top of the dough with a little milk and sprinkle a little sugar over it. Return the dish to the oven and continue baking until a toothpick inserted in the dough comes out clean, about 35 minutes. If the top becomes too brown, cover loosely with foil and continue to bake.

When the cobbler is done, remove it from the oven and allow to cool at least 1 hour. To serve, spoon onto a plate, fruit side up; top with sweetened whipped cream; garnish with cinnamon geranium leaves.

SERVES 8 TO 10

An old-fashioned cobbler of ripe summer fruits is enhanced with the subtle flavor of scented geraniums.

A SPONTANEOUS COOK

Like Jackie Rose and Pat and Bryan Webb, Jean Sherman is another longtime resident of Vermont. She moved from Chicago to Sugarbush with her husband and children about twenty-five years ago. "I really started cooking when I came to Vermont," she says. "In Chicago, I cooked when we entertained, but never did everyday cooking. Here it was a challenge; you had to scout around and be inventive because there were no gourmet items. And there were no herbs. Even a bunch of watercress was a treat in those days."

Eventually Jean planted some herbs in her garden and even though fresh herbs are now available locally, she continues to grow favorites like thyme, tarragon, and rosemary. And since Jean is so fond of Italian food, there are always patches of basil and oregano. "When you cook, herbs are the frosting on the cake," she says. "They make a recipe interesting. I enjoy spontaneous cooking most, putting meals together at the last minute," she adds. "Years ago I made a casserole with the vegetables and herbs left in the garden at the end of summer. It was wonderful and I didn't realize until much later that I'd reinvented ratatouille."

Vermont cheddar is a fitting accompaniment to the apple tart, *right*. Jean, *left*, picks apples from a tree in the backyard.

APPLE TART

This tart is traditionally cooked in a cast-iron skillet that can also be put in the oven. An enamel skillet with an ovenproof handle could be used instead.

    1   cup all-purpose flour
    ½   cup yellow cornmeal
    ½   teaspoon salt
    ½   cup vegetable shortening
    ¼   cup water
    1   cup sugar
    8   tart apples, peeled, cored, and quartered
    ½   cup (1 stick) unsalted butter, in pieces
    6   tablespoons chopped fresh lemon thyme

Preheat the oven to 350°F.

Combine the flour, cornmeal, and salt in a bowl. Cut in the shortening until mixture is the texture of coarse cornmeal. Gradually mix in the water with a fork. Shape the dough into a ball, wrap in waxed paper, and refrigerate.

Meanwhile, place ¾ cup of the sugar in a 9-inch cast-iron skillet and cook over medium heat until brown but not burned, about 5 to 10 minutes. Cool. Arrange the apples on top of the sugar, mounding them in the center. Sprinkle the remaining sugar on top and dot with the butter. Scatter the lemon thyme on top.

Roll the chilled dough into a circle large enough to fit the top of the skillet. Place the dough over the apples, tucking the edges into the skillet, and cut 3 holes in the crust to allow steam to escape. Bake until the crust is

The roast pork and squash arrayed on a buffet.

golden and the apples are tender, about 1 to 1½ hours. Cool for a few minutes, then run a knife around the edge of the tart; invert onto a plate.

MAKES 1 9-INCH TART

STUFFED SUMMER SQUASH

    8   yellow summer squash
    ½   cup (1 stick) butter
    ½   cup minced onion
    2   garlic cloves, minced
    ¾   cup chopped fresh mushrooms
        Salt and pepper to taste
    ¼   cup minced fresh parsley
    ¾   cup grated Gruyère cheese
    1   cup homemade bread crumbs

Preheat the oven to 350°F.

Cut the squash in half lengthwise and seed. Scoop the pulp out of the shells, reserving the shells, and chop coarsely. In a heavy pan, melt half the butter. Add the onion and garlic, and cook over medium heat until the onion is translucent, about 5 minutes. Add the mushrooms, chopped squash, salt and pepper; cook, stirring, for another minute. Stir in the parsley, cheese, and bread crumbs. Set aside.

Cook the squash shells in boiling water for 1 minute, then drain upside down on paper towels. Divide filling equally among the shells. Melt the remaining butter and pour over the filling. Bake until squash is tender and filling is golden brown, about 20 to 30 minutes.

SERVES 8

STUFFED LOIN OF PORK WITH THYME

This fruit-laden pork loin can be served warm, cold, or at room temperature.

    3   garlic cloves
    4   tablespoons (½ stick) butter, at room temperature
    1   (4-pound) boned loin of pork, butterflied
    6 to 8   dried prunes
    6 to 8   dried apricots
    8   or more sprigs fresh thyme
    1½ cups dry sherry
        Salt and pepper to taste

Preheat the oven to 350°F.

Mash the garlic and mix with 2 tablespoons of the softened butter. Spread the mixture over the butterflied loin. Alternate the prunes and apricots in a row 1½ inches from the edge of one long side of the loin. Carefully roll the loin up around the fruit and tie with kitchen twine every 2 or 3 inches to hold it closed. Transfer the pork to a roasting pan, seam side down. Spread the remaining butter on top and add half the thyme sprigs. Pour the sherry over the meat and roast for 1½ hours.

When roast is completely cooked (160°F. on a meat thermometer), place the roast on a serving platter. Decorate the top of the roast with the remaining thyme sprigs, and slice thinly.

SERVES 10 TO 12

England

The English have been enchanted with herbs ever since the Romans carried the fragrant plants of the Mediterranean north. And while the Dark Ages saw the use of herbs temporarily diminished—only monks had time to nurture herbs in their carefully tended monastery gardens, safeguarding them for the future—by the time the Renaissance was in full flower, it was hard to find a house without an herb garden. Herbs and flowers found their way into every dish: salads burst with the savory taste of sage, burnet, mint, balm, and deep purple violets; Queen Elizabeth I started her day with a cup of health bouillon brewed from parsley, thyme, mint, and balm; and large-leafed plants like calendula, known as potherbs, were cooked up as vegetables. The only herb the English didn't embrace was garlic, and even today its pungent flavor is less evident here than in many countries.

❦❦❦

A hillside garden overlooking the river Dart provides herbs for the Carved Angel.

177

Doreen Mead, *above*, puts the pungent leaves from the enormous bay tree in her front garden to good use in her kitchen.

❦

Opposite, Katrin Cargill sets poached peaches with bay-flavored custard sauce out in front of the fire. Cows graze in the Devon countryside, *below.*

Herbs continued to flourish in English gardens until the end of the nineteenth century. They enhanced the natural goodness of vegetables and fruits grown by small English gardeners of the time, farm cheeses, specially cured hams, and fish from the surrounding seas. Then the English kitchen went into a decline. Herbs were rarely used and English cookery based its reputation on such straightforward dishes as roast beef and Yorkshire pudding, boiled mutton and treacly puddings. Today English cookery is experiencing a renaissance and regaining its place in world cuisine. The English and their visitors pass up fancy French restaurants in favor of those that use local foods in ways reminiscent of other days—or ways totally of their own devising. The chefs who run these restaurants have encouraged small farmers to cultivate dozens of varieties of apples, to raise goats for special cheeses, to graze their lambs on the salt marshes, and to follow traditional ways of aging fine English hams. They serve John Dory and prawns pulled from the seas. Herb gardens grow outside kitchen doors and herbs and flowers bloom in salads.

The same cooks who inspire and are inspired by local foods are also intrigued by traditional recipes like gooseberry fool and elderberry fritters. They use old-fashioned herbs like lovage, let the fragrance of rose petals perfume desserts as they did in Victorian days, or challenge tradition and serve lamb with a mint pesto. Once again England has taken herbs into its kitchens and is showing others how to use them with taste and imagination.

LUNCH IN A COUNTRY COTTAGE

Although Katrin Cargill was born in Colorado and has lived all over the world, she is an Englishwoman at heart. While she was growing up, Katrin's family traveled from country to country, following her father, an American geologist, on his assignments. Somehow they always landed back in England, and Katrin fell in love with the English and their gentle way of life.

Even so, after training as an interior decorator in London, Katrin decided to try living in America. She established her own interior-design business in Texas, then moved on to New York and a job as decorating editor of *House Beautiful*. A change in staff found her doubling as food editor, a position for which she was superbly qualified. "My mother, father, and sister are all great cooks," she says, "and as we moved around I developed tastes for different kinds of food and a willingness to try things." When she realized she was spending all her money visiting London, Katrin decided it was time to go back to England. Now a decorating editor for *World of Interiors*, she indulges her passion for cooking on weekends in Derbyshire with her husband, David. They spend as much time as possible in the little country cottage Katrin has transformed into a charming retreat.

Weekend cooking sprees generally start with a shopping expedition to the butcher, bakery, and cheese store in the nearby town, followed by a brief stop in the local pub to catch up on village news. Back at the cottage, Katrin picks whatever herbs she'll need from the garden. Meals often include the mushrooms she is so fond of. "Most foods are so bland, they really need the pungency of herbs," she says. "But even wild mushrooms, with all their flavor, go hand in hand with herbs."

A coating of nettle ashes adds its special touch to a local cheese, *left*. A charming stone gatekeeper's cottage in Derbyshire, *right*, makes a perfect weekend retreat.

LAMB EN CROÛTE WITH MINT PESTO

In England, lamb and mint are a traditional pairing of tastes. Mint pesto served in place of the more expected mint sauce is a refreshing change. The mint pesto is also delicious spread on a butterflied leg of lamb before grilling or used with lamb and tomatoes on a pizza.

MINT PESTO
1 cup fresh mint leaves

1 garlic clove

¼ cup olive oil

½ teaspoon salt or to taste

12 loin lamb chops, 1 inch thick

1 (17-ounce) package frozen puff pastry, defrosted

1 egg yolk, beaten

Fresh mint, for garnish

Preheat the oven to 425°F.

To make the pesto, place the mint, garlic, oil, and salt in the bowl of a food processor and purée. Set aside.

Cut the lamb tenderloins from the bones and trim off all fat. (Save the bones and meat scraps for soup.) Roll out the puff pastry into a rectangle ⅛ inch thick. Trim the edges so they are straight and reserve the scraps. Cut the dough into 12 rectangles, each large enough to enclose a lamb medallion. Place 1 piece of lamb at the bottom half of each rectangle and top with a heaping tablespoon of mint pesto. Fold dough over to enclose the lamb and crimp the edges tightly to seal. Use the scraps of dough to cut out 24 "mint" leaves. Affix 2 leaves to the top of each dough package with beaten egg.

Brush each package lightly with beaten egg and place on a baking sheet. Cook in the oven until the meat is done and the pastry is golden brown, about 10 minutes for rare meat, 15 minutes for medium rare. If you want your meat well done, reduce the oven to 350°F. after 5 minutes and cook for an additional 15 minutes. Garnish with mint leaves.

SERVES 6

Lamb for Sunday dinner gets a nontraditional twist when coated with mint pesto and cooked in a crust. More breaking with tradition: bowls of nasturtiums and a potted lavender replace the usual floral centerpiece.

POACHED PEACHES WITH BAY CUSTARD SAUCE

Years ago, bay laurel was used frequently to flavor custards. It gives this custard sauce a delightfully spicy taste that complements the sweetness of the peaches. The poaching syrup can be saved in the refrigerator and used to flavor drinks or pour over fresh fruit.

The green of majolica plates enhances the peaches in their custard sauce.

❧

6 large or 12 small ripe peaches

3 cups water

2 cups sugar

Small fresh bay leaves, for garnish (optional)

BAY CUSTARD SAUCE

1¾ cups milk

2 bay leaves, fresh if possible

½ cup sugar

4 egg yolks

1½ teaspoons vanilla extract

Fill a large bowl with boiling water. Drop the peaches in and let sit for 2 to 4 minutes to loosen the skins. The riper they are, the less time this will take. Drain and carefully remove the skins. Set aside.

Combine the water and sugar in a large saucepan and bring to a boil over high heat. Once the sugar has dissolved, turn the heat down and simmer for a few minutes. Add the peaches to the syrup and continue to simmer gently until the fruit is tender but not soft, about 15 minutes. Again, the time will depend on the ripeness of the peaches. Re-move from the heat and cool in the syrup.

Make the custard sauce. Scald the milk with one of the bay leaves; set aside. Place the sugar and egg yolks in a medium bowl and beat with a whisk or electric beater until the mixture becomes pale yellow and forms a ribbon. Add the hot milk gradually, beating constantly, then pour the mixture into a non-aluminum saucepan. Add the second bay leaf and cook over low heat, stirring constantly, until the sauce thickens enough to coat a wooden spoon, about 15 to 20 minutes. Do not let the sauce come to a boil or it will curdle. As soon as the sauce is thick enough, remove it from the heat, stir briefly, then stir in the vanilla. Place a piece of waxed paper over the top to prevent a skin from forming as it cools. Remove the bay leaf before serving. If the sauce gets lumpy, strain it before using.

To serve, place a puddle of sauce on each plate, drain the peaches and set them on the sauce. Garnish each peach with 2 fresh bay leaves, if desired.

SERVES 6

An enticing display of elderflower vinegar, strawberries, and herbs preview the culinary pleasures to come.

THE SUBTLE TASTE OF FLOWERS

"I just enjoy cooking so. It's very satisfying," says Joyce Molyneux, chef-owner of the Carved Angel in Dartmouth. Before opening the Carved Angel, Joyce had spent many years working with the well-known English culinary expert George Perry Smith at the Hole in the Wall in Bath, eventually becoming his partner. She was also exposed to French cuisine by her French father. However, Joyce says she's most interested in very low-key, simple cooking using local ingredients—the kind of food you can eat twice a day.

The Carved Angel itself is simple but charming. Great bowls of herbs are gathered into country bouquets; bottles of elderflower vinegar sit on a shelf catching the sunlight that pours through the windows; and a glorious display of straw-berries and tarts is temptingly arrayed near the entrance. Joyce cooks in an open kitchen at the back of the small room. "I like being able to see the customers," she says, and she can also catch glimpses of the river and the bustling dockside through the restaurant's large, light-filled windows.

Many of the herbs she uses, including the borage flowers that decorate desserts, come from a tiny allotment high on a neighboring hillside overlooking the mouth of the river. Elder-flowers, when they are in season, might be gathered from the hedgerows by the woman who daily delivers strawberries to the restaurant or, on occasion, picked by Joyce herself. Even local roses lend their subtle fragrance to desserts when they are available. "Actually," says Joyce, "I use whatever seems nice."

SEA BASS IN LETTUCE PACKETS

- 4 (6-ounce) fillets of sea bass, skin removed
- Salt and pepper
- 4 teaspoons chopped fresh dill
- 4 teaspoons chopped fresh parsley
- 4 large, crisp lettuce leaves
- 2 tablespoons (¼ stick) unsalted butter
- ¼ pound shallots, finely chopped
- ⅔ cup dry vermouth
- ⅔ cup heavy cream

Preheat the oven to 275°F.

Season the fish with salt and pepper, then sprinkle with the chopped dill and parsley. Set aside. Place the lettuce leaves in a bowl and pour boiling water over them; after 1 minute, drain and refresh with cold water. Spread the lettuce leaves out on a tray and blot dry with a paper towel. Place a fish fillet in the center of each leaf; fold the lettuce leaf around the fish to enclose it in a neat parcel.

In a large, shallow ovenproof pan with a lip, melt the butter over low heat and add the shallots. Cook gently for 5 minutes. Place the fish packets in the pan; add the vermouth and salt and pepper to taste. Cover and cook in the oven for about 15 to 20 minutes. Use a sharp pointed knife to check and see if the fish is firm. When done, remove the fish from the pan and keep warm, reserving the juices.

Over high heat, reduce the cooking liquid slightly. Add the cream and continue to cook over medium heat, stirring until thick, about 5 to 8 minutes. Correct seasonings. To serve, place a puddle of sauce on each plate and set a packet of fish on top.

SERVES 4

To make elderflower vinegar, *above*, the blossoms must be gathered during their short flowering season. The busy river port is clearly visible from the restaurant, *below*.

Fresh elderflowers garnish a plate of crisply fried elderflower fritters.

ELDERFLOWER FRITTERS WITH GOOSEBERRY SAUCE

This dessert can only be enjoyed in early summer, when the elderberry bushes are in flower.

SAUCE
½ pound fresh gooseberries
½ cup sugar

BATTER
1 heaping cup all-purpose flour
Pinch of salt
2 tablespoons vegetable oil
½ cup water, approximately
1 egg white

Vegetable oil for frying
8 heads elderflowers
Confectioners' sugar

Wash the gooseberries and put them in a saucepan with the sugar. Cover tightly and cook gently over low-heat until tender, about 10 minutes. Purée in a blender or food processor or put through a food mill and set aside.

In a bowl, make the batter by mixing the flour, salt, and oil. Add water 1 tablespoon at a time to make a batter with the consistency of thick cream. In a separate bowl, whip the egg white until stiff but not dry, then fold it gently into the batter.

Heat 3 to 4 inches of oil in a large skillet over high heat. Rinse and dry the elderflowers. Dip each flower in the batter, shake off the surplus, and deep-fry for about 4 minutes on each side. Drain the fritters on paper towels. To serve, divide the sauce among 4 plates, arrange 2 fritters on top of each, and dust with confectioners' sugar.

SERVES 4

ROSE PETAL CREAM WITH STRAWBERRIES

Be sure to use a rose that has not been sprayed with any chemicals. The more fragrant the rose, the stronger the flavor it will impart to the cream.

2 pints fresh strawberries
1 fragrant dark red rose
⅔ cup light cream or half-and-half
1½ tablespoons confectioners' sugar
Squeeze of lemon juice
⅔ cup heavy cream

Wash, dry, and hull the strawberries. Set aside. Carefully separate the rose petals, remove the white heel from each petal, and wash and dry them on paper towels. Chop finely.

In a large bowl, combine the light cream, and the confectioners' sugar, lemon juice, and rose petals. Mix well and let stand, covered, in the refrigerator for at least 1 hour to blend the flavors. Strain if desired. Add the heavy cream and whip lightly.

Layer the strawberries with the rose petal cream in individual bowls.

SERVES 4 TO 6

A bright blue borage blossom punctuates the subtle rose petal cream topping lush strawberries.

The picturesque harbor at Padstow, *left*. On sunny days, patrons enjoy eating in the glassed porch, *below*, which overlooks the harbor.

FRESH SEAFOOD IN CORNWALL

When Rick Stein left university, he lived on the bay near the little fishing port of Padstow in Cornwall. Padstow is a charming town and Rick realized there was room there for a good seafood restaurant like those that dot the French coast just across the Channel. With this in mind, he went off to work in the kitchen of a big London hotel to gain experience in cooking and running a restaurant. When he returned to Padstow in 1975, he bought an old stone granary that overlooks the boat-filled harbor and opened the Seafood Restaurant.

He started modestly, offering only lobster and fish and chips. They were upscale fish and chips, however, made from sea bass rather than the usual plaice. These days, the Seafood Restaurant is considered one of the best in England. Rick's sons have now joined him as chefs, and Jill, his wife, looks after the front of the restaurant while Rick concentrates on the kitchen and works on a book called *English Seafood Cookery*. Recently, the Steins added several airy rooms above the restaurant where overnight guests can enjoy the sunny views of the town and harbor along with the Steins' hospitality.

The basic thrust of Rick's cooking is simplicity: fresh foods, well cooked and carefully seasoned. With an abundant supply of fresh seafood in the local market plus fresh herbs, "everything falls into place," he says. "Most sauces for fish are reductions of wine, butter, and cream. Herbs make the difference; they really sell the dish."

Rick uses sweet cicely and lovage, unfamiliar to most cooks, when they are in season and often blanches strong-flavored herbs like lovage to soften their flavor. Borage, hyssop, nasturtium, rocket, and chive flowers for salads are supplied by a nearby herb grower. Basic herbs for the restaurant are grown in Rick's home garden during the summer, but in winter they must be brought in from greenhouses or warmer climates. "That's one reason I'm so fond of chervil and parsley," he says. "Their season starts early and finishes late."

A GRILLADE OF SEAFOOD

Rick Stein recommends this dish for a warm summer's evening when you are planning to eat outdoors. Serve it with lots of French bread to mop up the dressing and a fairly robust wine, such as a chilled Retsina.

MARINADE

¼ cup olive oil

1½ teaspoons chopped fresh fennel leaves

3 fresh bay leaves, sliced, or 1 dried bay leaf, crumbled

Salt and freshly ground black pepper

2 teaspoons lemon juice

4 (4-ounce) monkfish steaks

4 steaks or fillets of gray mullet, conger eel, or shark, about 3 ounces each, or whole small mackerel, red snapper, small John Dory, *gurnard,* or sea bass

2 (1-pound) lobsters, cooked

24 Dublin Bay prawns, 12 Mediterranean prawns, or 36 North Atlantic prawns, cooked (see note)

4 lemon wedges

FENNEL DRESSING

¾ cup olive oil

3 tablespoons red wine vinegar

Salt and freshly ground black pepper to taste

1½ tablespoons chopped fresh fennel leaves

½ small onion, finely chopped

At least 1 hour before cooking, make the marinade. Combine the oil, herbs, salt and pepper, and lemon juice in a shallow dish. Add the fish and marinate for 1 hour, turning 2 or 3 times.

Prepare a charcoal grill at least 40 minutes before cooking. The coals will be ready when they are covered with a fine white ash.

While the fish is marinating, make the dressing. In a small bowl, combine the oil, vinegar, salt, pepper, fennel, and onion; mix well and set aside. Cut the lobsters in half lengthwise and crack their claws.

When the fire is ready, cook the fish steaks about 3 minutes on each side. Brush the lobster and prawn shells with the marinade and grill: 2 minutes per side for the lobsters, 1 minute per side for the prawns. (Because the lobsters and prawns are already cooked, they should be grilled just long enough to be warmed through and lightly char the shells, giving the grillade a spectacular aroma.) When done, place all the seafood on a large serving dish. Add any remaining marinade to the dressing and pour it over the fish. Serve with lemon wedges.

NOTE: 12 jumbo shrimp may be substituted for the prawns.

SERVES 4

The seafood grillade, *above.* One of the local fishing boats, *below,* at anchor in the harbor.

BRAISED FILLET OF JOHN DORY WITH LOVAGE

Lovage, with its strong celerylike flavor, should be used sparingly: 6 leaves are quite enough for this dish. Blanching them gives the leaves a more subtle, pleasing taste.

½ cup (1 stick) unsalted butter

¼ cup finely diced carrot

¼ cup diced onion

¼ cup diced celery

¼ cup diced leeks, white part only

3 tablespoons Vouvray or similar fruity dry white wine

4 fillets of John Dory or any firm-fleshed white fish, 6 ounces each

6 fresh lovage leaves

Lemon juice

Salt and ground white pepper

Preheat the oven to 375°F.

In a small pan, melt half of the butter. Add the vegetables and wine and cook over low heat until cooked through but still al dente and not at all browned, about 15 to 20 minutes. Spread the vegetables and any liquid on the bottom of a shallow flameproof baking dish. Place the fish fillets on top, skin side down; add the water.

Blanch the lovage leaves in boiling water for 1 minute; refresh in cold water. Chop 2 of the leaves and add to the vegetables around the fish. Place a leaf on each fish fillet. Cover with buttered aluminum foil and bake until the fish flakes easily, about 8 minutes.

Transfer the fish to a warm serving plate and bring the juices in the baking dish to a boil on top of the stove. Stir in the rest of the butter. Reduce the sauce slightly, season to taste with lemon juice, salt and pepper, and pour over the fish.

SERVES 4

Braising juices make this dish's light sauce.

MUSSEL AND CHERVIL SOUP WITH GREEN VEGETABLES

60 small mussels

¼ cup dry white wine

2½ cups fish stock (page 23)

1 small branch fresh lovage

2 celery stalks

½ onion, roughly chopped

2-inch strip lemon rind without pith

Flesh of ¼ lemon without pith

2 garlic cloves

Pinch of curry powder

Large pinch of saffron

12 snowpeas

2 ounces spinach, washed and stems removed

¼ cup heavy cream

½ cup (1 stick) unsalted butter

2 ounces zucchini, finely sliced

Large pinch of chopped fresh chervil

Large pinch of chopped fresh chives

Curry and saffron add an exotic touch to mussel soup.

Place the mussels in a large saucepan with half the white wine. Cook, covered, over high heat until the mussels open, about 5 to 8 minutes. As soon as they are open, remove from the heat and pour into a colander, reserving the cooking liquid. Strain the cooking liquid into a saucepan through a fine sieve and add the fish stock, lovage, celery, onion, lemon peel and flesh, garlic, the rest of the wine, curry powder, and saffron. Bring to a boil, lower the heat, and simmer the broth for 30 minutes. While the broth is cooking, remove the beards from the mussels. Leave 8 mussels in their shells; shell the remaining mussels and set aside.

Blanch the snowpeas in boiling water for 1 to 2 minutes until they are still crisp but tender; refresh in cold water. Blanch the spinach for 1 to 2 minutes and refresh. Strain the broth and return it to the saucepan. Stir in the cream and butter, and bring to a rapid boil over high heat, reducing slightly. Lower the heat. Add the zucchini, then the peas and spinach. Just before serving, add the mussels, including the 8 still in the shell. Cook just until heated through or mussels will toughen. Ladle into bowls and sprinkle with the chives and chervil.

SERVES 4 TO 6

FEUILLETÉE OF BLACKBERRIES WITH SORREL SABAYON

Blueberries may be substituted for the blackberries in this recipe.

½ pound puff pastry

1 egg, beaten

2 tablespoons sugar

2 tablespoons water

1½ cups blackberries or blueberries

　SORREL SABAYON

2 tablespoons water

¼ cup sugar

⅓ cup white wine, preferably a Chardonnay

½ cup sorrel leaves, washed and dried

3 egg yolks

½ cup (1 stick) unsalted butter, cut into small cubes

Preheat oven to 450°F.

On a smooth work surface, roll out the puff pastry into a sheet about ³/₁₆-inch thick. Using a sharp knife, cut 4 parallelograms, 2 × 4 inches, from the pastry. Brush them lightly with the beaten egg. Transfer the pastry to a baking sheet; set in the oven for 8 minutes or until golden brown and flaky. Let the pastry pieces cool, then cut them horizontally through the middle.

Place the sugar and water in a small saucepan and bring to a boil over high heat. Add the berries, lower the heat, and poach for 2 to 3 minutes or until the berries have just softened slightly. Set aside to cool.

To make the sabayon, place the water, sugar, and wine in a small saucepan and bring to a boil over high heat. Simmer about 5 minutes; then pour into a blender. Add the sorrel leaves and purée until smooth.

Set a copper bowl over a pan of boiling water (or use a non-aluminum double boiler). Add the sorrel purée and the egg yolks and whisk until the mixture becomes foamy. Do not let the egg mixture become too hot or it will curdle. If necessary, remove from the heat when it feels uncomfortably hot when tested with your little finger. When the sauce is thick and foamy, whisk in the butter a few pieces at a time. Be sure each addition of butter is incorporated into the sauce before adding any more. Keep warm over hot, not boiling, water.

To serve, place one piece of pastry on a plate, spoon ¼ of the berries on top, and cover with another piece of pastry. Spoon the sorrel sabayon onto the plate around the feuilletée.

SERVES 4

Rick Stein holds braised John Dory, *above.* **The stone houses and slate roofs of Padstow are in the background. For his luscious berry feuilletée,** *top,* **he adds the unexpected flavor of sorrel.**

A GLIMPSE OF ENGLISH COUNTRY LIFE

Gidleigh Park is situated amid rolling lawns on the edge of a river in the Devon countryside, the quintessential English country house–hotel. Surprisingly, it was two Americans, Paul and Kay Henderson, who created this luxurious retreat, where chintz-filled rooms with blazing hearths recall English country life as it might have been in Edwardian times. When the Hendersons bought the house in 1977, they had no experience in the restaurant or hotel fields, but their goal of turning Gidleigh into the sort of place where they would enjoy staying has been accomplished brilliantly.

The kitchen, one of the most respected in England, is presided over by Shaun Hill. An Irishman who trained in England's best hotels and restaurants, Shaun started cooking as a hobby. "Then it got out of hand," he laughs. His approach to food is down-to-earth. "It's important to celebrate food rather than ego," he says. The menu is very market oriented, and he calls the fish market each morning for the day's catch. "It's rash to plan ahead and then have to hunt for the ingredients you need," he says. Steamed or toss-fried samphire, a salty sea vegetable that grows on the banks of the river Dart and in nearby Wales, is often served with the local fish.

Shaun devotes a great deal of time to making the stocks and relishes that enhance his simply cooked dishes. Only fresh herbs are used in the kitchen. "Herbs should lend a fresh, natural taste to food," he says. An herb garden just outside the kitchen door supplies coriander, dill, fennel, marjoram, thyme, and sage, which grow well in the Devon soil and climate. "Those that thrive here seem to complement the local produce," he notes. "Tarragon, on the other hand, doesn't seem to have any taste when planted here." Basil for the pesto that sauces pasta and scallops must be raised in the hothouse. "I look forward to it; it's a taste of summer," says Shaun.

A section of the colorful gardens that surround the house.

SEA TROUT WITH SORREL AND WILD MUSHROOMS

Above, the sea trout with wild mushrooms. The gracious country house-hotel, *below.*

¼ pound mixed fresh wild mushrooms (girolles, morels, etc.)

1 sea trout, about 2 pounds

2 tablespoons fish stock (page 23) or dry vermouth

½ cup (1 stick) unsalted butter, in pieces

5 sorrel leaves, finely chopped

1 tablespoon heavy cream
Few drops of lemon juice
Salt

Carefully wash the mushrooms, removing all sand and dirt. Slice and set aside.

Clean and fillet the sea trout. Steam the fillets over boiling water for about 4 minutes, or until just cooked. Keep warm.

In a medium saucepan, boil the stock or vermouth over medium heat until reduced by half. Whisk in the butter, piece by piece, to thicken the sauce. Add the sorrel and mushrooms; cook for another 3 to 4 minutes until softened. Finally stir in the cream and lemon juice; season to taste with salt. Put half the sauce on each plate and top with the fish.

SERVES 2

LAMB IN MARJORAM CONSOMMÉ

2 small racks of lamb

CONSOMMÉ

6 cups water

2 leeks, chopped, green and white parts

1 onion, chopped

2 tomatoes, chopped

2 egg whites, lightly beaten

Salt and pepper

2 sprigs fresh marjoram, leaves only

Cut the racks into individual chops. Cut the eye out of each chop, saving all bones and trimmings separately, and set aside.

Make the consommé. Place the reserved lamb bones and water in a large saucepan and bring to a boil. Skim the surface, reduce to a simmer, and cook slowly for at least 1 hour. When the consommé is done, mince the reserved lamb trimmings and mix them with the chopped vegetables and the egg whites in a large saucepan. Pour the stock over the vegetable mixture and then simmer over low heat until the consommé is clear, about 10 to 15 minutes. Strain carefully and adjust the seasonings. Reserve 2½ cups of consommé for the lamb; any extra can be frozen for future use.

Bring the consommé to a boil and add the lamb pieces and the marjoram. Poach the lamb over low heat until pink and tender, about 1 to 3 minutes. Serve in soup plates.

SERVES 4

BABY VEGETABLES WITH MARJORAM

You can use any vegetable in this dish, even baby zucchini with their flowers. Just be sure to add the vegetables requiring the most cooking to the pot first.

3   tablespoons olive oil

1   garlic clove, chopped

1   teaspoon paprika

1   small bunch fresh marjoram, chopped

4   tomatoes, peeled and chopped

2   cups chicken or beef stock or tomato juice

½   pound baby fennel

½   pound finger carrots

½   pound baby turnips

½   pound baby leeks

½   pound small asparagus
    Salt and pepper

In a large saucepan with a lid, heat the oil over medium heat. Add the garlic and cook until it is golden, 3 to 5 minutes. Remove from the heat; stir in the paprika, then add the marjoram, tomatoes, and stock or juice.

Place a steamer in the pot and return the pot to the heat. Add the fennel, carrots, and turnips to steam, covered, for 4 minutes. Add the leeks and cook an additional 4 minutes; then add the asparagus and steam a few minutes more. When the vegetables are tender, arrange them in individual soup plates. Quickly reduce the cooking liquid over high heat and pour over the vegetables.

SERVES 4

Above, a splendid way to enjoy vegetables year-round. Silvery lamb's ears, *right*, provide a lovely contrast to deeper greens and colorful flowers in the garden. The chintz-filled sitting room, *opposite*, is the essence of English country living.

EASY COUNTRY DINING

Herbs have always been a part of Caroline Collis's life. As a child she remembers gargling with red sage to tame a throat infection. When her own children had chest colds, she eased their coughs with a jelly made from lotus-root flowers, hot water, and honey, an old Chinese herbal medicine she learned from friends.

Caroline's husband, Michael, a hair stylist, discovered another dimension of these useful plants. In the early seventies he began studying herb books, looking for substitutes for the harsh products women used to keep their highly stylized coifs in place. Soon he and Caroline were stirring up buckets of herbal shampoo in the back of their Molton Brown Salon. Customers were so delighted with the shampoo they asked to buy it for home use, and Michael obligingly packaged the shampoo in old medicine bottles. Finding himself besieged with requests for conditioners, lotions, and other herbal products, he realized he had started a business.

In order to expand and still retain complete control over the quality of their products, the Collises bought an old farm, Mott's Hall, in the countryside north of London. Now they have room to raise herbs for their products and for a small factory in the former barn. In addition to the fields of herbs, a traditional herb garden with culinary herbs was planted just outside the dining room. "I'd always admired other people's gardens and wanted one of my own," says Caroline. "I'm drawn to the sense of order."

The Collises and their children spend most weekends at the farm, and Caroline often finds herself cooking for weekend guests. "I try to cook things that are quick and easy to prepare," she says. "I resent spending time in the kitchen unless it's for a very special dinner party." The cooking at Mott's Hall reflects the Collises' mutual interest in healthful eating, and adapting Chinese cooking methods to her wholesome vegetable and grain dishes helps Caroline put meals together quickly. Herbs, generally in interesting combinations, are always an important part of the seasoning. "I use lots of ginger, garlic, parsley, chives, and tarragon," she says. "When I'm in the country, I just go into the garden and pick what I think will be nice."

Caroline Collis on the terrace surrounded by the fragrant potpourris made at Mott's Hall.

BROWN RICE SAUTÉ WITH PARSLEY AND SAGE

The secret of this recipe is not to cook any of the ingredients too long. You will then keep the bright color of the carrots and the parsley.

1½ cups short- or long-grain brown rice, preferably organic

3 tablespoons olive oil

2 onions, diced

4 carrots, shredded

1 tablespoon sesame seeds

Salt and pepper

1 large bunch fresh parsley, chopped

1 teaspoon dried thyme, or 1 tablespoon chopped fresh

2 teaspoons dried sage, or 2 tablespoons fresh, chopped

1 tablespoon soy sauce (optional)

Wash the rice well under cold water, then place in a saucepan with water to cover by ¼ inch. Bring to a boil over high heat, then turn the heat down low and cover tightly. Simmer until all water is absorbed, approximately 1 hour.

In a frying pan or wok, heat the oil and sauté the onions until golden brown or even a bit burnt, about 8 minutes. Add the cooked rice to the onions. Stir in the carrots, sesame seeds, salt and pepper to taste, and the herbs. Stir-fry lightly for about 5 minutes. Mix in the soy sauce just before serving, if desired.

SERVES 8

SIMPLE VEGETABLE RAGOUT WITH PARSLEY

3 or 4 dried cèpes or morels

1½ tablespoons sunflower oil

½ to 1 pound yellow onions, thinly sliced, or an equal amount of chopped shallots

2 garlic cloves, chopped

½ pound carrots, thickly sliced

1¼ cups chicken or vegetable stock

½ pound new potatoes, sliced

Salt and pepper

½ pound zucchini, sliced

½ pound fresh button mushrooms

½ pound shelled peas

1 heaping cup chopped fresh parsley

2 tablespoons chopped fresh mint

Soy sauce (optional)

Soak the dried mushrooms in hot water until they are soft, about 20 to 30 minutes.

In a large saucepan, frying pan, or wok with a cover, heat the oil and sauté the onions over medium heat until they are transparent but still maintain their shape, about 3 to 5 minutes. Add the garlic, carrots, and about ½ cup stock. Cover tightly and continue to cook until the carrots are tender-crisp, about 10 minutes.

Add the potatoes and cook an additional 15 minutes. If the ingredients seem too dry, add more stock. Season to taste with salt and pepper. Add the zucchini, cover again, and cook for another 5 minutes. Add the fresh and dried mushrooms and the peas. Simmer for another 5 minutes, until all the vegetables are lightly cooked. Stir in the parsley and mint. If desired, add a tablespoon or two of soy sauce just before serving.

SERVES 8

🌿

The appealing summer fruit compote, *opposite*, is a healthy yet delicious ending to a meal. The Aga stove, *below*, is a fixture of English country life. It helps heat the house, wet boots and mittens are set nearby to dry, and dogs luxuriate in its gentle warmth.

SUMMER FRUIT COMPOTE WITH MINT AND CINNAMON

This compote can be made with any combination of soft fruits. Remember to add the firmest fruit first, so all of them are soft but not mushy. If the fruit is very ripe, decrease cooking time accordingly.

2½ cups water

⅔ cup plum jam

2 sprigs fresh mint

1 cinnamon stick

1½ tablespoons raw sugar

1 lemon, quartered

1 pound peaches, peeled

1 pound nectarines, peeled

1 pound apricots, peeled

1 pound red plums, peeled

1 pound fresh black currants or 1 pint berries or a mixture of both

Fresh mint, for garnish

In a large saucepan, combine the water, jam, mint, cinnamon, sugar, and lemon. Bring to a boil, reduce the heat, and simmer for 15 minutes. Discard the mint and cinnamon.

Add the fruit in the order listed, simmering for 5 minutes between each addition. Continue until all the fruit except the currants or berries is lightly cooked, soft but still firm. Add the currants or berries last; they require no cooking.

Remove the compote from the heat, cool, and chill. Garnish with mint before serving.

SERVES 12

France

For many years, classic French cuisine was synonymous with gourmet cooking and herbs: the tarragon that flavors Bearnaise sauce and roast chicken; the essential bouquet garni of parsley, bay, and thyme used with soups, stews, and braised meats; the mixture of parsley, chives, chervil, and tarragon known as *fines herbes* are the cornerstones of that tradition. But in France, as elsewhere, today it is regional cooking that truly reflects the taste of the country. Dishes made from local produce cooked in the traditional way are respected by cooks everywhere. At the same time, creative young chefs are exploring ways of using the same ingredients in inventive new ways, adding another dimension to the food.

The lusty food of Provence is among the most distinctive of these regional cuisines. Based on olive oil from the olive trees that dot the landscape, it is generously

❦

Masses of fragrant lavender surround a typical Provençal farmhouse.

M. Rousselet gathers fresh herbs and vegetables in the garden of Les Bories.

❦

At the renowned Hostellerie du Château de la Chevre D'Or in the alluring village of Eze, crayfish are served with a salad of freshly gathered local herbs.

seasoned with garlic and the rosemary, thyme, savory, and hyssop that grow wild in the rugged mountains. The cuisine derives some of its vitality from the cheerful way the natives have embraced foreign products; ingredients such as tomato, eggplant, and basil have been so assimilated over the years as to have become symbols of Provençal cooking. The people of Provence love vegetables and have discovered delightful ways to use them: pistou, a basil-flavored vegetable soup, is a regional favorite. Mesclun, a tasty array of tender young greens that includes baby lettuces, chervil, purslane, dandelion, mâche, chickweed, and other herbs and greens, is a Provençal specialty now finding its way to the United States.

Farther north in Périgord, where the bare mountains that sheltered prehistoric peoples rise above green valleys, the judicious use of goose and pork fat or locally produced walnut oil replaces the olive oil of the south. Provence's largess with herbs is missing, but garlic, parsley, savory, and thyme are used with discretion. The taste of this land comes from the geese and ducks raised for both their livers and their flavorful meat, which is traditionally preserved in goose fat. The many rivers are filled with fish, and, in the fall, the woods are full of wild mushrooms and truffles; walnuts and chestnuts drop from trees that line the roads. The richness of the local larder is apparent in even the humblest fare: farm restaurants serve up delicious homemade foie gras, preserved goose, an omelet bursting with wild mushrooms, or a sweetly bitter walnut liqueur.

In Paris, where classic cuisine infused with dried herbs once reigned, *nouvelle cuisine* has made people aware of the many possibilities of fresh culinary herbs. Talented cooks buy them in the market or grow them in pots to enjoy their special flavor in every kind of dish, and as garnishes to make the food even more appealing. And so French cuisine, north or south, traditional or innovative, remains synonymous with herbs.

Typical of many towns in Périgord, Brantôme stretches along the banks of the quietly flowing Dronne.

LES BORIES

On the narrow, stone-walled road just outside the village of Gordes is a cluster of small, rounded stone structures called *bories*. Some of these strange-looking rustic buildings date from the fourteenth century and were last inhabited around the mid-1800s. Constructed without mortar from the area's abundant supply of flat rocks, these buildings sheltered humans and animals and held wine or community ovens. Close by, another large *borie* has been restored and incorporated into one of Provence's most delightful restaurants, Les Bories.

The restaurant is the passion of Gabriel Rousselet, a native of Provence, who began his long career as an apprentice chef in Gordes. "I lived for the cooking," he says. After a twenty-year stint in Avignon, M. Rousselet returned to the hilltop village of Gordes. "I prefer the mountains," he admits. "There's a freshness to the air and it's cooler. And we always have the best, the freshest products at hand in the garden for the highest quality."

M. Rousselet and his wife live at Les Bories. Several comfortable rooms permit a few guests to enjoy the same pleasure, breakfasting in the warm sun on the terrace or relaxing in the shade of a tree at the end of a day's sightseeing. Lavender blooms in profusion just below the terrace, and Mme. Rousselet's mother tends the herb- and vegetable-filled garden farther down the slope. Whatever cannot be supplied by the garden is bought fresh early each morning, when M. Rousselet drives to the local market in Cavaillon, although herbs such as thyme are often gathered from the mountains.

The cooking at Les Bories is basically traditional, but M. Rousselet's talents and intelligence adds an extra dimension to the food. The smooth lavender ice cream is a good example. "Most people just use lavender honey," he says. "I make a praline incorporating the lavender flowers themselves so the ice cream has a richer lavender flavor."

M. Rousselet, *left*, stands in the *borie* he transformed into a restaurant. Pistou, *right*, is a traditional Provençal soup, the recipe for which can be varied to accommodate what's in the garden or market.

SOUPE AU PISTOU

½ pound dried white beans

4 quarts water

½ pound shelled fresh cranberry beans

¾ pound flat green beans, cut in 2-inch pieces

1 leek, chopped fine, white and tender green parts

½ pound tomatoes, peeled and diced

½ pound carrots, chopped

1 zucchini, chopped

½ pound spaghetti

1 garlic clove, minced

Handful of fresh basil leaves, chopped

¼ cup olive oil

Salt and pepper

3½ ounces Parmesan cheese, freshly grated

Pick over the white beans and place in a stockpot with cold water to cover. Soak for 2 hours, drain, and return to the pot with the water. Bring to a boil, then simmer until just tender, about 2 hours. About 30 minutes before the beans are done, add the cranberry beans. Thirty minutes later, add the green beans, leek, tomatoes, and carrots; cook 10 minutes. Add the zucchini and spaghetti, and cook about 10 minutes more.

With a mortar and pestle or in a food processor, make a paste of the garlic and basil. Mix in the olive oil. Stir the basil mixture into the soup before serving. Season to taste and pass the Parmesan separately.

SERVES 6

MEDITERRANEAN PAGEOT GRILLED WITH FENNEL

The pageot is a fish native to the Mediterranean. You can substitute red snapper or any firm-fleshed white fish. M. Rousselet grills his fish with the scales still on to keep the moisture in; they are removed along with the skin when the fish is eaten. The bed of fennel subtly flavors the fish as it cooks.

1 *pageot*, 1½ to 2 pounds, cleaned but not scaled

Large bunch of fresh fennel, leaves and stalks

2 lemons, halved

Melted butter

Prepare a charcoal fire in the grill. The coals are ready when they are covered with a fine layer of white ash.

Place a thick bed of fresh fennel on one side of a hinged fish grill. Place the fish on top and cover with another layer of fresh fennel. Close the grill. Set the grill over the hot coals and cook 20 to 25 minutes, turning the fish often. When the fish is done, place on a platter and serve accompanied with lemon halves and melted butter.

SERVES 2

LAVENDER ICE CREAM

This ice cream must be made with fresh lavender—the flavor of dried lavender will be too strong.

LAVENDER PRALINE

¼ cup granulated sugar

1 tablespoon water

¼ cup fresh lavender flowers

3 cups milk

½ cup heavy cream

1 sprig fresh lavender

6 egg yolks

¼ cup honey, preferably lavender

Lavender flowers, for garnish

Combine the sugar and water in a heavy pan over medium heat. Cook until the sugar caramelizes, about 5 to 10 minutes, then stir in the lavender flowers and cook 1 minute more. Turn out onto a lightly oiled marble surface or baking sheet. After the praline hardens, about 10 minutes, crush as fine as possible with a rolling pin. Set aside.

In a heavy saucepan, combine the milk, cream, and lavender. Bring to a boil, then remove from the heat, cover, and let steep until cool.

❧

M. Rousselet discovered his unique method of grilling fish, *left and far left*, in an old Provençal cookbook. His mother-in-law, *top right*, tends the herb and vegetable garden. The lavender ice cream, *right*.

In a medium bowl, beat the egg yolks and honey until they are thick and form a ribbon. When the milk has cooled, remove the lavender and slowly stir the milk into the egg-yolk mixture. Return the milk-and-egg mixture to the pan and cook over moderate heat, stirring constantly with a stainless-steel slotted spoon, until it is thick enough to coat the back of the spoon, about 15 minutes. Do not let the mixture come to a boil. Remove from the heat and cool.

Pour the ice cream into an ice-cream maker and freeze according to manufacturer's instructions. When partially frozen, stir in the lavender praline and freeze until firm. Garnish with lavender flowers before serving, if desired.

MAKES APPROXIMATELY
1 QUART

A FAMILY AFFAIR

Entering the cool, dark interior of La Bonne Étape in Château Arneau, you sense the warmth and humor of the Gleize family—mother, father, and son—who run this *hostellerie* with such care. Since the eighteenth century, it has been an inviting retreat for travelers in Provence, first as a coach stop, then a station hotel, and now as a beautifully appointed inn with a critically acclaimed kitchen.

Arlette Gleize, whose father owned the hotel, grew up here and met her husband, Pierre, when his motorcycle broke down in front of the hotel. He soon returned to marry her and work alongside his father-in-law in the kitchen. Their son, Jany, apprenticed with top chefs in France and even spent some time at the Connaught in London before returning home to share the running of the kitchen with Pierre. While they tend to the seasonal menu, Arlette watches over the dining room, turns masses of flowers from the garden into beautiful arrangements, and transforms local fruits into special conserves that guests enjoy with their morning croissants.

The cooking at La Bonne Étape is basically Provençal, touched with Gleize creativity. "When you're in Provence you should feel it in the food," says Jany. To this end, much of the restaurant's produce is grown in the Gleizes' own garden or obtained from forty or so small suppliers close by. Pierre has patronized these farmers for over thirty years, and they often drop in to chat with Pierre and Jany over a drink.

Most of the herbs used in the kitchen come from the garden. Even purslane, considered a pesky weed by most but a favorite of Provençal cooks, is cultivated at La Bonne Étape. The crunchy and slightly lemony herb is used raw in salads or pickled to eat with pâtés or cold meats in place of the more expected cornichons. Other herbs are picked in the wild. "Local people know exactly when to gather the herbs at their peak of flavor," says Jany. "You have to know *where* to pick them, too; in the mountains some places have better herbs than others."

DAUBE D'AGNEAU EN GELÉE

If possible, prepare this dish the evening before you plan to serve it. Adding the hooves to the pot provides the gelatin that makes the cooking liquid set. Before discarding the hooves, put a few drops of the liquid on a saucer and refrigerate; if it does not set, cook 20 or 30 minutes longer. If you cannot get hooves, dissolve 1 packet of gelatin with 3 cups of strained cooking liquid.

2½ pounds boneless lamb, from the leg or shoulder

Salt and black pepper to taste

3 to 4 tablespoons olive oil

4 to 5 carrots, peeled and sliced

2 onions, coarsely chopped

3 to 4 garlic cloves, minced

4 lambs' hooves or 1 veal hoof, blanched

1 whole clove

1 bouquet garni (1 celery stalk; 1 sprig each chervil, thyme, savory, and rosemary)

4 cups dry white wine

1 cup beef bouillon or water

SAUCE

2 garlic cloves, peeled

2 tablespoons chopped fresh thyme

2 tablespoons chopped fresh savory

¼ cup chopped fresh parsley

½ cup olive oil

Trim all the fat from the meat and cut meat into 4 or 5 pieces; season with salt and pepper. Heat the oil in a 3-quart earthenware or enamel casserole over medium-high heat and brown the lamb on all sides. When it is done, remove and set aside.

In the same pot, brown the carrots, onions, and garlic lightly. Remove the vegetables with a slotted spoon and discard the oil. Return the lamb and vegetables to the pot and add the lambs' hooves, clove, and bouquet garni. Bring the wine and bouillon to a boil over high heat; add to the casserole. Cover and cook over low heat for about 1½ hours.

When the meat and the vegetables are done, remove them with a slotted spoon and let the hooves cook in the broth for an additional hour. Strain the sauce into a bowl, reserving the hooves; skim off all traces of fat from broth, then season to taste. Remove the meat from the hooves and set aside.

Spoon a thin layer of liquid into the bottom of a 2-quart terrine and let it set in the refrigerator. Arrange the pieces of lamb, vegetables, and hoof meat over the jelly in a pattern that will look attractive when the terrine is sliced. Pour the remaining liquid over the meat and chill until firm, at least 4 hours or overnight.

To make the sauce, blanch the garlic in boiling water for 2 minutes. Repeat with fresh boiling water. Make a paste of the garlic and herbs either by hand or in a miniprocessor. Blend in enough oil to make a sauce. Unmold the terrine just before serving, slice, and serve with sauce on the side.

SERVES 8

CHERRIES WITH LAVENDER FLOWERS

1½ cups water

½ cup sugar

2 tablespoons lavender flowers

2¼ pounds fresh cherries, stemmed

Lavender flowers, for garnish

Combine the water, sugar, and lavender flowers in a saucepan. Bring to a boil over high heat and boil for 10 minutes. Remove from the heat and let steep for 10 minutes, then strain, discarding the lavender. Return the syrup to the saucepan, add the cherries, and bring to a boil. Immediately remove from the heat, cover, and cool to room temperature, then chill in the refrigerator. Garnish with lavender flowers before serving, if desired.

SERVES 8

Purslane from the garden, *opposite*, is pickled in white wine vinegar boiled with salt and aromatic herbs, such as fennel, thyme, bay, parsley, and garlic. It is served with cold meats. The daube, *top left*. Lavender is the exotic flavoring for local cherries, *left*.

COLD VEGETABLE OMELET WITH TAPENADE

The tapenade accompanying this omelet can also be served with some crusty bread as an appetizer. If purple artichokes are not available, substitute fresh or canned green artichoke hearts.

⅓ pound fresh spinach, shredded

⅓ pound Swiss chard, shredded

½ cup (1 stick) unsalted butter

¼ teaspoon minced garlic

3 tomatoes, peeled and diced

1 shallot, finely chopped

Pinch of fresh oregano or wild marjoram

2 tablespoons olive oil

4 purple artichoke hearts, cooked and sliced

½ pound wild mushrooms (girolles, cèpes, etc.), chopped

12 eggs

2 teaspoons chopped truffles

Salt and pepper

1 teaspoon chopped fresh parsley

1 teaspoon chopped fresh chervil

1 teaspoon chopped fresh chives

Tapenade (recipe follows)

Red wine vinegar

Preheat the oven to 300°F.

Blanch the spinach and chard in boiling water for 1 minute; drain well. Heat 1 tablespoon of the butter in a sauté pan, add the greens and the garlic, and sauté over medium-low heat for 2 to 3 minutes. Set aside.

Heat 1 tablespoon of butter in a clean saucepan over medium-low heat. Add the tomatoes, shallot, and a pinch of oregano or marjoram; cook until the vegetables are soft but not mushy, about 5 minutes. Set aside.

Heat 1 tablespoon of oil in another saucepan over medium heat, add the artichoke hearts, and sauté for about 5 minutes. Set aside.

In a small saucepan, sauté the wild mushrooms in the remaining olive oil over medium heat. The mushrooms should be just tender. Set aside.

In a small bowl, beat 2 of the eggs. Stir in the truffles and season with salt and pepper. Melt 1 tablespoon of butter in a small skillet over medium heat and scramble the egg mixture until it is set but still soft. Spoon an even layer of the eggs into the bottom of a lightly greased 2-quart terrine. Repeat process with the spinach mixture, the tomatoes, the green herbs, the artichoke hearts, and the mushrooms in that order, using 2 eggs for each layer. Layer each batch into the terrine alternating the colors to make an attractive display. Place the terrine in the oven for 20 minutes. Cool. Slice and serve with Tapenade and an excellent wine vinegar.

SERVES 6 TO 8

TAPENADE

¾ cup pitted ripe olives

1 tablespoon capers

2 to 3 anchovies

2 teaspoons olive oil

Pinch of freshly ground black pepper

Finely chop the olives, capers, and anchovies by hand or in a food processor. Stir in the olive oil and season with pepper.

The warm and welcoming Gleize family, *left*, in front of La Bonne Etape. Served at room temperature, the vegetable omelet, *opposite*, is a good dish for entertaining.

LA CUISINE PROVENÇALE

Stephanie Demery leads a double life. By day she is in charge of product design at Soleiado, the famous manufacturer of classic Provençal fabrics founded by her husband, Charles. At night she watches over her restaurant, Le Café des Artistes, in Avignon, where the menu offers a lightened version of traditional Provençal cuisine. The same careful attention is lavished on meals prepared at home.

"I've always eaten well," says Stephanie of her interest in food. "I grew up in Provence and my mother was an excellent cook. I like to eat well, too, so I entertain often. The meals are *fêtes*." One day to pass the time she decided to gather her recipes together for a book, something friends had been suggesting she do for a long time. When her recipe collection was mentioned in an *Elle* magazine interview, an offer came from a publisher within days.

The resulting book, *La Cuisine Provençale Traditionnelle*, concentrates on the authentic cuisine Stephanie prefers. "It's a cuisine of olive oil and little or no butter," she notes. "Provence is a magic region where you can find all the vegetables, fish, and herbs you want. When you're Provençal, you know each herb has a definite purpose—thyme, savory, and fennel are good for grilling, for example—and that you can't mix strong herbs like rosemary and sage." Lavender, rarely used for cooking in other parts of France, is popular in Provençal kitchens. Says Stephanie, "Lavender with chocolate is sublime."

The entire Demery clan often gathers at this country house for a festive lunch in the shade of a vine-covered arbor, *right*. Stephanie Demery, *left*.

EGGPLANT PROVENÇALE

PROVENÇALE TOMATO SAUCE

¼ to ½ cup olive oil

2 garlic cloves, crushed

2 whole cloves

1 tablespoon chopped fresh thyme

1 bay leaf

1 tablespoon chopped fresh savory

2 tablespoons chopped fresh basil

2 to 2½ pounds ripe tomatoes, seeded and quartered, or 1 (2-pound) can peeled and crushed tomatoes

Salt and pepper

6 small eggplants

Salt

2 cups olive oil

¼ cup chopped fresh parsley

¼ cup chopped fresh basil

In a pan, warm ¼ cup oil over low heat. Add the garlic, cloves, herbs, and tomatoes. Season to taste with salt and pepper and cook, covered, over low heat for at least 50 minutes, until the sauce thickens slightly. Keep the sauce warm while you cook the eggplant. (If you want a slightly thicker sauce, put the tomato sauce through a food mill. Heat another ¼ cup of olive oil in a pan, add the purée, and cook over medium heat until further reduced.)

Cut the eggplants lengthwise into thin slices. Salt the slices and let them rest 1 hour while the bitter juices drain out. Dry the eggplant with paper towels. Heat ¼ cup of the oil in a skillet over high heat. When the oil is hot, lower the heat and sauté the eggplant in batches until it is golden brown and tender, adding more oil as needed. Drain on paper towels.

Place a layer of eggplant on a platter and cover with tomato sauce. Continue layering the eggplant and sauce, ending with the sauce. Sprinkle parsley and basil on top and serve immediately.

SERVES 6

Eggplant Provençale combines the lusty flavors typical of this region.

The delicate zucchini loaf is garnished with whole basil leaves and surrounded with a hearty tomato sauce.

ZUCCHINI LOAF WITH GARDEN HERBS

TOMATO SAUCE

¼ cup olive oil

2 to 2½ pounds tomatoes, peeled, seeded, and cut in small dice, or 1 (2-pound) can tomatoes

1 onion, finely chopped

3 garlic cloves
   Handful of fresh thyme

1 bay leaf

4 leaves fresh basil

1 sprig fresh parsley
   Salt and pepper

6 zucchini, about 1¼ pounds total

1 tablespoon olive oil

1 cup chopped fresh basil

1 sprig tarragon, leaves chopped

6 chive stalks, chopped

1 tablespoon bread crumbs
   Pinch of grated nutmeg
   Salt and freshly ground black pepper

6 eggs

1 cup heavy cream
   Basil leaves, for garnish

To make sauce, heat the oil in a heavy pan. Add the tomatoes, onion, garlic, and herbs. Season with salt and pepper. Reduce the heat to low, cover, and cook gently for about 50 minutes.

Preheat the oven to 475°F.

While the sauce is cooking, prepare the loaf. Trim the ends from the zucchini and cut them into large dice. In a large pan, heat the oil, add the zucchini, and cook for 10 minutes. Stir in the basil, tarragon, and chives. Simmer gently 10 minutes more; the zucchini should be barely cooked. Stir in the bread crumbs and season to taste with nutmeg, salt, and pepper.

In a bowl, beat the eggs and cream together until thoroughly blended. Stir in the zucchini mixture. Butter a 9 × 5 × 3-inch loaf pan and pour in the zucchini mixture. Set the pan in a larger pan and fill halfway up the sides with hot water. Bake for 30 to 35 minutes, or until the loaf is set.

Carefully unmold the zucchini loaf onto a cutting board. Spoon the tomato sauce on a long platter. Cut the loaf in thin slices and arrange them on the warm tomato sauce. Garnish with several fresh basil leaves.

SERVES 6

STUFFED LAMB (L'AIADO)

Have the butcher bone the lamb, leaving it in one piece so that it can be rolled around the stuffing. Reserve the bone for the sauce. Stephanie serves this lamb with sautéed potatoes flavored with thyme.

STUFFING
- 1 white onion, finely chopped
- 4 shallots, finely chopped
- 6 garlic cloves, finely chopped
- 2 cups fresh parsley, finely chopped
- ¼ cup finely chopped fresh basil
- 2 sprigs fresh thyme, leaves only
- ½ teaspoon finely chopped fresh rosemary
- ½ cup bread crumbs
- 3 tablespoons olive oil
- Salt and pepper

- 2½ pounds boned lamb from the leg or shoulder, bones reserved

COOKING LIQUID
- 3 small carrots, peeled and diced
- 1 small onion, diced
- 1 sprig fresh thyme
- 1 small sprig fresh rosemary
- 1 bay leaf

- ¼ cup olive oil
- 3 tablespoons fresh thyme, or 1 tablespoon dried
- Salt and pepper

The stuffed lamb is served with potatoes perfumed with thyme.

In a large bowl, mix the onion, shallots, garlic, herbs, and bread crumbs. Stir in the oil and season to taste with salt and pepper. Spread the stuffing on the lamb, roll it up, and tie with string in several places to hold it closed.

To prepare the cooking liquid, place the carrots, onion, herbs, and lamb bones in a deep pot. Barely cover with water and cook over high heat for about 35 to 40 minutes. Strain, reserving the bones.

Preheat the oven to 425°F.

Pour the cooking liquid into a large roasting pan; add the bones. Place the lamb on top and douse with the olive oil and sprinkle with thyme. Season to taste with salt and pepper. Roast the lamb for 15 minutes, reduce the heat to 350°F., and continue to cook for another 25 minutes for medium rare. To serve, cut in quarter-inch slices.

SERVES 6

CITRUS TERRINE WITH LEMON VERBENA SYRUP

The fruit for this terrine must be prepared the night before serving.

- 5 small oranges
- 5 small grapefruits
- 2 packages gelatin
- ¼ cup water
- ½ cup sugar

LEMON VERBENA SYRUP
- 2 cups water
- 6 sprigs fresh lemon verbena
- 2½ cups sugar
- 2 lemons, juice and zest

Lemon verbena and strawberries, for garnish

Peel and section the fruit, removing membrane, over a bowl to collect any juice. Place a wire rack over the bowl, put the sections on the rack, and let them drain overnight in the refrigerator. Reserve the accumulated juice and cut the sections into small dice; set aside.

In a medium saucepan, combine the gelatin, water, and approximately 2 cups of juice saved from the fruit. When the gelatin has softened, stir in ½ cup sugar and cook over medium heat until the sugar and gelatin dissolve.

Layer the oranges and grapefruit in a 9 × 5 × 3-inch loaf pan until three-fourths full. Pour the gelatin mixture over the fruit and place in the freezer for 1–1½ hours.

To make the syrup, bring water to a boil in a saucepan. Remove from the heat, add the lemon verbena, cover, and steep for 30 minutes. Stir in the sugar and bring to a boil over high heat. Cook, uncovered, until the syrup thickens, about 5 minutes. Remove the lemon verbena and stir in the juice and zest of the lemons. Cool.

To serve, pour some of the syrup onto a deep platter. Carefully unmold the terrine, cut it into rather thick slices, and place on the syrup. Garnish with fresh lemon verbena and strawberries, and serve with crisp cookies.

SERVES 5 TO 6

Lemon verbena sauce complements the cold citrus terrine.

THE ESSENCE OF PROVENCE

The essence of Provence envelops visitors to Nathalie Waag's simple house on a plateau near Bonnieux. An extraordinary woman, she is as unpretentious and welcoming as Provence itself. Nathalie came here with her two children more than twenty years ago, leaving a photographic career and a husband behind in Paris. When she first arrived, funds were short; an elderly neighbor taught Nathalie the basics of Provençal cooking, and friends introduced her to the wild thyme, rosemary, and savory that grew around the house. She discovered that rice cooked with herbs was a very satisfying dish; and at times she even foraged whatever she could and cooked it in a pot hanging over the fireplace.

Eventually Nathalie opened a small restaurant in Vence. Since the restaurant had no stove, all the food was cooked at home. "Everything had to be prepared ahead, so I cooked grandmother food—lamb stews, daube. It was a nice experience," she says, "because friends gathered round and I had some wonderful regular customers." One of these customers was responsible for Nathalie's meeting Alice Waters. Eventually she spent a year at Chez Panisse, which in turn led to her hosting small groups that come to share Nathalie's Provence for a week. Together they tour the small town markets, then watch Nathalie improvise as she turns the ingredients they've chosen into a meal that is simple, honest, but superbly flavored. "It's a question of imagination and common sense," notes Nathalie.

Adept at seasoning with herbs, Nathalie warns against overwhelming the taste of food. "People here make fun of Parisians; when they come to Provence and cook," she says, "there is such an abundance of herbs available, they use too many. Often just the subtle taste produced by burning a few twigs of juniper or savory—or even lavender—in the fire when grilling meat is enough." Like her friend Alice Waters, Nathalie is convinced that preparing food with love and care adds its own indefinable seasoning to the final dish.

The ingredients for garlic soup, *opposite*, a Provençal standby, sit on Nathalie's windowsill. This simple but comforting medley of water, garlic, sage or bay, and a little salt, is poured over a piece of French bread. Sometimes a poached egg is added. *Below*, Nathalie picks wild herbs near her house.

HERBED POTATOES

3 tablespoons olive oil

2 garlic cloves, unpeeled

2 pounds small potatoes, skins on

Coarse sea salt to taste

3 to 4 sprigs fresh rosemary

3 to 4 sprigs fresh thyme

Heat the oil in a large skillet over medium-high heat. Add the garlic, potatoes, salt, and herbs. Cook, turning often, until the potatoes are browned all over and nearly done, about 20 minutes. Cover, reduce heat to medium, and cook an additional 5 minutes. Uncover; cook a few minutes more before serving.

SERVES 4

A typically simple lunch is served in the yard outside the old stone house, *above and right.* A sprig of mint makes a bottle of icy cold water even more refreshing. Thyme and rosemary, *far right,* from the hills around the house.

EGGS AND ZUCCHINI WITH MINT

6 zucchini

3 sprigs fresh mint, leaves
only

8 eggs

2 tablespoons (¼ stick)
butter

Salt and pepper

Trim the ends from the zucchini, peel 3 of them, then cut
all into several large pieces each.
Place the zucchini and mint in a
saucepan with water to cover,
and cook over medium heat until the zucchini are just tender,
about 10 minutes. Drain well,
press dry with a towel, then
transfer to the bowl of a food
processor and purée, or chop
very fine by hand.

In a bowl, beat the eggs well.
Stir in the zucchini-mint purée.
In a large saucepan melt the
butter over low heat. Add the
zucchini-egg mixture and cook,
stirring frequently, until the
eggs have the texture of soft
scrambled eggs, about 8 to 10
minutes. Season to taste with
salt and pepper.

SERVES 4

A PROVENÇAL SENSIBILITY

Eugene Mayard grew up in a family where serving people good food was a way of life. As a child he watched farmers bring grain to his parents' mill in the morning. While it was ground into flour, they played boule and drank pastis. When the wait was long enough, they also enjoyed food cooked and served by Eugene's grandmother, and, later, his mother, in a small home restaurant. As Eugene grew up, he knew he wanted to continue this tradition, but on a grander scale. His first undertaking, a hotel in Beaumes-de-Venise, was an enormous success that soon became a demanding way of life.

Nearly thirty-five years ago, Eugene sold the hotel and moved to Gordes in order to live more simply. At that time running water, electricity, telephones, and tourists were far from commonplace, and many buildings were still unrestored. Eugene was able to buy a splendid place that is now La May-anelle, a small hotel perched on the side of the hill, with a long terrace that overlooks red tile roofs and the rugged Provençal countryside. "I wanted to create a family atmosphere," he says, "not a commercial hotel. Something like a family pension, only better. It is best to stay simple but offer people a good ambience, a chance to sample the 'art de vivre français', which all the world tries to copy."

A Provençal sensibility, and his instinct for making people comfortable and feeding them well, has brought many people to La Mayanelle. But in spite of his success and a Cordon Bleu given him as an ambassador of French cuisine, Eugene Mayard wants nothing more than to stay himself. "You have to remain honest, what you are," he says. His cooking reflects this honesty. Regional in character, it centers on the splendid local produce seasoned with local herbs. "Cooking with herbs is an art. Each person has his own touch, like an artist with colors. It's a very human activity that can't be done by machine."

TAPENADE

3 cups pitted black olives

3 garlic cloves

2 tablespoons drained capers

3 cornichons

2 tablespoons olive oil

5 anchovy fillets

Place the olives in the bowl of a food processor and pulse on and off until chopped quite fine. Do not purée. (Alternately, chop the olives by hand.) Transfer the chopped olives to a bowl. Place the garlic, capers, and cornichons in the processor bowl and chop finely. Stir into the olives. In a small skillet, heat the olive oil, add the anchovies, and allow them to "melt" into the oil. Stir the anchovies into the olive mixture. Serve at room temperature.

MAKES APPROXIMATELY
2 CUPS

The makings of tapenade are arranged on a ledge of the terrace. This traditional Provençal dish derives its name from *tapen*, the Provençal word for *caper*.

SCALLOPS MAYANELLE

8 sea scallops, with coral if possible

Flour for dredging

2 tablespoons (¼ stick) unsalted butter

1 garlic clove, minced

¼ cup chopped fresh parsley

2 small tomatoes, peeled, seeded, and diced

8 fresh mushroom caps

Salt and pepper

Preheat the oven to 350°F.

Wash and dry the scallops. Coat them lightly with flour. In an ovenproof pan, melt the butter over high heat and quickly brown the scallops; they should not be completely cooked. Reduce the heat to medium, add the garlic and parsley, and cook for 2 minutes. Then add the tomatoes and mushroom caps, season to taste with salt and pepper, and place in the oven for 5 minutes.

SERVES 2

The old stone walls of Gordes frame a slice of the surrounding countryside and scallops seasoned with those Provençal favorites, parsley and garlic.

HERBED TERRINE

2¼ pounds fresh spinach

2¼ pounds boneless pork, with the fat from the shoulder

1 pork liver

3 tablespoons chopped garlic

1 tablespoon chopped fresh sage

1 tablespoon fresh thyme

Pinch of grated nutmeg

Salt and freshly ground pepper

¼ pound pork fat, thinly sliced

Beef aspic and cornichons, for garnish

Preheat the oven to 350°F.

Wash the spinach thoroughly, remove the tough stems, and place in a saucepan with a tight lid. Cover and cook in the water clinging to the leaves for 5 minutes. Drain and chop.

Chop the pork and pork liver in a food processor or put them through the medium or fine blade of a meat grinder. In a bowl, mix the meat, chopped spinach, garlic, herbs, and nutmeg. Season with salt and pepper. Pack the mixture into a terrine and top with a few slices of pork fat. Place the terrine in the oven and cook until the juices are clear, about 2 hours. Cool and serve at room temperature; garnish with beef aspic, if desired.

SERVES 10 TO 12

ROAST QUAIL WITH SAVORY AND ROAST TOMATOES

2 tomatoes

1 tablespoon fresh thyme

1 tablespoon chopped fresh savory

2 tablespoons bread crumbs

2 tablespoons olive oil

4 quail

Salt and pepper

12 sprigs fresh savory

1 red bell pepper, sliced vertically

8 fresh mushrooms

Fresh thyme and savory, for garnish

Remove the tops from the tomatoes and core. In a small bowl, mix the thyme, savory, bread crumbs, and 1 tablespoon oil. Divide the herb mixture among the tomatoes, then set them in a small baking pan.

Preheat the oven to 425°F.

Wash and dry the quail. Rub the birds inside and out with salt and pepper, then place 3 savory sprigs in the cavity of each. Set on a rack in a roasting pan and roast for approximately 25 minutes. The birds should be golden brown all over. If they are cooked but not brown, run them under the broiler.

After the quail have cooked for 10 minutes, put the tomatoes in the oven. Coat the pepper strips and mushrooms with the remaining oil and place them in the oven 5 minutes later. The vegetables should be cooked tender, but not soft, when the quail is ready. Season with salt and pepper and place 2 quail on each serving plate. Garnish with thyme and savory.

SERVES 2

❦

The herbed terrine, *top left*. Thyme and savory from the nearby hills add their pungent flavor to the local quail, *below*.

DINING AT A RESTORED MILL

Once, the large water wheel that dominates Moulin du Roc powered the presses that squeezed oil from the region's vast, crop of flavorful walnuts. Abandoned, the mill slowly fell into disrepair and was overgrown with weeds. Working long hours and with no professional help, Solange Gardillou and her husband, Lucien, reclaimed the sixteenth-century mill, transforming it into a handsome, antiques-filled restaurant and inn.

Solange grew up on a local dairy farm, where she learned to prepare regional Périgordian dishes from her mother. Her talent for cooking might never have developed further if one of the restaurant's former chefs, overcome one day by his weakness for alcohol, hadn't threatened Solange with a chopper. He was summarily dismissed, but since it was the height of the season, no replacement was available and Solange took over in the kitchen. From this dubious start she became a two-star chef known for the subtlety and originality of her cooking.

Solange's recipes often start with local ingredients, to which she applies her own imaginative twists, frequently adding aromatic herbs or changing the traditional method of cooking. Foie gras, for example, is served with chives; and the wild mint that grows close to the river adds its cool touch to a rich chocolate dessert. "I really like the marriage of mint and chocolate," she says. Herbs as well as some vegetables are grown in a small kitchen garden across the road from the hotel, and a few are tucked in among the flowers in the charming hedged garden that welcomes guests when they arrive.

Incredibly organized and filled with energy, Solange not only cooks and supervises the mill's kitchen but spends hours at home preserving seasonal foods and making jam for the breakfast trays. This small and dainty woman doesn't look as though she'd have the stamina to take on this huge work load. "Sometimes," she says, "people are surprised to see me in the kitchen. But you know, years ago it was always women who cooked in country restaurants. Now they are chefs."

Minty chocolate pavé is as refreshing as the river rushing through the mill's waterwheel.

BITTER CHOCOLATE PAVÉ WITH ITS RIVER OF WILD MINT

The pavé, or paving stone, is a very rich mousse/cake. If there is no wild mint growing where you live, substitute apple mint or spearmint.

MINT CRÈME ANGLAISE

4 ⅓ cups milk

1 bunch fresh wild mint, about 1 cup chopped

8 egg yolks

1 cup sugar

7 tablespoons green crème de menthe

10 ounces semisweet chocolate

10 ounces unsweetened chocolate

½ cup (1 stick) unsalted butter

2 cups heavy cream, whipped

Chocolate shavings, for garnish

Confectioners' sugar

Mint leaves, for garnish

To make the cream, place the milk and mint in a saucepan and bring to a boil over high heat. Meanwhile, in a bowl beat the yolks and sugar together until they are pale and thick. Pour the boiling milk into the egg mixture, stirring constantly. Return the sauce to the saucepan and cook over medium-low heat, stirring constantly, until thickened, about 15 minutes. Do not allow the sauce to boil. Cool to room temperature, covered, then stir in the crème de menthe and pass through a fine strainer to remove any lumps. Set aside.

Melt the chocolates in a double boiler over hot but not boiling water. Stir in the butter. Cool to barely warm, then fold in the whipped cream. Pour the pavé into a lightly greased rectangular mold, and refrigerate until firm, about 4 to 6 hours or overnight.

To serve, unmold the *pavé* and slice about 1 inch thick. Place a slice in the middle of each plate, then surround with large chocolate shavings and a sprinkle of confectioners' sugar. Spoon the sauce around the cake. Chop several mint leaves and sprinkle over the cake and sauce, then decorate with whole leaves.

SERVES 8

ROUGETS WITH WALNUT OIL

SAUCE

3 tomatoes, peeled and finely diced

Salt and pepper

Juice and zest of 2 lemons

1 shallot, chopped

½ tablespoon shredded fresh basil

½ tablespoon chopped fresh tarragon

1 teaspoon chopped fresh parsley

1 teaspoon chopped fresh chervil

1 teaspoon chopped fresh chives

Pinch of fresh thyme

7 tablespoons walnut oil

2 tablespoons olive oil

12 small rougets or red snapper, filleted

Place the tomatoes in a bowl and season to taste with salt and pepper. Blanch the lemon zest in boiling water for 1 minute. Drain. Add the juice of the lemons and a little of the zest to the tomatoes. Stir in the shallot and the herbs, then the walnut oil. Set aside to marinate for 1 hour.

When you are ready to eat, heat the olive oil in a large skillet over medium-high heat and sauté the fillets until done, about 3 minutes per side. While the fish is cooking, warm the sauce. Place the fillets on a plate and spoon the sauce around them.

SERVES 6

Walnut oil adds a distinctive taste of Périgord to sauteed rougets.

A DESIGNING COOK

Laurence Lafont is a talented designer of linens, china, and other housewares. Since 1979, she has also been fashioning stylish eyeglass frames for her husband, whose family owns one of the most prominent eyeglass firms in Europe.

The Lafonts spend weekends in the country, but workdays find them in their charming house in St.-Cloud, on the outskirts of Paris. Running two households, a family, and working full time means that Laurence doesn't have much time to cook. "During the week we eat family food—roast meat, a green vegetable, salad, fruit and cheese. But on the weekends," she says, "I really like to make more interesting dishes." Since her husband, Philippe, also enjoys cooking, they often share the chores, especially when they entertain. "We each have certain desserts or entrees that are our specialties."

Laurence constantly reads cookbooks and magazines for new recipes. "I always cook the recipe the way it's written the first time," she says. "After that I alter it to make it mine." Altering the recipe may entail substituting or adding herbs. In the country, herbs grow in the garden; in St.-Cloud, most grow in pots outdoors or on a sunny windowsill. "I try to have herbs growing year round so I can go outside and cut a leaf whenever I need it."

Laurence in the kitchen, *above,* **which reflects her sense of design. An arch in the hedge,** *right,* **seems to lead to a secret garden, where the Lafonts often entertain,** *left,* **on warm sunny days.**

CHERVIL NASTURTIUM SOUP

2 quarts water

Salt

2 cups fresh chervil

1 cup nasturtium leaves

1 cup watercress leaves, large stems removed

1 pound potatoes, peeled and quartered

1 cup heavy cream

1 tablespoon butter

Nasturtium leaves, for garnish

In a large pot, bring the water to a boil over high heat. Add salt, reduce the heat to medium-low, and add the chervil, nasturtium and watercress leaves, and potatoes. Simmer gently for 1 hour. Purée the soup in a food processor or blender in several batches.

Just before serving, stir in the cream and, if the soup has cooled, reheat gently. Place the butter in the bottom of a tureen and pour the hot soup over it. Garnish with nasturtium leaves, if desired.

SERVES 8

A cluster of nasturtium leaves garnish the soup.

BRILL WITH HERBS

Brill is a large, flat European fish. If it is not available, you can substitute sole.

6 leeks (white parts only)
Salt
½ cup (1 stick) butter
6 fillets of brill, about 2½ pounds total
3 cups heavy cream
2 egg yolks
½ cup chopped fresh parsley
½ cup chopped fresh chervil
½ cup chopped fresh tarragon
½ cup chopped fresh chives

GARNISH
24 nasturtium leaves
6 nasturtium flowers
6 chive spears

Preheat the oven to 425°F.

Cut the leeks into 1-inch pieces and place in a saucepan. Season with salt, add 1 tablespoon of butter, cover with water, and cook over medium heat for 20 minutes. When they are done, the water should be gone and the leeks should have a light coating of butter. Set aside and keep warm.

Meanwhile, place the fillets in an ovenproof dish. Pour all but 6 tablespoons of the cream over them and bake until done but still firm, about 8 minutes. Transfer the fish to a plate, reserving the cooking liquid, cover, and keep warm.

Combine the reserved cooking liquid, the egg yolks, and remaining 6 tablespoons cream in a saucepan; beat well. Cook over medium heat, stirring, until the sauce has thickened slightly. Transfer the sauce to the bowl of a food processor or a blender, add the chopped herbs, and purée.

To serve, place some leeks, a fillet napped with the sauce, and a bouquet of 4 nasturtium leaves and 1 flower tied with a chive on each plate.

SERVES 6

The fish, *left*, is garnished with a small nosegay of nasturtiums and served on plates of Laurence's design, inspired by the garden. Herbed cheeses are arrayed on the buffet, *right*.

A LAKESIDE FEAST

"I like meals to be a feast," says Aude Clément, owner of one of Paris's most intriguing housewares stores, Au Bain Marie. Aude's love of food goes back to her childhood, when birthdays were occasions for a splendid meal at Fernand Point's celebrated restaurant. "My father always drank good wine," she adds, "and he always gave me a taste."

Aude has pursued her love of food in her work as well, developing articles on cooking for leading French magazines, then styling them for photography. While searching for interesting props, she became intrigued with the beautiful but useful antiques related to preparing and serving food. Eventually she amassed enough of them to open a shop devoted to the table.

As busy as she is, Aude still manages to find time to cook. Every Saturday morning she searches the weekly market in Lac d'Enghien, the small spa town near Paris where she lives, for the best produce, fish, and meats. "I like everything that's good," she says. Arriving home, the morning's purchases are unpacked on the long counter to inspire her. Any fish is washed, dried, then lightly salted. "It's a trick I learned from the Japanese," says Aude. "The fish keeps better and the flesh is firmer."

"I cook by smell," she notes. "When you can smell pasta, it's too late. It will already be overcooked." The fragrance of herbs is always an important consideration in her cooking. Basil is a favorite, "but I never cook it," she notes.

On weekends, Aude often creates a "feast" for a few close friends, but she also tries to cook for the entire week. "When I get home after work, it's 7:30 or 8 o'clock. If I have frozen food on hand I can thaw it in the microwave in just a few minutes. I'm a modern woman," she adds. "I work quickly in the kitchen. Maybe it's not always the best way, but it's the way."

Aude, *left*, shops in the local market. She uses her collection of antiques and her sense of fantasy to create a striking centerpiece, *right*.

RABBIT EN GELÉE

The liquid in which the rabbit cooks becomes a delicious aspic in this appealing terrine.

- 1 young hare or 2 fleshy rabbits, about 4 pounds total
- 2 envelopes unflavored gelatin
- ¼ cup water
- 6 carrots, peeled
- 1 bottle dry white wine
- 1 tablespoon white wine vinegar

   Zest of ½ lemon

   Freshly ground black pepper
- 2 bay leaves
- 3 sprigs fresh thyme
- 6 sprigs fresh Italian parsley
- 1 onion, halved
- 1 head garlic, peeled
- 24 small onions
- 6 to 8 whole French green beans
- ¼ cup white Madeira wine

   Pinch of ground cinnamon
- 12 pickled onions
- 2 tablespoons chopped fresh chives
- ¼ cup fresh chervil leaves
- 2 tablespoons chopped fresh fennel leaves

   Salt

   Fresh Italian parsley, for garnish

   Poppyseeds, kiwi, or black currants, for garnish

Cut the legs from each rabbit, then split the body into 2 pieces. In a small bowl, soften the gelatin in the water. Slice 2 of the carrots. Place the rabbit, gelatin, wine, vinegar, lemon zest, a few grinds of pepper, bay leaves, thyme, parsley, sliced carrots, onion, and garlic in a large pot. Bring to a boil over high heat, then reduce the heat to medium-low and simmer until the meat falls from the bones, about 1½ to 2 hours.

While the rabbit is stewing, in separate saucepans cook the remaining whole carrots and the small onions in boiling water until just tender, about 15 minutes. In another pot, cook the beans for 5 minutes. Drain the vegetables, rinse under cold running water, and set aside.

When done, remove the rabbit and vegetables from the pot with a slotted spoon. Strain the cooking liquid into a bowl, stir in the Madeira, and set aside.

Remove the rabbit meat from the bones and cut any large chunks into bite-size pieces. Sprinkle with a little cinnamon. Slice the crisp-tender carrots and small onions and reserve separately. Let all ingredients cool to room temperature.

Coat the inside of a shallow round 2-quart mold with a layer of the cooking liquid and let it set. Arrange crisp-tender carrot slices over the bottom and around the sides of the mold. Then layer the rabbit pieces, remaining carrots, cooked onions, garlic cloves, pickled onions, beans, and herbs in the mold, arranging them so they will look appealing when it is cut. Season with salt and pepper, and pour the remaining cooking liquid into the mold to cover the meat and vegetables. Place in the refrigerator to set, 4 to 6 hours.

Carefully turn the mold out onto a platter and gently press Italian parsley leaves into the aspic before serving. You can decorate it further with poppyseeds as shown, or kiwi slices or fresh black currants.

SERVES 6

The rewards of a trip to the market are spread out in the kitchen to inspire the cook.

PIGEON IN RED WINE SAUCE

To make this sautéed pigeon into a feast, Aude serves it with peeled, roasted, and sliced figs and slices of sautéed fresh foie gras.

4 pigeons (squab), about 1 pound each

4 cups chicken stock

4 cups red Burgundy wine

1 onion, chopped

1 bay leaf

1 sprig fresh thyme

3 sprigs fresh Italian parsley

1 sprig fresh curly parsley

1 small sprig fresh rosemary

6 to 8 garlic cloves

1 teaspoon coriander seeds

3 scallions (white and green parts), chopped

Black pepper to taste

6 tablespoons (¾ stick) unsalted butter

4 cups mixed greens and herbs

Wash and dry the pigeons; with a pair of kitchen shears, clip the wing tips and the ends of the legs from each bird. Cut the leg and thigh joints, wings, and breast meat from the carcasses and set aside. Reserve the carcasses for the sauce.

In a large nonaluminum saucepan, combine the carcasses, stock, wine, onion, herbs, garlic, and scallions over high heat. Reduce heat and simmer, uncovered, for 1 hour to allow the sauce to absorb all the flavors. If it seems to be reducing too quickly, add a little water. After 1 hour, increase heat and boil hard until the sauce is reduced by half; strain, season with pepper, and set aside.

In a large skillet, melt three tablespoons of the butter over medium-high heat. Sauté the legs and wings, turning until they are golden on all sides, about 10 to 15 minutes. Pour the strained sauce over the pigeon, cover, and bring to a boil. Reduce heat and simmer until the pigeon pieces are tender when pricked with a fork, about 30 to 40 minutes. Remove the pigeon and stir 2 tablespoons of butter into the sauce.

A few minutes before serving, sauté the boned breasts in the remaining three tablespoons of butter for 2 minutes on each side; they will be rare.

Mound the mixed greens and herbs on each plate and top with a pigeon piece that has been cooked in the sauce. Slice the breast and serve beside the greens with roasted figs and sautéed foie gras, if desired. Pass the sauce separately.

SERVES 4

A gala luncheon of pigeon, *left,* is served on the awninged terrace overlooking Lac d'Enghien. A typical French market, *right.*

Italy

In Italy, the refined dishes of the nobility have gradually merged with the simple cooking of the humbler classes to produce an honest, flavorful cuisine as rich and varied as its fertile countryside. The dishes indigenous to each of Italy's provinces make the most of the local bounty: wild mushrooms and game, lush fruits and vegetables, fragrant olive oils and robust wines, plump chickens, tender veal and Tuscan beef, and a plethora of pastas. And each region has its favorite herbs for seasoning.

At one time the only Italian food Americans experienced was the heavy tomato-based fare of southern Italy: pizza and pastas with long-cooked red sauces redolent of dried oregano and garlic. But in the past decade we've become familiar with the cream-based sauces and veal dishes savored in northern Italy; and pesto, that heady blend of olive oil, basil, garlic, pine nuts, and Parmesan

❧

A series of Marcella Hazan's flavorful dishes at her Venetian apartment.

Cypress trees, *above*, line the drive to Locanda del Amorosa. The square, *opposite*, surrounded by the chapel and other buildings.

The Trattoria Santina, *below*, like many simple country restaurants, serves deliciously honest foods such as succulent herb-roasted chicken.

cheese that's a staple of Genoese kitchens, is an old favorite. Recently the fresh and flavorful cooking of Tuscany, with an emphasis on fine local produce and grilled or roasted meats, one of the inspirations for California cuisine, has been making culinary headlines.

In every part of the country, herbs play an important role in the kitchen. Parsley (the flat-leafed variety, of course) is probably the most popular. Frequently combined with other herbs, it's found in every area of the country and is the basis of gremolata, a pungent mixture of parsley, lemon peel, and garlic that recurs in numerous Italian dishes. Rosemary, bay leaf, thyme, sage, and garlic are used with different degrees of intensity from region to region. Surprisingly, mint, little appreciated in American cooking, appears often in Italian recipes. It seasons pork, snails, and frittatas in the Marches; tomato sauce or artichokes in Rome; and vegetables in Tuscany. Nepetella, a wild mint whose taste is a cross between mint and marjoram, is a traditional flavoring for the porcini gathered in Tuscan forests.

Along the Adriatic and in Sicily, wild fennel complements fish, pork, and rabbit; and in Sardinia cooks even combine myrtle leaves with suckling pig or game birds. Herbs are mixed into breads and pastas, added to sauces and marinades, stirred into vegetables and risottos, and stuffed into fish and meat, subtly adding their flavor to the appetizing cooking of Italy. And as Marcella Hazan, Italy's most erudite cook, says in *Marcella's Italian Kitchen*, "All that matters in food is its flavor."

The garden, a mixture of formal plantings and containers, can be enjoyed from the loggia.

A FLORENTINE VILLA

The Villa Villoresi, on the outskirts of Florence, was built in the twelfth century as a military structure. During the Renaissance, when such protection was no longer necessary, it was enlarged and turned into a charming country house filled with art and surrounded by gardens. In the eight centuries the building has been in existence, only six families have lived there.

Christina Villoresi de Loche, Villa Villoresi's current owner, converted the villa into an elegant small hotel in the 1960s. It is entered through a long gallery cleverly lined with swan-neck settees of diminishing size that give the hall even greater perspective. Upstairs, elegantly furnished bedrooms open onto a sunny Renaissance logia, originally a communications passage for soldiers, that overlooks the charming Italian-style formal garden.

After dinner, guests can sit in the villa's garden and sip a small glass of chedrena, the delicious lemon-flavored liqueur Christina makes from the lemon verbena bushes that flourish around the edges of the garden. Culinary herbs for use in the kitchen also grow in the small garden, adding their delightful fragrance to that of the roses and citrus trees around them.

COUNTRY BREAD WITH TOMATOES

3 tomatoes

½ small onion, finely chopped

10 large fresh basil leaves, finely chopped

Salt and pepper

1 garlic clove

6 large or 12 small slices country bread

3 tablespoons olive oil

Dip the tomatoes in boiling water for a few seconds to loosen the skins, then peel. Chop the tomatoes very fine in a food processor or by hand, then transfer to a bowl; stir in the onion and basil. Season to taste with salt and pepper.

Halve the garlic clove in half and rub the cut side over one side of each slice of bread. Spread a little oil on each slice, then top with a few spoonfuls of tomato mixture. Serve immediately.

SERVES 6

GREEN HERB SAUCE

Christina serves this sauce with poached salmon, but it can be used with any fish, boiled meat, or hard-cooked eggs.

1 slice white bread

2 tablespoons white wine vinegar

¼ cup chopped fresh parsley

¼ cup chopped fresh basil

2 tablespoons chopped fresh mint

2 anchovy fillets with a little of their oil

1 hard-cooked egg, finely chopped

1 teaspoon drained capers, or to taste

¼ to ½ cup olive oil

Tear the bread into small pieces and combine in a small bowl with the vinegar. When bread has absorbed the vinegar, add the herbs and the anchovies with their oil; mash together well. Stir in the egg and capers, then slowly add the oil until the mixture has a saucelike consistency.

MAKES ABOUT 1 CUP

❧

A palm grows in a Tuscan pot outside one of the villa doors, *top left*. *Right*, a favorite Italian dish, country bread with tomatoes, is served on the Renaissance loggia.

BEACHSIDE DINING

Except for a short sojourn in New York, Marco Giacchetti has spent his whole life in Portonovo di Ancona, a small resort on the Aegean coast. The curving beach is dotted with humble fish restaurants, and the lifestyle is easy.

Until a few years ago, Giacchetti's, the restaurant owned by Marco's family, was as rustic as the others. Then Marco remodeled, and now an imposing modern structure with a broad, table-filled deck overlooks the beach where the simple beachside restaurant once stood. Inside, however, the menu still concentrates on incredibly fresh and simply cooked fish. Grilled fish—stuffed with a mixture of parsley, garlic, bread crumbs, and olive oil—is accompanied by bread toasted on the grill; fresh tomatoes, potatoes, carrots, and oil enhance the flavor of fish cooked on the stove. "The combination of fish and vegetables is traditional here," says Marco. "The people who farm in the mountains have always traded with the fishermen."

Shellfish is usually served in a fresh tomato sauce seasoned with parsley and marjoram. Among Marco's favorites are *ragosa*, a tough snail-like creature, and *balleri*, mollusks indigenous to the region. *Balleri* make their home in the area's mud, a unique substance that eventually becomes rock-hard; the only way to gather the shellfish is to walk the shoreline at low tide and break open the chunks of hardened mud with a mallet. Since *balleri* have become an endangered species, it is unlawful to harvest them commercially, and Marco's customers must content themselves with clams or mussels instead. But, sitting in the warm Italian sun, enjoying honestly cooked fish and robust wines while music floats overhead, no one minds.

❦

Mario, *left*, gathering *balleri*, a local shellfish rarely available in other areas. They are served with a simple tomato sauce, *right*, that works equally well with littleneck clams or mussels.

SHELLFISH IN TOMATO SAUCE

½ cup plus 2 tablespoons olive oil

1 onion, finely chopped
   Salt and pepper

3 pounds tomatoes, diced

1 celery stalk, diced

1 carrot, diced

1 teaspoon dried marjoram, or 1 tablespoon fresh

1 tablespoon red wine vinegar

3 tablespoons butter

4 pounds *balleri*, or littleneck clams, or 2½ pounds mussels

3 tablespoons chopped fresh parsley

In a large saucepan, heat ½ cup of the olive oil over medium heat. Add the onion and cook until transparent, about 5 minutes. Season to taste with salt and pepper, then add the tomatoes, celery, carrot, dried marjoram (if using fresh marjoram, add it with the shellfish and parsley), and vinegar. Reduce the heat to medium-low, and simmer for 1½ hours. Stir in 1 tablespoon of the butter and set aside.

Wash the shellfish well under running water. Transfer it to a large heavy pot, cover with the sauce, then add the remaining oil and butter, parsley, and fresh marjoram, if used. Cover and cook over medium heat for 15 minutes. Discard any shells that have not opened. Serve topped with the sauce.

SERVES 4

The main house's sweeping steps, *above*. A working garden, *opposite*, supplies the restaurant with herbs and vegetables.

A TUSCAN RETREAT

Long rows of cypress trees line the drive to Locanda dell' Amorosa, ending at the arch of a medieval tower that once protected this tiny walled village perched at the edge of the Sienese hills. Beyond the arch, the original fourteenth-century square still exists, enclosed by the elegant family villa built during the Renaissance, the private chapel, buildings where farm laborers lived, and the old stables that once housed a herd of Tuscany's famous white cattle. For many years this handsome cluster of buildings has been the family farm of Don Carlo dei Marchesi Citterio, who returned permanently in 1968, when youth riots were disrupting city life. At first he considered living in the country an amusing respite, but eventually he decided to settle in and start a business. Now Locanda dell' Amorosa is a renowned restaurant and country inn that offers travelers the opportunity to enjoy Don Carlo's Tuscan hospi-

tality while exploring the surrounding countryside.

"It's not commercial," says Don Carlo. "It's a private house that's not private, a hotel that is not a hotel. Everything I do is because it's what *I* like . . . and although not everyone will like what I like, I think there are enough who will." Indeed, it would be difficult not to appreciate the charming spot he has created.

Although Don Carlo no longer presides over the kitchen, he supervises the menu as artfully as he does the hotel's ambience. The restaurant concentrates on simple Tuscan foods. "It's important to use local foods," he says, "because they give an idea of the country. Native ingredients are easy to use well, but it's important to make sure they are well balanced and, above all, to use the herbs of the region." Tarragon is a favorite. "Most people don't realize tarragon was originally from Siena," he says. "Catherine de' Medici took it to France from Florence."

Grilled trout is served with turned cucumbers.

MINTED GREEN BEAN SALAD

1 teaspoon baking soda

1½ pounds green beans, trimmed

¼ cup extra-virgin olive oil

1½ tablespoons lemon juice

Salt and pepper

15 fresh mint leaves, coarsely chopped

In a large pot, bring an abundant amount of unsalted water to a boil. Add the baking soda and beans, and cook until just crisp-tender, about 15 minutes. Then cool under running water, drain, and place in a serving bowl.

In a small bowl, mix the olive oil and lemon juice until well blended; season with salt and pepper. Pour the dressing over the beans, sprinkle with the mint, and toss gently.

SERVES 4

FILET MIGNON WITH HERBS

A club steak can be substituted for the filet mignon.

¼ pound bacon fat or lard

1 cup freshly grated bread crumbs

2 tablespoons finely chopped fresh parsley

1 tablespoon finely chopped fresh thyme

2 teaspoons finely chopped fresh rosemary

1 tablespoon butter

2 filet mignons, about 7 ounces each

In a bowl, mix the bacon fat or lard, bread crumbs, and herbs until they form a paste. Spread the paste on a plate in a thin layer, cover with plastic wrap, and place in the refrigerator for about 45 minutes.

Preheat the oven to 300°F.

In a skillet, melt the butter over high heat and brown the meat quickly on both sides. Remove from the heat and transfer to a well-buttered ovenproof pan. Spread the paste over the meat and bake until cooked rare, about 15 minutes. Serve very hot.

SERVES 2

TROUT FILLETS WITH CUCUMBERS

4 brook trout, about 1 pound each

Salt and pepper

½ cup (1 stick) unsalted butter

2 tablespoons dry white wine

1 large seedless European cucumber, peeled and trimmed into 1-inch ovals

1 small tomato, peeled, seeded, and diced

6 fresh basil leaves, julienned

Fresh basil, for garnish

Clean, scale, and fillet the trout. Wash and dry the fillets and season to taste with salt and pepper. In a large skillet, melt 2 tablespoons of the butter over high heat. Add the fillets and cook for 5 minutes on each side. Remove the fillets to a plate with a slotted spoon; keep warm. Add the wine and cucumber to the pan and boil for 1 minute, then stir in the remaining butter, cut in small pieces, the tomato, and the basil. Cook for another minute, and season with additional salt and pepper. To serve, place 2 fillets on each plate and spoon some sauce over them. Garnish with fresh basil, if desired.

SERVES 4

Opposite, **an old well in the center of the courtyard frames the frescoed chapel behind it. The arched gallery of the old stables,** *below,* **which now house charming rooms and the restaurant.**

COUNTRY DINING IN TUSCANY

Dania Luccharini has a passion for food, a passion she has been sharing for the past eight years with those who dine at the delightful restaurant she and her husband, Umberto, run in the Tuscan countryside. A former lawyer, Dania originally moved to the country with Umberto to restore an old family farm. Once the farmhouse was done, the couple found themselves with free time and energy and a desire to start something new. They bought a sprawling old stone farmhouse on a hill overlooking a Tuscan valley and opened La Chiusa.

Dania has taken charge of the kitchen, and although she has no formal training as a chef, she does have an innate sense of good food, gleaned perhaps from time spent with friends like Roger Vergé. Under her direction, La Chiusa's menu emphasizes local produce and authentic fare that has been updated but still reflects the flavors of Tuscany. "The traditional way of cooking uses too much fat," she says. "I've lightened it up."

The olive oil that dresses salads is made in the old olive press the Luccharinis found in the basement, and overnight guests are offered La Chiusa's own honey and marmalade for breakfast. The herbs used in the kitchen come from a hillside garden below the terrace, supplemented by *nepetella*, the wild mint that grows throughout the region. Its subtle taste, a combination of mint and marjoram, is a traditional complement to porcini and artichokes. "I use sage and rosemary more than any other herbs," says Dania. "I can't cook without herbs, and I mix them. I pick a few fresh ones every morning. When you get them at the market, they are not really fresh and their aroma is not as good."

≪≪≪

Rabbit flavored with chives, *far right*, **is served on the flower-bedecked terrace. Dania Luccharini,** *left*. **The view over the Tuscan hills from La Chiusa,** *right*.

VEAL CARPACCIO WITH MARJORAM

¾ pound boneless veal loin, cut from the center, thinly sliced

¼ cup chopped fresh marjoram

MARINADE

½ cup olive oil

2 tablespoons lemon juice

Salt to taste

2 tablespoons olive oil

1 tomato, peeled, seeded, and diced

1 zucchini, thinly sliced

2 tablespoons chopped fresh marjoram

Salt and pepper

½ cup chopped fresh chives

Pound the veal slices until they are just ⅛ inch thick, and place them in a single layer on a platter. In a small bowl, combine the marinade ingredients. Pour over the veal slices, then sprinkle with the marjoram. Cover with plastic wrap and allow to marinate at least 1 hour before serving. (If you are preparing the meat ahead of time, set it in the refrigerator.)

While the meat is marinating, heat the oil in a small skillet over medium heat. Add the tomato and cook for 5 minutes, then add the zucchini and marjoram, and cook for an additional 3 minutes; the vegetables should be barely cooked. Season with salt and pepper and cool.

To serve, divide the veal among 4 plates, and place a few pieces of tomato and zucchini on top. Sprinkle with the chopped chives.

SERVES 4

STUFFED SQUASH BLOSSOMS

To make her tomato sauce, Dania Luccharini cooks down some ripe tomatoes with a little oil until she has a thickish purée. If you would prefer a more traditional sauce, use the recipe on page 251. To enhance the fresh herbal flavor, serve a green sauce, such as the one below, on the side.

8   large squash or zucchini blossoms

1   cup ricotta cheese

1   egg yolk, beaten

2   tablespoons grated Parmesan cheese

2   tablespoons finely chopped fresh parsley

2   cups tomato purée or light tomato sauce

    Parsley, for garnish

    GREEN SAUCE

4   tablespoons mayonnaise, preferably homemade

2   tablespoons chopped fresh parsley

2   tablespoons chopped fresh chives

2   tablespoons heavy cream

A beautifully presented stuffed squash blossom is served in the mellow dining room.

The savory rabbit.

Preheat the oven to 350°F.

Remove everything from the interior of the flowers, then carefully wash them inside and out under cold running water; drain on paper towels.

In a small bowl, beat the ricotta until it is smooth, then beat in the egg yolk, Parmesan, and parsley. With a spoon, stuff the squash blossoms with the ricotta mixture, dividing it equally among the flowers. Spoon the tomato sauce into a small baking pan, arrange the blossoms on top of the sauce, and bake, covered, until they are heated through, about 10 minutes.

While the blossoms are baking, purée the ingredients for the green sauce in a blender or miniprocessor.

To serve, place 1 blossom on each plate, top with a little tomato sauce from the baking dish, and garnish with parsley. Spoon a little green sauce alongside.

SERVES 8

RABBIT WITH CHIVES

The rabbit meat must be marinated at least 8 hours before cooking, so plan accordingly.

  1 rabbit, about 2 pounds
  ½ cup olive oil
  ½ cup chopped fresh chives
  ½ cup dry white wine
  ½ cup sliced zucchini

Bone the rabbit and cut the meat in small pieces. Place in a bowl with the oil and ¼ cup of the chives and refrigerate for at least 8 hours or overnight.

When ready to cook, place the meat and the oil in which it has marinated in a large skillet. Cook over medium heat, turning and basting, for 30 minutes; do not brown. Add the wine, cover, and cook for 15 minutes longer. Uncover, add the zucchini and 1 tablespoon chives, and cook 3 to 4 minutes, until zucchini is tender and sauce is slightly reduced. Serve very hot, garnished with the remaining chives.

SERVES 2

MUSHROOM SALAD

Porcini mushrooms and nepetella, the wild mint that grows in the Tuscan countryside, give this salad a special flavor. Using a mixture of three parts apple mint or spearmint to one part marjoram will give a close approximation of the taste of nepetella.

  1 pound small fresh porcini mushrooms
     Salt and freshly ground black pepper
  ½ cup olive oil
  2 tablespoons chopped fresh *nepetella*
  4 sprigs *nepetella*, for garnish

Trim the stems of the porcini, being sure to remove any part with traces of dirt. Wash the mushrooms well under cold running water, being careful not to damage them. Dry the mushrooms and slice thinly. Divide the mushrooms among 4 plates, arranging them in overlapping circles. Season to taste lightly with salt and pepper, drizzle some oil over them, and sprinkle with chopped *nepetella*. Garnish with *nepetella* sprigs, if desired.

SERVES 4

Porcini are traditionally cooked with nepetella, a wild mint that grows abundantly in the countryside.

THE QUINTESSENTIAL ITALIAN COOK

"I'm in love with very simple foods," says Marcella Hazan, the woman who has done so much to introduce Americans to the true cuisine of Italy. "Taste is important. I'm trying to teach people what Italian taste is. After all, the same foods taste different in New York and Italy. We must try to translate. In the States if I can't find radicchio, I use Belgian endive. And I can take any fish and make it taste Italian by seasoning it with the garlic, parsley, and oil I would use to cook clams in Italy. It won't be a traditional Italian dish, but it will *taste* Italian."

Between the thousands of classes she has given over the years and her successful books, Marcella has probably taught more people about Italian cuisine than anyone. A former doctor of biology, paleontology, and geology, Marcella never cooked until she married. She started teaching quite by accident when her fellow students in a Chinese cooking class in New York, where she and her husband, Victor, spend half of each year, wanted to learn about Italian food. One class led to another until an interview with Craig Claiborne finally pushed her into the public eye. Victor, an expert on wine, has his own acute sense of taste and a predilection for bitter things: he loves radicchio and digestifs of soft, unripened walnuts or those made in monasteries from a mixture of herbs.

A few years ago the Hazans decided to spend as much time as possible in their cool, roomy Venice apartment. "Venice is beautiful," says Marcella. "It's very small—human size." Each morning the Hazans saunter down to the produce-laden boats that dock at the foot of the Rialto Bridge. Although they buy herbs from the barge, they also grow a few pots of chives, mint, and rosemary on their terrace as a convenience. "Don't mix too many herbs together," Marcella advises. "Two, three, or possibly four is enough." Eventually, she believes, one gets a feeling for what each herb does. Rosemary, for example, is good with roast meat; basil suggests pesto; sage, game; and oregano, pizza. "Parsley is used with everything, so when an Italian sees someone turning up everywhere he's quite apt to greet him with 'You're just like parsley,'" she laughs.

PASTA WITH SIMPLE TOMATO SAUCE

This sauce can be cooked several hours in advance and reheated, but add the basil just before serving. Marcella Hazan tears the basil rather than cutting it, because a knife blade tends to darken the leaves.

⅓ cup extra-virgin olive oil

2 garlic cloves, sliced very thin

1½ cups canned peeled Italian plum tomatoes, cut into large pieces, with their juice

1 pound dried pasta (spaghetti, rigatoni, ziti, etc.)

Salt and freshly ground black pepper

10 fresh basil leaves, torn into small pieces

Additional basil, for garnish

Place the oil and garlic in a saucepan and cook over medium heat until the garlic is pale gold, about 5 minutes. Add the tomatoes and reduce the heat to very low. Cook, uncovered, until the oil separates from the tomatoes, about 20 minutes.

❦

The Hazans' apartment on the top floor of a nineteenth-century building overlooks the rooftops and one of Venice's many squares, *left*. Pasta sauced with fresh tomatoes and basil, *top*.

Meanwhile, bring a large pot of water to a boil and cook the pasta until al dente, 7 to 9 minutes; drain. Season the sauce with salt and pepper and cook for another 2 to 3 minutes, stirring from time to time. Remove from the heat, stir in the basil leaves, and toss immediately with the hot pasta. Garnish with additional basil, if desired.

SERVES 4

PORCINI WITH PARSLEY

1 pound fresh porcini mushrooms

⅓ cup extra-virgin olive oil

Salt and freshly ground black pepper to taste

2 teaspoons chopped garlic

2 tablespoons chopped fresh parsley

Trim from the mushrooms any part with soil attached. Wash the mushrooms quickly under running water and dry gently but thoroughly with paper towels. Detach the stems from the caps, then slice both stems and caps.

Place 1 tablespoon of oil in a skillet over medium-low heat and add the mushrooms. Cook 5 to 7 minutes, then turn the mushrooms over and sprinkle with salt and pepper. Cook for a few more minutes, until the mushrooms release their liquid. Turn the heat to high to evaporate the liquid, then lower the heat to medium. Add the remaining oil, the garlic, and the parsley, and cook for another 2 to 3 minutes.

SERVES 4

❦

Porcini require nothing more than a bit of oil, some parsley, and a hint of garlic.

VICTOR'S HOUSE COCKTAIL

1 cup well-chilled Campari

½ cup chilled vodka

½ cup chilled, aromatic sweet white wine (Riesling or Sauternes)

2 long stems fresh mint

¼ cup fresh orange juice, blood orange if possible

Combine Campari, vodka, and wine in a pitcher. Use 1 sprig of mint as a stirrer to mix the ingredients. Leave the mint in the pitcher, cover it with plastic wrap, and refrigerate for 30 minutes to allow the flavors to mellow.

When ready to serve, remove the pitcher from the refrigerator, add the orange juice, and stir several times with the mint. Discard the mint and replace with a fresh mint "stirrer."

SERVES 4 TO 6

To accompany the house cocktail, *opposite*, the Hazans often mince garlic and rosemary into a paste and then stir in some olive oil and dribble it over *carasau*, a crisp Italian bread sometimes called *foglio di musica*.

TOMATOES STUFFED WITH GOAT CHEESE AND CHIVES

9 large plum tomatoes

½ pound mild, creamy goat cheese (chèvre)

Heaping ⅓ cup chopped fresh chives

¼ cup extra-virgin olive oil or more, depending on the creaminess of the goat cheese

Freshly ground pepper

18 (2-inch) chive spears, for garnish

Cut the tomatoes in half lengthwise and scoop out all the seeds and inner membranes. Place them cut side down in a colander and drain for at least 30 minutes.

Place the cheese, chives, oil, and a generous grinding of pepper in a bowl, and mash together to form a smooth, creamy mixture. Divide the cheese mixture evenly among the tomato halves, mounding it if there is enough. Lay 2 chive spears across each mound. Serve at room temperature.

SERVES 6 TO 8

Venetians market at barges that dock along the canals, *above*. Plum tomatoes, *top right*, are stuffed with goat cheese and chives. *Right*, Marcella Hazan makes pasta sauce.

A SAGE OF THE ITALIAN KITCHEN

When he's not crossing the United States teaching Italian cooking or traveling through Italy doing research for one of his books, Giuliano Bugialli lives in a gracious old apartment in the heart of Florence. Once a convent, the apartment has belonged to his family for years and is entered through two rooms that were part of the convent's guard tower. The spacious kitchen occasionally accommodates his combination hands-on and demonstration classes that attract professional chefs as well as amateur cooks.

Giuliano first came to the United States as a language teacher, but soon started cooking and giving lessons. "My teaching is not *nouvelle*," he says. "That cooking is fake, more decoration than cooking. Food should be for eating—otherwise why not buy a painting? People in the United States think using herbs is exotic, while in Italy it's normal," he claims.

Giuliano finds fault with people who rely exclusively on a favorite herb. "You cannot assume the same herb will go well with fish, meat, and vegetables. Otherwise you destroy the flavor rather than enhance it," he says. "You must respect the idea that some herbs are strong, others light."

The pungent flavor of sage adds interest to pasta and a hearty loaf of bread, *right*. Giuliano Bugialli in his kitchen, *left*.

SAGE PASTA

(Pasta alla Salvia)

This sage pasta is a typical recipe from the Chianti region of Tuscany. If you cannot get fresh sage, substitute leaves that have been preserved in salt. Preserved leaves cannot be used for garnish.

PASTA

2 cups all-purpose flour

3 extra-large eggs

Pinch of salt

½ teaspoon freshly ground black pepper

25 large fresh sage leaves, stems completely removed, torn into small pieces

Coarse salt to taste

SAUCE

½ cup (1 stick) unsalted butter

¼ cup freshly grated Parmesan cheese

Freshly ground pepper

4 to 6 tablespoons freshly grated Parmesan cheese

4 to 6 fresh sage leaves

Mound the flour in the center of a pastry board. Make a well in the center, then put the eggs, salt, pepper, and sage in the well. With a fork, mix the ingredients in the well, then begin incorporating the flour from around the sides. When all the ingredients are blended, knead the dough by hand until it becomes elastic. Continue to knead for another few minutes or put the dough through a pasta machine on successively lower settings. Finally stretch the pasta about ¹⁄₁₆ inch thick by hand or in the pasta machine set at one setting before the last. Cut into ¼-inch-wide tagliatelle noodles, and let them rest on a cotton dish towel until needed.

To serve, bring a large pot of cold water to a boil over medium heat. Place a large serving dish over the pot, and add the butter to the dish to melt. When the water reaches a boil and the butter is completely melted, add coarse salt to the water, then add the pasta and cook for 1 to 3 minutes, depending on how dry it is. Drain the pasta and transfer it to the prepared dish. Sprinkle with the Parmesan, mix well, and serve immediately. Each portion should be garnished with black pepper, 1 tablespoon of Parmesan, and 1 whole sage leaf.

SERVES 4 TO 6

SAGE BREAD WITH GREEN OLIVES

(Pane alla Salvia con Olive)

The sponge for this bread must be prepared the night before you are planning to bake it. If fresh sage leaves are not available, substitute leaves preserved in salt.

SPONGE

2 cups plus 1 tablespoon all-purpose flour

2 ounces fresh compressed yeast, or 4 packages active dry yeast

2 cups lukewarm or hot water, depending on the yeast

Pinch of salt

20 large green olives in brine, drained

30 large fresh sage leaves

7½ cups all-purpose flour

2 cups lukewarm water

1 teaspoon salt

½ teaspoon freshly ground pepper

To make the sponge, place 2 cups of the flour in a large bowl and make a well in the center. In a small bowl, dissolve the yeast in the water, stirring with a wooden spoon. Put the dissolved yeast and a pinch of salt in the well and mix in gradually with a wooden spoon until all the flour is incorporated. Sprinkle with the remaining tablespoon of flour, cover the bowl with a cotton dish towel, and let it rest overnight in a warm place away from any drafts.

The next morning the sponge is ready. Before starting the bread, pit the olives and cut them into ½-inch pieces. Tear the sage leaves into small pieces. Set aside.

Mound the flour on a pasta board, make a well in the center, and place the sponge in the well. Add the lukewarm water, mixing continuously with a wooden spoon and incorporating some of the flour until the consistency is that of a thick batter. Add the salt, pepper, olives, and sage, then begin mixing with your hands, absorbing the flour from the inside rim of the well little by little. Keep mixing until all but 1 cup of the flour is incorporated into the mound of dough. Sift the unused flour to clean it, then start kneading the dough with the palm of your hand, in a folding motion, until it is homogenous and smooth (about 10 minutes), incorporating almost all the flour. Shape the dough into a long loaf and place it on a floured dish towel. Wrap the towel loosely around the loaf, put it in a warm place away from drafts, and let it stand until doubled in size, about 1 hour.

Line the middle or bottom shelf of the oven with ovenproof unglazed terra-cotta tiles or a pizza stone. Preheat the oven to 400°F.

When the dough has doubled in size, quickly remove it from the towel and immediately place it in the oven, directly on the tiles. Bake the bread for about 1 hour and 15 minutes. It is fully baked when the crust is thick and the inside airy. The bread must cool for at least 3 hours before slicing.

MAKES 1 LOAF

FRIED SAGE SANDWICHES

(Salvia Imbottita)

The batter for these pungent sand-wiches must be prepared 2 hours in advance.

BATTER

Scant 2 cups all-purpose flour

½ teaspoon salt

¼ teaspoon freshly ground pepper

3 tablespoons olive oil

2 extra-large eggs, separated

¼ cup vodka

1 cup cold water

8 slices white bread

4 ounces mozzarella cheese

16 large fresh sage leaves

About ½ cup cold milk

1 to 1½ quarts vegetable oil

Salt to taste

1 lemon, cut into wedges

To make the batter, sift the flour into a large bowl. Make a well in the flour, then add, one at a time, the salt, pepper, olive oil, egg yolks, vodka, and water. As each ingredient is added, mix it thoroughly with a little of the flour before adding the next. When all the ingredients are incorporated, beat with a wooden spoon until the batter is smooth. Let stand, covered, in a cool place for about 2 hours.

Cut the bread slices in half and the mozzarella into 8 slices. To prepare "sandwiches," place 1 sage leaf on top of 8 of the bread half-slices, top each with a slice of mozzarella, another sage leaf, and finally another half-slice of bread. Place all the prepared sandwiches on a large platter, sprinkle a few drops of the cold milk over them, then turn the sandwiches and sprinkle the other side. Gently press each sandwich so the layers adhere well to one another. (The sandwiches can be covered and refrigerated until needed at this point.)

Heat the oil in a deep-fat fryer or deep skillet to about 375°F.

Just before the oil is ready, beat the egg whites, preferably with a wire whisk in a copper bowl, until stiff but not dry. Very gently fold them into the batter with a wooden spoon until completely incorporated.

Line a serving dish with paper towels. Dip each sandwich in the batter and gently place it in the hot oil. Cook, turning if necessary, until lightly golden

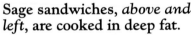

Sage sandwiches, *above and left*, are cooked in deep fat.

❦

on both sides (about 1 minute), then use a strainer-skimmer to transfer them to the prepared dish. When all the sandwiches are cooked, sprinkle with salt, remove the paper towels, and serve with lemon wedges.

SERVES 6 AS AN APPETIZER

❦

Bread, *opposite*, is always baked directly on a tile to create the effect of a brick oven.

Spain and Morocco

 In the eighth century Arabs from Morocco conquered Spain, and for centuries afterward there was a lively cultural exchange between the two countries. You can still see hints of an Arabian heritage in Spain's sweet desserts or trace the chick-peas in a Moroccan couscous back to Spain. But the way herbs are used in these two countries points up some interesting differences as well.

Many flavors associated with Spain's lusty cuisine come from herbs. Paella, that glorious mélange of rice and seafood, and *arroz con pollo*, rice with chicken, both depend on saffron; zarzuela, a shellfish stew, has a garlicky sauce, while roast suckling pig is enhanced with thyme.

A customer buys some chamomile for tea during the annual Barcelona herb fair.

259

Sacks of dried herbs in a Moroccan market.

A Moroccan shopper choosing juicy oranges in the souk.

Barcelona is a lively Mediterranean port whose gentle weather encourages leisurely strolls up and down Las Ramblas, the main thoroughfare dotted with outdoor cafés and kiosks selling birds and flowers. Just off Las Ramblas is the Mercat de Sant Josep, a large covered market where lobsters, prawns, and cod are displayed next to geese, ducks, and rabbits. Wild mushrooms, eggplants, and red peppers are mounded in the stalls next to beans, chick-peas, and rice. And herb growers display bay, thyme, rosemary, oregano, mint, and chamomile. All these ingredients come together deliciously in the unpretentious cuisine of Catalan.

Farther north, San Sebastian sits on the Bay of Biscay, just below Basque country. Fish like salt cod, hake, tuna, crabs, and tiny eels play an important part in the regional cuisine, often in stews and casseroles. Parsley is the most important herb of this region, along with garlic.

The cooking of Morocco is as exotic as the country itself. It derives its special flavor from lemons preserved in salt, olives, and unusual seasonings. Gum arabic scents sweet pastries, while stews and couscous are sparked with *ras el hanout*, a blend of as many as thirty herbs and spices, which might include lavender, belladonna, and orris root, as well as the more common cayenne, cloves, turmeric, and allspice. Herb seeds such as cumin and coriander and spices are everyday seasonings, but of the green herbs, only parsley, cilantro, and mint play a major role in the kitchen. Parsley and cilantro are indispensable to the endless varieties of stews known as *tajines*; to *bastilla*, the incredible concoc-

tion of flaky pastry, pigeon, eggs, and almonds; to couscous, the light grain served with lamb, chicken, or spicy sausage and a variety of vegetables; and to *chermoula*, a pungent sauce used in the preparation of fish. Mint is used to brew the national drink, mint tea, and also as a seasoning.

At La Roserie outside of Marrakesh, a jumble of roses cascades over arbors.

There is both simplicity and a sophistication about Moroccan food. Even those dishes prepared by desert dwellers evince the unique blend of flavors that characterize Morocco's most elaborate cooking. But whether a dinner is served in an intricately carved and tiled palace room or a tent on the sands, the food will be plentiful and Moroccan hospitality will abound.

A BARCELONA CLASSIC

Since Reno was founded by Antonio Juliá Rafecas in 1945, it has been one of Barcelona's most respected restaurants. From the first it was a meeting place for the city's political, financial, and artistic population, who came to dine on classic dishes influenced by French and Italian cooking, an international cuisine that was representative of fine Spanish cooking of the time. Today Antonio's two sons run the restaurant, maintaining the same high standards he insisted upon.

The kitchen is under the sure hand of José Juliá Bertrán, who received his training at his father's side and in some of France's best restaurants. He has kept the traditional cuisine his father favored, but adapted it to contemporary preferences for lighter foods. "We use less oil, less flour in sauces," he says. Since he must eat a lot for business, when he has a choice José prefers simple foods like salads and grilled meats seasoned with herbs. "You must use just enough herbs," he cautions. "Too much is bad." Tarragon is one of his favorites; fish is frequently seasoned with fennel; and sage is a surprising accent to a dish that combines flounder with noodles.

José is pleased to find a wider variety of people eating in his restaurant. "Once just the rich came," he says. "Now everyone comes, and they are all ready to experience new tastes."

❦

Shrimp boats, *left,* **returning to the docks in Blanes, a port north of Barcelona. The lively fish market where the catch is sold,** *opposite.*

BROCHETTE OF SHRIMPS AUX FINES HERBES

At Reno, these brochettes are served with rice pilaf.

Sea salt to taste

1 carrot, peeled and diced

1 onion, diced

1 bay leaf

4 sprigs fresh parsley

20 fresh large shrimp or prawns, about 1¾ pounds total

2 tablespoons olive oil

3 cups fresh bread crumbs

10 tablespoons (1¼ sticks) unsalted butter

1 shallot, chopped

1 tablespoon chopped fresh tarragon

1 tablespoon chopped fresh chervil

1 tablespoon chopped fresh parsley

Juice of 1 lemon

Place the salt, carrot, onion, bay leaf, and parsley in a large pot of water and bring to a boil. Add the shrimp or prawns and boil about 4 minutes, then drain and run under cold water to stop the cooking. Peel, leaving on the heads of the prawns, or the tails of the shrimp.

Prepare a charcoal fire and let it burn down to medium heat or preheat the broiler. Thread 5 shrimps on each skewer. Brush them with oil and coat with bread crumbs. Grill gently until the crumbs have browned, about 3 minutes per side, taking care that they do not burn. Baste with additional oil if needed. Transfer the skewers to a warmed plate.

Melt the butter in a pan over medium heat. Add the shallot, and when the butter has turned a nice brown color, add the herbs. Pour the herbed butter sauce over the skewered shrimp and sprinkle with a few drops of lemon juice. Serve immediately.

SERVES 4

At Reno, shrimp, *top and right*, are grilled with fresh herbs and butter.

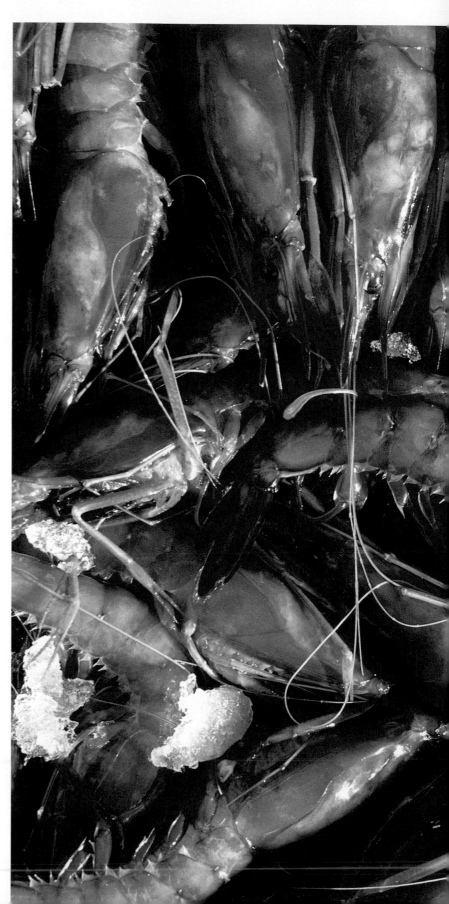

SOLE AND NOODLES WITH FRESH SAGE

Bottled hollandaise sauce can be found in good markets.

- 1 tablespoon oil
- 1 pound green fettuccine
- 12 fillets of sole, about 2 pounds total
- 6 tablespoons (¾ stick) butter
- 2 cups fish stock (page 23)
- 2 cups heavy cream
  Salt and pepper
- ¼ cup hollandaise sauce, preferably homemade
- ¼ cup chopped fresh sage
  Cayenne pepper

Preheat the oven to 350°F.

Add the oil to a large pot of water and bring to a boil. Add the fettuccine and cook until just barely done, about 8 or 9 minutes. Stop the cooking by running pasta under cold water. Drain and set aside.

Put the fillets in a baking dish with 2 tablespoons butter, 1 cup each of fish stock and cream, and salt and pepper to taste.

Cover with aluminum foil and bake until done, 8 to 10 minutes. Set cooked fish aside and keep warm.

Combine the remaining stock and cream in a saucepan and reduce over high heat until thickened. Remove from the heat, pass it through a sieve, and stir in the hollandaise sauce. Season to taste with salt, pepper, and cayenne.

Heat the remaining 4 tablespoons of butter in a skillet and add the fettuccine; sauté over medium heat. Season to taste with salt and chopped sage. Preheat the broiler.

Arrange a ring of pasta on each plate and place 3 fillets in the middle of each. Cover the fish with the sauce and glaze quickly under the broiler. Serve immediately.

SERVES 4

Pasta, not normally associated with Spanish cooking, has been a staple of Catalan cuisine since a short time after its introduction to Italy.

A DEVELOPING STYLE

Miguel Ezcurra's thirst for culinary knowledge began when he was very young, watching his mother cook. At 16 he worked in a restaurant during school vacations and by the time he was 18 he was cooking professionally, including a stint in France. Now just past 30, Miguel is the chef-owner of two restaurants: Ariatza, a commercial fish restaurant in Bilbao, and Beltxenea, a first-class establishment in Barcelona. The latter is where his passion lies, serving as a laboratory for developing innovative recipes and for refining his culinary style.

This impressive establishment is located in a beautiful old house whose handsomely detailed rooms overlook a lovely garden. It had previously housed another prestigious restaurant, where Miguel had been chef. When the restaurant was put up for sale, he bought it, changed the name, and set about creating his own restaurant. Miguel aspires to quality in food, service, and surroundings. "I don't do this to earn money," he says, "or I would do something else." He continues to work in the restaurant sixteen hours a day because he likes to cook, although with two chefs on staff he no longer needs to.

Miguel describes his cooking as traditional but modern. "During the past eight years my style has changed a lot," he notes. "I've made discreet innovations and made things lighter." At Beltxenea, herbs are used as much for their aroma as for their taste. "When you present a customer with a dish, the aroma of the herbs as the dish is set down makes it more appetizing."

"In order to experiment with traditional cooking, it's necessary to have a firm training in the basics first. Only then can you change it." Miguel himself continues to experiment and develop his cuisine. "In one year," says Miguel, "I will cook totally my own way."

Narrow streets are piled high with herbs at Barcelona's annual herb fair.

Diners can enjoy a view of the garden while eating cod fish with a garnish of roasted garlic.

SALTED CODFISH WITH GARLIC

Salted codfish is a staple of the Spanish diet. It must be soaked for 24 hours before using.

2¼ pounds dried salted codfish, cut in 6 even slices
¼ cup olive oil
6 garlic cloves, peeled
1 sprig fresh fennel, finely chopped

Place the codfish in a large bowl and cover with cold water. Soak for 24 hours, changing the water at least 3 times. When it is desalted, dry the fish with paper towels and debone.

In a large saucepan (preferably a clay pot that can be used over a burner), heat the oil over medium heat. Add the garlic cloves and brown on all sides. Remove with a slotted spoon and set aside. Place the codfish in the pan, skin side up, and add the fennel. Cook for 15 minutes; the fish should still be firm but easily flaked.

Remove the oil from the pan with a spoon and reserve. With a wooden spoon, move the fish around in the pan for a few minutes, then slowly return the oil to the pan, stirring to make a sauce. Serve immediately, garnished with the reserved garlic cloves.

SERVES 6

≪≪≪

The delightful formal garden behind the restaurant.

BEEF WITH TARRAGON

2 cups beef stock
1¾ pounds beef tenderloin, cut in 4 equal slices
Salt
¼ cup olive oil
¼ cup cognac
2 tablespoons chopped fresh tarragon, or 1 tablespoon dried
1 cup heavy cream
4 slices white bread
Fresh tarragon, for garnish

Place the stock in a small saucepan and reduce by half over high heat.

Meanwhile, season the beef with salt. Place 2 tablespoons of oil in a skillet over high heat. When the oil is hot, add the steaks and quickly brown on both sides, about 1 to 2 minutes per side. As soon as they are browned, add the cognac to the pan and ignite. After the flame has died, reduce heat to medium and add the tarragon, reduced stock, and cream. Cook until the steaks reach the desired state of doneness, about 5 minutes for rare, 8 minutes for medium-rare. Set aside and keep warm. Continue cooking the sauce until slightly thickened, 5 to 7 minutes longer.

While the sauce is cooking, heat the remaining oil in another skillet over medium heat and fry the bread.

When the sauce is ready, place 1 steak on each plate, then top with a slice of bread and a sprig of fresh tarragon, if desired. Pour some sauce, which should be very hot, over the bread.

SERVES 4

Miguel cooks beef tenderloin on top of the stove, then combines it with an unexpected tarragon cream sauce.

≪≪≪

AN ARCHITECT IN THE KITCHEN

San Sabastian, nestled close to the mountains of Basque country, is a gay seaside resort during the warm months of the year. More important, it is the home of Arzak, one of Spain's most renowned restaurants. Founded in the early 1900s, the restaurant is run by Juan Mari Arzak, the third generation to preside over its kitchens. Although originally Juan Arzak decided to forgo the restaurant business for architecture, the spell of the kitchen was too strong to resist: He gave up architecture and went home to the family restaurant business.

Now Arzak has earned a worldwide reputation for his updated Basque cooking. "I do *nouvelle cuisine* Basque," he says. "It's traditional but renewed," combining, for example, local ingredients like lobster with rose petals in a salad. Because of its proximity to the sea, there is an emphasis on fish at the restaurant. Herbs for seasoning are grown in a small kitchen garden at the Arzaks' house nearby and are harvested twice a day for the restaurant. "The most important herb in Basque cuisine is parsley," he says. "It's always mixed with other herbs." He also enjoys experimenting with rose petals, herb flowers, and less traditionally Spanish herbs like chives and sage. "Inhabitants of the Basque country eat like they are or are like they eat," says Arzak, "and when you do a new recipe, you must think of the people in the country."

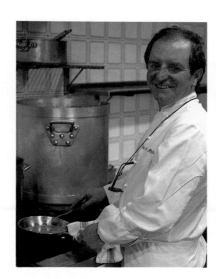

Arzak, *right*, and the intimate dining room of his restaurant, *far right*.

Arzak sometimes serves the salad with a creamy *salsa rosa*.

LOBSTER SALAD WITH ROSE PETALS

2 lobsters, 1 pound each

6 tablespoons peanut oil

2 tablespoons sherry vinegar

Salt and pepper

3 to 4 cups mixed lettuce, endive, and watercress

½ cup julienned leeks and chives

Fresh chervil and rose petals, for garnish

Place the lobsters in a large pot filled with cold salted water. Bring the water to a boil over high heat, then continue to boil for 5 minutes. Remove the lobsters from the pot and allow to cool. When they are cool enough to handle, cut the lobsters in half and remove the meat from the tail and the claws, keeping the claws intact if possible. Reserve the legs and heads for garnish if desired. Slice the tail meat and place it in a bowl with the claw meat. Combine the oil, vinegar, and salt and pepper to taste; pour half the vinaigrette over the lobster meat and set aside.

Tear the lettuce and endive into bite-size pieces and place in a bowl. Add the watercress, stems removed, and toss with the remaining vinaigrette. Divide the greens between two plates, mounding them in the center. Add the lobster pieces, the leeks, and chives. Garnish with chervil and rose petals, and decorate the plates with the reserved lobster legs and heads.

SERVES 2

HAKE IN GREEN CLAM SAUCE

1 teaspoon minced garlic

1 tablespoon minced fresh parsley

6½ ounces of shucked whole baby clams or coarsely chopped large clams

1 teaspoon flour

3 tablespoons water

4 hake fillets, about 6 to 7 ounces each

Salt and pepper

Chopped fresh parsley, for garnish

In a clay casserole that can be used on top of the stove, heat the oil over medium heat. Add the garlic and half the parsley and sauté until the garlic turns golden, about 3 to 5 minutes. Add the clams, flour, and water, and stir briefly.

Season the hake fillets with salt and pepper to taste and place in the casserole, skin side up. Cover the casserole and cook for 3 minutes over medium heat. Turn the fillets, shake the casserole to blend the sauce, and scatter the remaining parsley on top. Shake again, re-cover, and cook an additional 3 minutes.

Place one cooked fillet on each plate and surround it with the clams. Shake the casserole to blend the sauce thoroughly, then pour it over the fish. Garnish with chopped parsley.

SERVES 4

Hake, a popular regional fish, in a tasty green clam sauce.

GRILLED SQUID WITH ROSEMARY

4 squid, under 1 pound each, with ink sacs

3 shallots, chopped

1 cup olive oil

½ cup chopped fresh parsley

SAUCE

7 tablespoons olive oil

1½ onions, sliced

2 green peppers, seeded and sliced

2 tomatoes, sliced

2 garlic cloves, minced

¼ cup dry red wine

Few sprigs of rosemary

7 tablespoons olive oil

2 onions, julienned

4 green peppers, julienned

VINAIGRETTE

1 tablespoon red wine vinegar

1 tablespoon herbed vinegar

1 garlic clove, crushed

½ cup cognac

3 tablespoons olive oil

Fresh basil leaves or rosemary sprigs, for garnish

To clean the squid, hold the body in one hand and pull the tentacles from the body. Keeping the tentacles in one piece, cut them from the head. Remove and discard the beak. Reserving the ink sac, discard any waste material. Take off the fins and set aside for the sauce. Remove skin from the body under running water. Wash the squid thoroughly, inside and out, pat dry, and split lengthwise. Score one side of the squid in a dia-mond pattern, then marinate along with the tentacles in a mixture of the shallots, oil, and parsley for approximately 12 hours.

Prepare a fire in the grill or preheat the broiler.

Combine the oil, onion, peppers, tomatoes, garlic, and rosemary in a heavy saucepan and stir thoroughly. Add the fins and simmer over medium heat until the onion is cooked, 10 to 15 minutes. Add the red wine and simmer an additional 5 minutes. Remove the fins, stir in the ink, and pass the sauce through a sieve. Set aside and keep warm.

In a small bowl, combine the ingredients for the vinaigrette and mix thoroughly; reserve.

Warm the olive oil in a skillet over medium heat. Add the onions and peppers and sauté until tender, about 10 to 15 minutes.

While the vegetables are cooking, thread the squid bodies and tentacles on a skewer. Grill or broil for a few minutes, until golden brown. Turn carefully and baste with the vinaigrette.

To serve, divide the sauteed vegetables among the serving plates and top with the squid removed from the skewers. Spoon the sauce around the squid and decorate with fresh basil leaves or with a sprig of rosemary.

SERVES 4

❧

For a touch of whimsy, Arzak garnishes the squid with whole basil leaves to make it resemble a fish.

Felipe Rojas-Lombardi offers twenty-four hot and twenty-four cold tapas each day on the long bar at The Ballroom.

A TASTE FOR TAPAS

Felipe Rojas-Lombardi, a Peruvian, has cooked from the time he was a child. "From the moment I fell into a sack of garlic, I was in love with the kitchen," he says.

Although it is in New York, Rojas-Lombardi's restaurant, the Ballroom, was modeled after the tapas bars of Spain. Since dinner is served late in Spain, people customarily visit a tapas bar in the early evening to sip sherry and sample tidbits of delicious hot and cold dishes designed to postpone the pangs of hunger. Inspired by his happy memories of traveling in Spain, his fondness for small plates of food, and above all the restaurant's splendid long bar, where an enticing array of tapas could be set out, he decided it was time New York had an opportunity to enjoy Spain's savory treats.

Felipe's food is not bound by tradition. "The food at the Ballroom is a mixture of cultures, like New York," he says. "All food is related, and what I try to do is create layers of taste on the palate." The result is an interesting mix of foods with influences from Spain and Spanish South America, the Peruvian Indians, Creoles, blacks—even Morocco, for the Arabs at one time ruled Spain. Nor does Felipe hesitate to give a classic sauce like hollandaise a facelift by adding chopped hot peppers.

"Actually, I use a tremendous quantity of herbs," Felipe says. "We have a stable of herbs in the kitchen, and they're always fresh." Felipe also uses strong twigs of woody plants as skewers or soaks dried stems of rosemary or wild fennel in water, then sets them in a pan to form a rack for the food. More soaked stems are placed on top of the food before cooking. The herbs char slightly but impart a wonderfully subtle taste.

CHICKEN ESCABECHE

Escabeche, a method of "cooking" foods by marinating them in vinegar or wine with herbs and oil, is popular in both Peru and Spain, as well as at the Ballroom. Part of this chicken's distinctive taste comes from achiote oil flavored with annatto seeds, a popular South American seasoning. Both annatto seeds and prepared achiote oil can be found in Spanish or Mexican markets, gourmet stores, or health food stores.

- 1 (3½- to 4-pound) chicken, cut into 10 pieces (do not include the back)
  Salt
- 12 to 15 sprigs fresh thyme, or 1 tablespoon dried
- ¾ cup Achiote Oil (recipe follows)
- 12 large garlic cloves
- 12 small onions (1½ inches in diameter), peeled
- 3 fresh serrano peppers
- 4 bay leaves
- 1 teaspoon cayenne pepper
- ¼ cup coarse salt
- 3 carrots, cut into batons 2½ inches long and ¼ to ½ inch wide
- 4 cups red wine vinegar
- 2 cups dry red wine
- 4 celery stalks, cut on the diagonal 1½ inches thick
- 2 red bell peppers, stems, seeds, and ribs removed, cut into 1½-inch triangles
- 2 green bell peppers, stems, seeds, and ribs removed, cut into 1½-inch triangles
  Thyme sprigs and leaves, for garnish

Sprinkle the chicken parts with a pinch or two of salt and the dried thyme leaves if fresh thyme is not available. (The fresh thyme is added later.)

Heat the Achiote Oil in a large skillet over medium-high heat, add the chicken parts, and brown all over. Reduce the heat and continue cooking until tender, about 10 to 15 minutes. Remove chicken with a slotted spoon and set aside. Lower the heat, add the garlic cloves and onions, and cook until golden, about 5 minutes. Add the serrano peppers, bay leaves, cayenne, coarse salt, and fresh sprigs of thyme, if used. Cook for 1 minute, then add the carrots, vinegar, and wine. Bring to a boil and boil gently for 15 minutes. Add the celery and cook for 10 minutes longer. Add the red and green pepper pieces and cook for another 3 minutes. Pour the vegetables and sauce over the chicken and cool. Serve at room temperature garnished with extra fresh thyme.

SERVES 6 TO 8

ACHIOTE OIL

- 1 cup vegetable or olive oil
- ½ cup annatto seeds
- 1 dried serrano pepper, crumbled
- 1 bay leaf

Combine the ingredients in a saucepan and bring to a slow boil over low heat. Lower the heat and barely simmer for 5 minutes. Allow to cool, then strain through a fine sieve or cheesecloth. Discard the seeds and bay leaf. The oil is ready to use; refrigerated, it will keep for up to 1 year.

MAKES ABOUT 1 CUP

The chicken escabeche is flavored with achiote oil, a popular South American flavoring.

MOROCCAN EGGPLANT

3 eggplants, approximately 1 pound each

½ cup plus 2 tablespoons olive oil

1 teaspoon finely chopped garlic

1 teaspoon finely chopped fresh ginger

1 teaspoon finely chopped jalapeño

2 teaspoons ground cumin

7 cups tightly packed cilantro leaves

2 tablespoons lemon juice

1 tablespoon coarse salt or to taste

2 lemons, thinly sliced, for garnish

Cilantro sprigs, for garnish

Preheat the oven to 450°F.

Prick the eggplants several times all around with a fork. Rub thoroughly with 1 tablespoon of the olive oil, place on a rack, and bake until soft, approximately 1 hour and 15 minute. Remove from the oven and allow to cool.

Meanwhile, place ¼ cup of olive oil, the garlic, ginger, jalapeño, and cumin in the bowl of a food processor and blend until smooth. Without stopping the machine, start adding the cilantro leaves. When you have added about 4 cups of leaves, add the lemon juice, salt, and another ¼ cup of olive oil.

The spicy Moroccan eggplant.

❧

Add the rest of the cilantro leaves. Process until smooth. Add more salt, if necessary.

With a paring knife, peel the skins from the eggplants, starting from the stem and pulling downward, but leaving the stems attached. Slice the peeled eggplants lengthwise from the bottom into 3 sections each, leaving them attached at the stem end. Using a teaspoon, carefully remove most of the seeds. Place the eggplants on a baking sheet and broil until their surface is golden and slightly charred around the edges, about 6 to 8 minutes. Brush them with the remaining tablespoon of oil, transfer to a serving platter, slightly fan them, and brush again with olive oil.

With a tablespoon or a pastry bag, fill the slits in the eggplants with the cilantro sauce. Garnish the platter with thin slices of lemon and sprigs of cilantro. Serve at room temperature.

SERVES 6 TO 8

QUINOA EN SALPIÇON

Quinoa (pronounced KEEN-wa) is an extremely nutritious grain that somewhat resembles cracked wheat and can be found at health food stores. It expands during cooking; 1 cup of raw quinoa yields 2 cups cooked.

2 cups raw quinoa

8 cups water

1 cup peeled, seeded, and diced cucumber

1 cup seeded and diced tomato

½ cup finely sliced scallions, white and green parts

⅓ cup chopped fresh Italian parsley

⅓ cup chopped fresh mint leaves

Salt and white pepper

VINAIGRETTE

¼ cup fresh lime juice

¼ teaspoon ground white pepper

1 fresh chile, seeded and minced

1 teaspoon coarse salt

½ cup olive oil

Rinse the quinoa under running water and drain. Place the quinoa and water in a large saucepan, cover, and bring to a boil over high heat; this should take about 5 minutes. Remove the cover and lower the heat; simmer 10 minutes longer. Drain the quinoa and cool.

While the quinoa is cooking, make the vinaigrette. In a bowl, whisk together the lime juice, pepper, chile, and salt. Gradually add the olive oil, stirring constantly. Set aside.

When the grain has cooled, assemble the salad. In a bowl place the quinoa with the cucumber, tomato, scallions, parsley, and mint. Toss to mix the ingredients, then add the vinaigrette and toss thoroughly. Season to taste with salt and white pepper.

SERVES 6 TO 8

❧

Quinoa, a grain well known for its nutritional value in South America, is now becoming popular in other countries.

Sturdy sprigs of rosemary do double duty as skewers and seasoning in this kidney dish.

VEAL KIDNEYS ON ROSEMARY SKEWERS

MARINADE

1 garlic clove
1 tablespoon coarse salt
½ teaspoon ground cumin
Pinch of cayenne pepper
1 tablespoon red wine vinegar
¼ cup olive oil

2 cups cold water
¼ cup coarse salt
2 veal kidneys, peeled and trimmed of fat
2 thin slices bacon
6 strong rosemary stems (with leaves)
Olive oil for basting

With a mortar and pestle, mash the garlic and salt to a paste. Mix in the cumin and cayenne, then add the vinegar and stir thoroughly. Add the olive oil and mix again until thoroughly blended.

Combine the water and salt in a small bowl. Peel off the membrane surrounding the kidneys, remove excess fat, and place the kidneys in the salted water. Soak the kidneys for about 15 minutes, then remove, drain, and wipe well. Discard the water.

Cut each kidney into 9 bite-size pieces, rub with the prepared marinade, and allow to sit at room temperature for 1 hour.

Cut the bacon into 18 small pieces. Sharpen the ends of the rosemary sprigs a bit and thread with alternating bacon and kidney pieces, 3 of each per skewer. Brush the skewers with olive oil and grill or sauté in a frying pan over high heat, turning to cook all sides. This should not take longer than 5 to 8 minutes. Serve immediately.

SERVES 6

FROM THE SOUKS OF CASABLANCA

Casablanca is a modern city built around and upon tradition. It boasts both extraordinary old homes, their cool dark rooms lined with intricate tilework and beautifully carved wood, and intriguing modern structures. Nezha Ben Hallem and her husband, like many of Casablanca's citizens, live in one of these modern houses, but they still eat traditional Moroccan food. Nezha has been buying herbs and spices from the same merchant for many years. "The space in the marketplace is passed down from generation to generation," she explains.

The herb and spice markets are busy spots. Fresh cilantro and parsley, mint, and scented geraniums are heaped in piles beside bins of dried rosemary and thyme, verbena, and common and uncommon seasonings like gum arabic and rosewater. Other herbs are sold only for medicinal purposes: dill to help jaundice or sticks of licorice to ease sore throats. Occasionally a turtle is offered for sale. "It's considered lucky to have a turtle in your garden," notes Nezha. "They eat the insects."

Nezha often buys bunches of fresh cilantro and parsley and heads of garlic so that her housekeeper can make *chermoula*, a classic Moroccan marinade. This pungent sauce imparts such extraordinary flavor to fish that it is used in every preparation from the simplest fried fillets to more complex dishes that combine the fish with potatoes and tomatoes.

Fried fish marinated in *chermoula*, *right*, a combination of garlic, cilantro, and parsley, is the Moroccan version of fish and chips and is even sold by street vendors throughout the country. Nezha often serves additional *chermoula* on the side. The smallest piece of land may be used to grow mint, *left*.

MOROCCAN FISH WITH *CHERMOULA*

In Morocco, fish is often marinated in chermoula, a pungent sauce whose main ingredient is cilantro, before cooking. In some areas, parsley is combined with the cilantro to temper its exotic taste, as in this version.

MARINADE (CHERMOULA)

- 1 cup fresh cilantro leaves
- 1 cup fresh parsley
- 12 garlic cloves
- 1 teaspoon salt
- Juice of about 2 lemons, or 6 to 8 tablespoons vinegar
- 2 to 3 tablespoons peanut oil
- 1 tablespoon paprika
- 1 tablespoon ground cumin
- Pinch of cayenne pepper

FISH

- 3 pounds fish fillets (hake, sea bass, snapper, shad, etc.)
- Flour for dredging
- Vegetable oil for frying

Place the cilantro, parsley, garlic, salt, lemon juice or vinegar, and oil in the bowl of a food processor or blender and purée. Stir in the paprika, cumin, and cayenne. Cut the fillets into 3-inch pieces and arrange them in a single layer in a shallow pan. Pour the *chermoula* over the fish and marinate for several hours.

Drain the fish and dredge lightly in flour. Heat the vegetable oil to 375°F. in a deep-fryer or a deep skillet. When the oil is the proper temperature, cook the fish pieces a few at a time until they are golden, about 6 to 8 minutes.

SERVES 6

Many fresh herbs such as dill are for medicinal use only.

Couscous may well be the national dish of Morocco, with each region—and family—preparing it their own special way.

A MOROCCAN KITCHEN PRIMER

Like all young brides, when Latifa Bannani-Smires married she wanted to make her husband happy. Since he liked good food, she learned to cook, asking family and friends question after question until she could flawlessly prepare the classics of Moroccan cuisine. Soon Latifa was providing the same information for other young brides just starting to find their way in the kitchen. "I realized everyone needed the same information," she says, "but there was no basic book to turn to." Latifa decided to write a primer on how to cook the enchanting, sometimes exotically seasoned food of Morocco. The book, *Moroccan*

Cooking, was eagerly received and eventually translated into English. In the process, Latifa discovered she enjoyed teaching others about her native cuisine; she is now at work on a second book focusing on the country's regional cookery.

"To cook Moroccan food successfully, you must like to cook," says Latifa. "Then you must know about the amounts. But perhaps most importantly, you must know how to make the sauce that is so important to many Moroccan dishes. No matter what the ingredients, the sauce must have the right consistency: not too light, not too heavy, or the dish won't taste right."

BIDAOUI COUSCOUS WITH SEVEN VEGETABLES

Couscous is made most easily in a couscousière, a special two-part pot with a steamer on top. You can improvise your own couscousière using a large pot with a steamer that fits snugly into the top: the couscous in the steamer must not touch the broth and vegetables cooking below. Harissa, an exceedingly hot pepper sauce sometimes served with couscous, can be found in ethnic markets or gourmet food shops.

2¼ pounds meat from a veal knuckle or shoulder of lamb, cut into 2-inch pieces

2¼ pounds onions

1 medium Savoy cabbage, cut in pieces

1 cup (2 sticks) plus 2 tablespoons butter

½ teaspoon saffron threads

Salt to taste

1 tablespoon black pepper

2¼ pounds couscous

4 to 5 tomatoes, peeled, seeded, and quartered

1¾ pounds eggplant, quartered

1¼ pounds carrots, peeled and cut in 2-inch pieces

¾ pound turnips, peeled and quartered

2 dried chiles

1 cup chopped fresh cilantro

¾ pound medium potatoes, peeled and quartered

1¼ pounds pumpkin, peeled and cubed

In the bottom of the couscousière or in a large pot, place the meat, 2 pounds of the onions (sliced), the cabbage, 1 stick plus 1 tablespoon of the butter, saffron, salt and pepper. Cover with 5½ quarts of water and bring to a boil over high heat.

Place the couscous in the steamer and set it over the steaming broth. Seal the seam between the steamer and the pot with a thick paste of flour and water so no steam can escape except through the couscous. Reduce the heat to medium and continue to steam for 30 minutes. Remove from the heat. Pour the couscous into a large shallow dish, pressing gently with a wooden spoon to break up any lumps. Allow the couscous to cool, then sprinkle it with about 1 cup of cold water, allowing the grains to absorb as much as they will. Let the grains rest for 10 minutes, then sprinkle with up to another cup of cold water. At this point the couscous can be set aside, covered, until you are ready for the final steaming.

One hour before serving, return the meat and broth to a boil, lower the heat to medium, and add the tomatoes, eggplant, the remaining onions (peeled and quartered), carrots, turnips, chiles, and cilantro. Simmer for 30 minutes. Meanwhile, in a separate pot, cook the potatoes and pumpkin over medium heat in a little of the broth from the pot until tender, about 20 to 30 minutes. Keep warm.

After thirty minutes, taste the broth for seasoning. Return the couscous to the steamer and seal as before. Steam the couscous for 20 minutes, then remove from the heat and spread out in the large shallow dish. Stir in the remaining butter and as much broth as the couscous will absorb.

To serve, heap the couscous in the center of a large round dish, make a well in the center, and fill it with the meat and vegetables. Serve the remaining broth separately. Offer harissa on the side to mix into the broth.

SERVES 10

The famed Koutoubia minaret dominates the skyline of Marrakesh.

GRILLED KEFTA

Highly seasoned ground meat, grilled on a skewer, is a common Moroccan dish. Use meat with a relatively high fat content so the kefta do not dry out in cooking.

1½ pounds ground beef or lamb

1 teaspoon of ground cumin

2 teaspoons paprika

1 pinch cayenne pepper

2 cups fresh parsley leaves, minced

2 cups fresh cilantro leaves, stemmed and minced

1¼ teaspoons ground cinnamon

2 tablespoons minced fresh mint

1 onion, minced

Salt to taste

Place the meat in a large bowl. Add the remaining ingredients and mix well. Knead the meat mixture thoroughly, then set aside in the refrigerator to rest for 1 hour.

Wrap a chunk of the meat mixture about the size of an egg around a skewer, shaping it into a sausage about 4 to 5 inches long. Make sure the ends are pressed firmly onto the skewer so the meat will rotate with the skewer as it is cooked.

Prepare a charcoal fire, allowing the coals to burn down until they are covered with a fine white ash. Place the kefta on the grill. Cook, turning frequently, for about 8 minutes.

SERVES 6 (18 SKEWERS)

Kefta make a delicious substitute for American hamburgers.

FISH WITH CHERMOULA AND TOMATO

Many Moroccan fish dishes, of which this is typical, start with fish marinated in chermoula. A tajine is a round earthenware plate with a conical cover, but any large shallow casserole with a cover can be substituted. And although it will not taste exactly the same, if you do not have a preserved lemon, you can substitute an equal amount of lemon zest that has been boiled in salted water until somewhat softened.

4½ pounds of whiting, mullet, snapper, or sea bass, whole or cut in 2 × 3-inch pieces according to their size
Chermoula (page 279)

5½ pounds tomatoes, peeled, seeded, and cut in large dice

1 teaspoon powdered ginger

1 teaspoon saffron threads

½ teaspoon ground red chiles

1 garlic clove, peeled and crushed

½ cup peanut or olive oil
Salt

1 preserved lemon, the zest cut in pieces (recipe follows)

6 to 7 large mid-ripe California olives

1 cup chopped fresh parsley

In a shallow glass dish, marinate the fish in *chermoula* (reserving ¼ cup for later use), refrigerated, for several hours.

Place the tomatoes in a large heavy saucepan. Add the ginger, saffron, chiles, garlic, oil, salt to taste, and the reserved *chermoula*. Cook over moderate heat, stirring often to prevent the tomato from sticking, until all the liquid has evaporated, about 15 to 20 minutes. The tomato will have become a purée. Stir in the lemon zest, olives, and parsley, and continue to cook for another few minutes, stirring constantly.

Preheat the oven to 425°F.

Place a few pieces of reed or some wooden chopsticks in the bottom of the *tajine* and set the fish on top. (This will keep the fish off the bottom of the pot and prevent it from burning.) Pour the *chermoula* marinade and the tomato purée over the fish, setting the olives and pieces of lemon zest on top as garnish. Cover and simmer on medium-low heat for 3 to 4 minutes, then transfer to the oven, still covered, and cook for another 45 minutes.

If the sauce is too thin, pour it into a saucepan, add a spoonful of flour mixed with a little water, and bring to a boil. Cook, stirring, until it thickens, then return it to the *tajine*, pouring it over the fish. Serve hot or cold.

SERVES 8 TO 10

PRESERVED LEMONS

Lemons

Salt

Wash the lemons and cut into quarters, leaving the sections joined at the stem end. Salt the insides carefully, then press the sections back together and place in a clean preserving jar. Fill the jar to the top with warm water. Put a clean stone or weight on the fruit, cover the jar, and store in a cool, dry place for 1 month before using. To use, remove and discard the lemon pulp. Rinse the peel in cool water, and use the zest only.

Preserved lemons add a distinctive Moroccan taste to many tajines.

TEA AT THE MAMOUNIA

Old Marrakesh is Morocco's fairy-tale city, the manifestation of a romantic vision of this mysterious country. The old city is set amid arid plains surrounded by snow-capped mountains, its sprawling souk packed with stalls offering carpets and copper, teapots and kaftans, colorful spices and aromatic herbs. Story-tellers and snake charmers vie for attention in the busy Djemma el Fna square, while in the narrow streets of the medina blank façades hide charming courtyards and cooling fountains.

Just outside the old town stands the legendary Hotel Mamounia, surrounded by lush gardens planted with colorful roses, fragrant rosemary, sprawling nasturtiums, and heady night-blooming jasmine. There, the Moroccan ritual of sipping a glass of mint tea is observed with great elegance. The ingredients come to the dining room on a silver tray in gleaming silver containers. They are then brewed in an ornate and distinctively shaped teapot. But Moroccan mint tea is not a simple pepper-mint infusion. It starts with strong black tea brewed with handfuls of fresh mint and a goodly amount of sugar to make a beverage almost too sweet for many non-Moroccans. Many people add a stem or two of another herb—marjoram, lemon verbena, wormwood (absinthe), or scented geranium, per-haps—to give an extra bit of flavor. At the Mamounia, lemon verbena adds distinction.

❧

Morocco's beloved mint tea is served with great elegance at the Hotel Mamounia, *right*. A variety of tea herbs, *left*, can be found in the souk.

MINT TEA HOTEL MAMOUNIA

Moroccans serve mint tea after meals or when visitors drop in. It's a sweet affair that varies from house to house because another herb is often added to lend a subtle overtone to the mint.

- 4 teaspoons Chinese green tea
- 9 sugar cubes
- 3 sprigs fresh mint
- 1 small sprig fresh lemon verbena
- 4 cups boiling water

Place the tea, sugar cubes, and herbs in a tea pot and pour the boiling water over them. Stir to dissolve the sugar and bruise the herbs, releasing their flavor. Cover and steep for 5 minutes before serving.

SERVES 4

Mounds of mint tempt shoppers in the souk in Marrakesh.

DIRECTORY

This directory lists sources for herb seeds and plants, dried culinary herbs, and special chiles or other ingredients you may need for some of these recipes. A notation in each listing indicates which of the categories is available from that particular source. Many of the sources also carry other things herbal, such as wreaths, potpourris, vinegars, honeys, and so on.

The code letter (R) indicates a retail store; (R)(MO), a retail store that sells mail order; (MO), a mail-order-only operation; (W), that they also sell wholesale. Stores vary widely in their hours and some may only be open seasonally; it is therefore wise to check by telephone before making a special trip. Many mail-order operations charge for their catalogue. We have indicated the charge where we know it; but in writing to others, be sure to include a stamped, self-addressed envelope so they will be able, if necessary, to send you further information.

ALABAMA

BIRMINGHAM BOTANICAL
GARDENS
2612 Lane Park Road
Birmingham, AL 35223
(205) 879-1227
Seeds, plants, dried culinary herbs, other. (R)

ARIZONA

EARTHSTAR HERB GARDENS
P.O. Box 1022
Chino Valley, AZ 86323
(602) 636-4910
Seeds, plants. (R)(MO)

NATIVE SEEDS/SEARCH
3950 West New York Drive
Tucson, AZ 85745
(602) 327-9123
Seeds, dried culinary herbs. (MO)
Catalogue $1.

ARKANSAS

CLEMENT HERB FARM
Rt. 6, Box 390
Rogers, AR 72756
(501) 925-1603
Plants, dried culinary herbs, other. (R)(MO)
Catalogue $1.

CALIFORNIA

BAY LAUREL FARM
West Garzas Road
Carmel Valley, CA 93924
(408) 659-2913
Dried culinary herbs, other. (R)(MO)
Brochure $1.

BOUNTIFUL GARDENS
19550 Walker Road
Willits, CA 95490
Seeds, other. (MO)

THE HERB GARDEN
109 North Montgomery Street
Ojai, CA 93023
(805) 646-7065
Seeds, plants, dried culinary herbs, other. (R)

J. L. HUDSON SEEDSMAN
P.O. Box 1058
Redwood City, CA 94064
Seeds. (R)(MO)
Catalogue $1.

PARADISE FARMS
1101 Eugenia Suite B
Carpinteria, CA 93013
(805) 684-9468
Fresh cut herbs and edible flowers. (MO)(W)

REDWOOD CITY SEED CO.
P.O. Box 361
Redwood City, CA 94064
(415) 325-7333
Seeds. (R)(MO)
Catalogue $1.

ROSES OF YESTERDAY AND
TODAY
802 Brown's Valley Road
Watsonville, CA 95076
(408) 724-2755
Old, rare, and unusual roses. (R)(MO)
Catalogue $3.

SHEPHERD'S GARDEN SEEDS
6116 Highway 9
Felton, CA 95018
(408) 335-5311
Seeds, plants. (R)(MO)

TAYLOR'S HERB GARDEN
1535 Lone Oak Road
Vista, CA 92084
(619) 727-3485
Seeds, plants. (R)(MO)

CONNECTICUT

CAPRILANDS HERB FARM
Silver Street
Coventry, CT 06238
(203) 742-7244
Seeds, plants, dried culinary herbs, other. (R)(MO)

CATNIP ACRES HERB FARM
67 Christian Street
Oxford, CT 06483
(203) 888-5649
Seeds, plants, other. (R)(MO seeds only)

GILBERTIE'S HERB
GARDENS, INC.
Sylvan Lane
Westport, CT 06880
(203) 227-4175
Seeds, plants, dried culinary herbs, other. (R)(W)

LOGEE'S GREENHOUSES
55 North Street
Danielson, CT 06239
(203) 774-8038
Plants. (R)(MO)

NORTH GUILFORD HERBARY
57 Whitfield Street
Guilford, CT 06437
(203) 453-2753
Seeds, plants, dried culinary herbs. (R)(MO)

SASSAFRAS
132 Washington Street
South Norwalk, CT 06854
(203) 838-2499
Dried culinary herbs, other. (R)

DISTRICT OF COLUMBIA

THE HERB COTTAGE
Washington Cathedral
Mount Saint Alban
Washington, D.C. 20016
(202) 537-8982
Seeds, dried culinary herbs, other. (R)(MO)

FLORIDA

KANAPAHA BOTANICAL
GARDENS
4625 Southwest 63 Boulevard
Gainesville, FL 32608
(904) 372-4981
Seeds, plants, other. (R)

McCRORY'S SUNNY HILL
NURSERY
Star Rt. 3, Box 844
Eustis, FL 32726
(904) 357-9876
Plants. (R)(MO)

GEORGIA

JAS. JIRKLAND LTD.
12 West Harris Street
Savannah, GA 31401
(912) 238-3902
Plants, dried culinary herbs, other. (R)(MO except plants) (W)

IDAHO

HIGH ALTITUDE GARDENS
Box 4238
Ketchum, ID 83340
(208) 726-3221
Seeds. (MO)

NORTHPLAN/MOUNTAIN SEED
P.O. Box 9107
Moscow, ID 83843
(208) 882-8040
Seeds. (MO)

ILLINOIS

FRAGRANT FIELDS
128 Front Street
Dongola, IL 62926
(618) 827-3677
Plants, other. (R)

MARI-MANN HERB CO., INC.
North End of St. Louis Bridge
  Road
RR #4, Box #7
Decatur, IL 62521
(217) 429-1404 or 429-1555
*Plants, dried culinary herbs, other.
(R)(W)*

SHADY HILL GARDENS
803 Walnut Street
Batavia, IL 60510
(312) 879-5665
*Plants. (R)(MO)
Catalogue $2.*

INDIANA

DAVIDSON-WILSON
GREENHOUSES
Rt. 2, Box 168, Dept. 26
Crawfordsville, IN 47933
(317) 364-0556
Seeds, plants. (R)(MO)(W)

GREENFIELD HERB GARDEN
Depot and Harrison, P.O. Box 437
Shipshewana, IN 46565
(219) 768-7110
Seeds, plants, other. (R)(MO)

THE HERB FARM
13182 Pierce Road
Hagerstown, IN 47346
(317) 886-5193
*Plants, dried culinary herbs, other.
(R)*

KRIDER NURSERIES
303 West Bristol P.O. Box 29
Middlebury, IN 46540
(219) 825-5714
Seeds, plants. (R)(MO)

IOWA

EARL MAY SEED AND
NURSERY
208 North Elm
Shenandoah, IA 51603
(712) 246-1020
Seeds, plants. (R)(MO)

FOX RIDGE HERBS
4918 Red School Road
Central City, IA 52214
(312) 438-6687
Plants, other. (R)(W)

HENRY FIELD SEED &
NURSERY CO.
407 Sycamore
Shenandoah, IA 51603
(605) 665-9391
Seeds, plants. (MO)

THE HERB AND SPICE
COLLECTION
Box 118
Norway, IA 52318
(800) 365-4372
*Dried culinary herbs, other.
(R)(MO)*

KANSAS

COOK'S GERANIUM NURSERY
712 North Grand
Lyons, KS 67554
(316) 257-5033
*Scented geranium plants.
(R)(MO)*

KENTUCKY

DABNEY HERBS
Box 22061
Louisville, KY 40222
(502) 893-5198
*Seeds, plants, dried culinary herbs,
other. (R)(MO)*

THE HERB MARKET
Jail Street
Washington, KY 41096
(606) 759-7815
*Seeds, plants, dried culinary herbs,
other. (R)*

WINDING WAY FARM
2595 West Mount Zion Road
Crestwood, KY 40014
(502) 241-4609
*Plants, dried culinary herbs, other.
(R)(MO)*

LOUISIANA

GOOD SCENTS
11655 Highland Road
Baton Rouge, LA 70810
(505) 766-3898
*Dried culinary herbs, other.
(R)(MO)*

THE HERB PLACE
120 Anita Drive
Monroe, LA 71202
(312) 322-3527
*Plants, dried culinary herbs, other.
(R)(MO)*

MAINE

BLACKROCK FARM
P.O. Box 19
Cape Porpoise, ME 04014
(207) 967-5783
Plants, other. (R)(MO)

THE CHAMOMILE SHOP INC.
Stephens Road
P.O. Box 619
Rangeley, ME 04970
(207) 864-5261
*Dried culinary herbs, other.
(R)(MO)(W)*

HEDGEHOG HILL FARM
RFD 2 Box 2010
Buckfield, ME 04220
(207) 388-2341
*Plants, dried culinary herbs, other.
(R)(MO)*

JOHNNY'S SELECTED SEEDS
299 Foss Hill Road
Albion, ME 04910
(207) 437-9294
Seeds. (MO)

MERRY GARDENS
Mechanic Street, P.O. Box 595
Camden, ME 04843
(207) 236-2121
Plants. (R)(MO)

RAM ISLAND FARM HERBS
Ram Island Farm
Cape Elizabeth, ME 04107
(207) 767-5700
Dried culinary herbs, other. (MO)

UNITED SOCIETY OF SHAKERS
Sabbathday Lake
Poland Spring, ME 04274
(207) 926-4597
*Plants, dried culinary herbs, other.
(R)(MO)*

MARYLAND

D. LANDRETH SEED COMPANY
180 West Ostend Street
Baltimore, MD 21230
(301) 727-3922
Seeds. (R)(MO)(W)

MARIA PRICE'S WILLOW OAK
FLOWER AND HERB FARM
8109 Telegraph Road
Severn, MD 21144
(301) 551-2237
*Plants, dried culinary herbs, other.
(R)(MO)*

THE MEYER SEED COMPANY
600 South Caroline Street
Baltimore, MD 21213
(301) 342-4224
Seeds. (R)(MO)(W)

SMILE HERB SHOP
4908 Berwyn Road
College Park, MD 20740
(301) 474-8791
*Seeds, plants, dried culinary herbs,
other. (R)(MO)*

STILLRIDGE HERB FARM
10370 Rt. 99
Woodstock, MD 21163
    Also: Ellicot City, MD
          Savage Mill, Savage MD
          Woodstock, MD
(301) 465-8348
Plants, dried culinary herbs, other.
(R)(MO)

ST. JOHN'S HERB GARDEN
7711 Hillmeade Road
Bowie, MD 20715
(301) 262-8661 or 262-5302
Seeds, plants, dried culinary herbs,
other. (MO)(W)

MASSACHUSETTS

BETSY WILLIAMS/THE PROPER
SEASON
68 Park Street
Andover, MA 01810
(508) 470-0911
Plants, other. (R)(MO)

CRICKET HILL HERB
FARM LTD.
Glen Street
Rowley, MA 01969
(508) 948-2818
Seeds, plants, dried culinary herbs,
other. (R)(MO)
Catalogue $1.

HANCOCK SHAKER VILLAGE
P.O. Box 898
Pittsfield, MA 01262
(413) 442-8381
Dried culinary herbs, other. (R)

THE HERB PATCH, INC.
Concord, MA
    Also: Belmont Center, MA
(617) 369-1948 or (508) 263-2405
Plants, dried culinary herbs, other.
(R)

NAOMI'S HERBS
11 Housatonic Street
Lenox, MA 01240
(413) 637-0616
Plants, dried culinary herbs, other.
(R)(MO)

OLD HILL HERBS
29 Norman Street
Marblehead, MA 01945
(617) 631-4323
Plants, dried culinary herbs, other.
(R)

STOCKBRIDGE HERBS &
STITCHES
Stockbridge Road Box 95
South Deerfield, MA 01373
(413) 665-4633
Dried culinary herbs, other. (MO)

WOLF HILL FARM
30 Jericho Hill Road
Southborough, MA 01772
(508) 485-5087
Plants, other. (R)

MICHIGAN

FAR NORTH GARDENS
16785 Harrison
Livonia, MI 48154
Seeds. (R)(MO)

FOX HILL FARM
440 West Michigan Avenue,
    Box 9
Parma, MI 49269
(517) 531-3179
Seeds, plants, fresh and dried
culinary herbs, other.
(R)(MO)(W)

GARDEN GATES HERBS
RR #2 Box 158
Bellaire, MI 49615
(616) 377-7336
Plants, dried culinary herbs, other.
(R)(MO)

THE HERB COTTAGE
700 Anderson Road
Niles, MI 49120
(616) 663-8952
Seeds, plants, dried culinary herbs,
other. (R)

THE SASSAFRAS HUTCH HERB
FARM
11880 Sandy Bottom NE
Greenville, MI 48838
(616) 754-9759
Plants, dried culinary herbs, other.
(R)(MO)

SUNSHINE FARM AND GARDEN
2460 North Wixom Road
Milford, MI 48042
(313) 685-2204
Seeds, plants, dried culinary herbs,
other. (R)

WILLOW TREE HERB FARM
3886 Butterworth Southwest
Grand Rapids, MI 49504
(616) 453-6134
Plants, dried culinary herbs, other.
(R)(MO)

WOODLAND HERBS
7741 North Manitou TR, West
Northport, MI 49670
(616) 386-5081
Seeds, plants, dried culinary herbs,
other. (R)(MO, except plants)

MINNESOTA

RED SAFFRON
3009 16th Avenue South
Minneapolis, MN 55407
(612) 724-3686
Dried culinary herbs, other. (MO)

RICE CREEK GARDENS
1315 66 Avenue Northeast
Minneapolis, MN 55432
(612) 574-1197
Plants. (R)(MO)
Catalogue $2.

SHADY ACRES NURSERY
7777 HIghway 212
Chaska, MN 55318
(612) 466-3391
Plants. (R)(MO)

MISSOURI

HERB GATHERING INC.
5742 Kenwood Avenue
Kansas City, MO 64110
(816) 523-2653
Seeds, fresh and dried culinary
herbs, other. (MO)(W)
Catalogue $2.

MISSOURI BOTANICAL
GARDEN
4344 Shaw Boulevard
St. Louis, MO 63110
(314) 577-5125
Seeds, plants, other. (R)

MONTANA

LOST PRAIRIE HERB FARM
805 Kienas Road
Kalispell, MT 59901
(406) 756-7742
Plants, other. (R)(MO)

NEW HAMPSHIRE

PICKITY PLACE
Nutting Hill Road
Mason, NH 03048
(603) 878-1151
Seeds, plants, dried culinary herbs,
other. (R)(MO)

STRAWBERRY MEADOW HERB
FARM, INC.
RFD #3 Box 3689
Pleasant Street
Pittsfield, NH 03263
(603) 435-6132
Plants, dried culinary herbs.
(R)(MO)(W)
Catalogue $1.

NEW JERSEY

HERBALLY YOURS
Changewater Road
Changewater, NJ 07831
(201) 689-6140
Dried culinary herbs, other.
(R)(MO)(W)

WELL-SWEEP HERB FARM
317 Mt. Bethel Road
Port Murray, NJ 07865
(201) 852-5390
Seeds, plants, dried culinary herbs,
other. (R)(MO)

WHISKEY RUN HERB FARM
RD 2 Box 281
Locktown-Flemington Road
Flemington, NJ 08822
(201) 782-1278
Plants, other. (R)

NEW MEXICO

BLUE CORN CONNECTION
3825 Academy Parkway South
  NE
Albuquerque, NM 87109
Blue cornmeal. (R)(MO)

CASADOS FARMS
P.O. Box 1269
San Juan Pueblo, NM 87566
(505) 852-2433
Chiles, corns, flours, spices. (MO)

CHILI SHOP
109 East Water Street
Santa Fe, NM 87501
(505) 983-6080
*Mild and hot chili powders.
(R)(MO)*

GREEN CHILI FIX COMPANY
P.O. Box 5463
Santa Fe, NM 87502
(505) 471-3325
*Dried green chiles, green chili
powder. (MO)*

LYTLE FARMS
P.O. Box 310
Salem, NM 87941
(505) 267-4168
*Fresh green chiles, dried chopped
red chiles, chili powder. (MO)*

PLANTS OF THE SOUTHWEST
1812 Second Street
Santa Fe, NM 87501
(505) 983-1548
Seeds, plants. (R)(MO)

NEW YORK

APHRODISIA
282 Bleecker Street
New York, NY 10014
(212) 838-6878
Dried culinary herbs. (R)(MO)

ASTER PLACE HERBS
RD #1 Box 24B
Poland, NY 13431
(315) 845-8099
Plants, other. (R)(MO)(W)

BACK OF THE BEYOND
7233 Lower East Hill Road
Golden, NY 14033
(716) 652-0427
*Plants, dried culinary herbs, other.
(R)(MO)*

FRESH HERB FARM
Pitcher Lane RD3 Box 466
Red Hook, NY 12571
(914) 758-5595
*Plants, fresh and dried culinary
herbs, other. (R)(MO)*

FROG PARK HERBS
Frog Park Road
Waterville, NY 13480
(315) 841-8636
*Seeds, plants, dried culinary herbs,
other. (R)(MO)*

THE GREEN HOUSE
24 Grove Street
Massena, NY 13662
(315) 769-2840
*Dried culinary herbs, other.
(R)(MO)(W)*

THE HERB CUPBOARD
Box 375 Route 163
Fort Plain, NY 13339
(518) 993-2363
*Plants, dried culinary herbs, other.
(R)(MO)*

HERB HOLLOW
Safford Road
East Otto, NY 14729
(716) 257-5105
*Seeds, plants, dried culinary herbs,
other. (R)(MO)*

LATIN AMERICAN PRODUCTS
142 West 46th Street
New York, NY 10036
(212) 302-4323
*Dried herbs, dried chiles, flours,
beans. (R)(MO)(W)*

PECONIC RIVER HERB FARM
310-C River Road
Calverton, NY 11933
(516) 369-0058
Plants, other. (R)

PECOS VALLEY SPICE
COMPANY
500 East 77th Street
New York, NY 10162
(212) 628-5374
Ground and crushed chiles. (MO)

RUE JA'S HERB COLLECTION
1849 Woodard Road
Webster, NY 14580
(716) 265-0169
Plants, other. (R)

THISTLE HILL
59 Evans Street
Mayville, NY 14757
(716) 753-7692
*Plants, dried culinary herbs, other.
(R)(MO)(W)*

NORTH CAROLINA

CHARLOTTE'S GREENHOUSE
Valle Crucis, NC 28604
(704) 963-5974
*Plants, fresh herbs and edible
flowers. (R)*

DOVECOTE
Fearrington Village Center
Pittsboro, NC 27312
(919) 542-1145
*Plants, dried culinary herbs, other.
(R)*

RASLAND FARM
NC 82 at US 13
Godwin, NC 28344
(919) 567-2705
*Plants, dried culinary herbs, other.
(R)(MO)(W)
Catalogue $2.*

SANDY MUSH HERB NURSERY
Rt. 2 Surrett Cove Road
Leicester, NC 28748
(704) 683-2014
*Seeds, plants, other. (R)(MO)
Catalogue $4; list SASE*

OHIO

BACKYARD HERBS AND
THINGS
4101 Canfield Road
Canfield, OH 44406
(216) 793-8326
*Dried culinary herbs, other.
(R)(MO)*

BITTERSWEET FARM
6294 Seville Road
Seville, OH 44273
(216) 887-5293
Plants, other. (R)(MO)

BLUESTONE PERENNIALS, INC.
7211 Middle Ridge Road
Madison, OH 44057
(800) 852-5243
Plants. (MO)

COMPANION PLANTS
7247 North Coolville Ridge
Athens, OH 45701
(614) 592-4643
*Seeds, plants. (R)(MO)(W)
Catalogue $2.*

COUNTRY HERBS
P.O. Box 128
189 East South Street
Lithopolis, OH 43136
Seeds, plants, other. (R)(MO)

THE HERBARY
3550 New Hudson Road
Orwell, OH 44076
(216) 437-5107
*Plants (R only); dried culinary
herbs, other. (R)(MO)*

THE HERB HOUSE CATALOG
340 Grove Street
Bluffton, OH 45817
(419) 358-7189
*Dried culinary herbs, other.
(R)(MO)*

LEWIS MOUNTAIN HERBS &
EVERLASTINGS
2345 Street Rt. 247
Manchester, OH 45144
(513) 549-2484
Plants, other. (R)

LILY OF THE VALLEY HERB
FARM
3969 Fox Avenue
Minerva, OH 44657
(216) 862-3920
Plants, dried culinary herbs, other.
(R)(MO)
Catalogue $2.

THE LINDEN TREE SHOP
Cox Arboretum
6733 Springboro Pike
Dayton, OH 45449
(513) 434-9005
Plants, other. (R)

THE OLD GREENHOUSE
1415 Devil's Backbone Road
Cincinnati, OH 45233
(513) 941-0337
Plants, other. (R)

THE PARSLEY POT
697 Country Road 1302 Rt. 2
Ashland, OH 44805
(419) 281-7514
Plants, dried culinary herbs, other.
(R)

SHAKER HERB FARM
11813 Oxford
Harrison, OH 45030
(513) 738-2939
Plants, other. (R)

SWISHER HILL HERBS
4089 Swisher Road
Urbana, OH 43078
(513) 653-8730
Seeds, plants, dried culinary herbs,
other. (R)

A TOUCH OF WILLIAMSBURG
2725 Dogwood Drive
Youngstown, OH 44511
(216) 792-5846
Dried culinary herbs, other.
(R)(MO)

WOODEN ONION
6810 Thompson Road
Cincinnati, OH 45247
(513) 385-9026
Plants, other. (R)

WOODSPIRITS HERB SHOP
1920 Apple Road
St. Paris, OH 43072
(513) 663-4327
Seeds, dried culinary herbs, other.
(R)

OKLAHOMA

SEQUOYAH GARDEN AND
GIFTS
Rt. 1 Box 80
Gore, OK 74435
(918) 487-5849
Plants, other. (R)

OREGON

GOODWIN GREEK GARDENS
P.O. Box 83
Williams, OR 97544
(503) 846-7357
Seeds, plants, other. (R)(MO)
Catalogue $1.

THE HERBERY
HC 83 Box 4010
Coquille, OR 97423
(503) 396-5356
Plants, other. (R)(MO)(W)

NICHOL'S GARDEN NURSERY
1190 North Pacific Highway
Albany, OR 97321
(503) 928-9280
Seeds, plants, dried culinary herbs,
other. (R)(MO)

SARESSENCE HERBS AND
AROMATICS
669 Hudson Road
Gold Hill, OR 97525
(503) 855-9921
Plants, other. (R)(MO)(W)

PENNSYLVANIA

DILLY DUO HERBS
2015 Potshop Road
Norristown, PA 19403
(215) 539-7371
Plants, other. (R)

THE DILWORTH TOWN
COUNTRY STORE
275 Brintons Bridge Road
West Chester, PA 19382
(215) 399-0560
Plants, dried culinary herbs.
other.(R)

THE ERBE SHOPPE
158 East Union Street
Somerset, PA 15501
(814) 443-2016
Seeds, plants, dried culinary herbs,
other. (R)(MO)

FOUR-LEAF CLOVER HERB
FARM
R.D. #1 Ridge Road
Natrona Heights, PA 15065
(412) 224-5125
Plants, fresh and dried culinary
herbs, other. (R)

GIUNTA'S HERB FARM
R.D. #1 Box 706
Todd & White School House
Roads
Honey Brook, PA 19344
(215) 273-2863
Plants, dried culinary herbs, other.
(R)(MO)

GOOD'S GREENHOUSE, INC.
R.D. #2 Box 2565
Mohnton, PA 19540
(215) 445-6055
Seeds, plants, other. (R)

HALCYON GARDENS HERBS
P.O. Box 124
Gibsonia, PA 15044
(412) 443-5544
Seeds. (MO)

THE HERB BARN
Box 31, Bodines Road
Bodines, PA 17722
(717) 995-9327
Plants. (R)(MO)(W)

THE HERB MERCHANT, INC.
70 West Pomfret Street
Carlisle, PA 17013
(717) 249-0970
Seeds, plants, dried culinary herbs,
other. (R)(MO)

NATURE'S HARMONY
2240 Pinetown Road
Lewisberry, PA 17339
(717) 697-0580
Plants, other. (R)

PARSLEY PORCH
39 Manor Avenue
Millersville, PA 17551
(717) 872-2006
Plants, dried culinary herbs, other.
(R)(MO)(W)

THE ROSEMARY HOUSE, INC.
120 South Market Street
Mechanicsburg, PA 17055
(717) 697-5111
Seeds, plants, dried culinary herbs,
other. (R)(MO)

SCARBOROUGH FAIRE
2B West Pittsburgh Street
Delmont, PA 15626
(412) 468-5252
Seeds, plants, dried culinary herbs,
other. (R)

SHANTI GARDENS
R.D. #2, Box 68
Birdsboro, PA 19508
(215) 582-4334
Plants. (R)

TIMBER ROCK FARMS
R.D. #2 Box 290E
Emporium, PA 15834
(814) 486-7685
Dried culinary herbs, other.
(R)(MO)(W)
Catalogue $1.

W. ATLEE BURPEE & CO.
300 Park Avenue
Warminster, PA 18974
(215) 674-4900
Seeds, plants. (R)(MO)

RHODE ISLAND

MEADOWBROOK HERB
GARDEN
Route 138
Wyoming, RI 02898
(401) 539-7603
Seeds, plants, dried culinary herbs,
other. (R)(MO)

SOUTH CAROLINA

PARK SEED COMPANY, INC.
P.O. Box 46 Cokesbury Road
Greenwood, SC 29648
(803) 223-7333
Seeds. (MO)

WOODLANDERS, INC.
1128 Colleton Avenue
Aiken, SC 29801
(804) 648-7522
Plants. (MO)

TENNESSEE

HYSSOP HILL HERBS
Box 1082 418 Lewisburg Pike
Franklin, TN 37064
(615) 790-6454
Dried culinary herbs, other. (R)

SASSAFRAS HERBS, INC.
P.O. Box 50192
Nashville, TN 37205
(615) 244-8711
*Dried culinary herbs, other.
(R)(MO)*

TEXAS

ANTIQUE ROSE EMPORIUM
Rt. 5, Box 143
Brenham, TX 77833
(409) 836-9051
*Antique rose and herb plants.
(R)(MO)(W)
Catalogue $3.*

THE HERB BAR
200 West Mary
Austin, TX 78704
(512) 444-6251
*Seeds, plants, dried culinary herbs,
other. (R)(MO)*

LUCIA'S GARDEN
2213 Portsmouth
Houston, TX 77098
(713) 523-6494
*Plants, dried culinary herbs, other.
(R)(MO)*

VARNEY'S CHEMIST LADEN
242 West Main Street
Fredericksburg, TX 78624
(512) 997-8615
*Seeds, plants, dried culinary herbs,
other. (R)(MO)*

VERMONT

THE CAMBRIDGE HERBARY
Tower Road 7
Cambridge, VT 05444
(802) 644-2480
Plants, other. (R)

LE JARDIN DU GOURMET
West Danville, VT 05873
Seeds, plants. (R)(MO)

RATHDOWNEY LTD.
3 River Street
Bethel, VT 05032
(802) 234-9928
*Seeds, plants, dried culinary herbs,
other. (R)(MO)(W)*

VERMONT BEAN SEED
COMPANY
Garden Lane
Fair Haven, VT 05743
(802) 265-4212
Seeds, other. (R)(MO)

VIRGINIA

CHICK COVE HERB FARM
P.O. Box 468 Rt. 33
Deltaville, VA 23043
(804) 776-6470
Herb plants, other. (R)(MO)

EARTHWORKS HERB GARDEN
NURSERY
923 North Ivy Street
Arlington, VA 22201
(703) 243-2498
Plants. (R)

SOUTHERN EXPOSURE SEED
EXCHANGE
P.O. Box 158
North Garden, VA 22959
Seeds. (MO)

T. DEBAGGIO ROSEMARY &
LAVENDER
923 North Ivy Street
Arlington, VA 22201
(703) 243-2498
*Plants: Rosemary for Christmas,
lavender in the spring. (MO)*

WHITE OAK NURSERIES, INC.
12521 Lee Highway
Manassas, VA 22110
(703) 754-2222
Plants, other. (R)

YESTERDAY'S HERB FARM
Rt.1 Box 104
Dugspur, VA 24325
Seeds, other. (MO)

WASHINGTON

ABUNDANT LIFE SEED
FOUNDATION
P.O. Box 772 1029 Lawrence
Port Townsend, WA 98368
(206) 385-5660
Seeds, other. (R)(MO)

CEDARBROOK HERB FARM
986 Sequim Avenue South
Sequim, WA 98382
(206) 683-7733
*Seeds, plants, dried culinary herbs,
other. (R)(MO)*

WEST VIRGINIA

WRENWOOD OF BERKELEY
SPRINGS
Rt. 4 Box 361
Berkeley Springs, WV 25411
(304) 258-3071
*Plants, dried culinary herbs, other.
(R)(MO)(W)*

WISCONSIN

HEISE WAUSAU FARMS
2805 Valley View Road
Wausau, WI 54401
(715) 675-3256
*Plants, dried culinary herbs, other.
(R)(MO)*

J. W. JUNG SEED COMPANY
335 South High Street
Randolph, WI 53957
(414) 326-3121
Seeds, plants. (MO)

KAVANAUGH HILL SPICE SHOP
1244 North Glenview Avenue
Wauwatosa, WI 53213
(414) 258-7727
Dried culinary herbs, other. (R)

PRAIRIE SEED SOURCE
P.O. Box 83
North Lake, WI 53064
*Seeds. (MO)
Catalogue $1.*

SUNNYPOINT GARDENS
6939 Highway 42
Egg Harbor, WI 54209
(414) 868-3646
Plants, other. (R)

CANADA

ASHBY'S SEEDS
R.R. 2, Cameron
Ontario, Canada KOM 1GO
(705) 359-1115
*Seeds, plants (MO) or by
appointment July–September*

THE HERBAL TOUCH
30 Dover Street
Otterville, Ont NOJ 1RO
(519) 879-6812
*Plants, dried culinary herbs, other.
(R)*

OTTO RICHTER & SONS, LTD.
Box 26
Goodwood, Ontario
Canada, LOC 1AO
(416) 640-6677
Seeds, plants, other. (R)(MO)

SANCTUARY SEEDS
2388 West 4th Avenue
Vancouver, British Columbia
Canada V6K 1P1
(604) 733-4724
Seeds, other. (R)(MO)

INDEX